THE SCIENCE OF A LOST MEDIEVAL GAELIC GRAVEYARD

The Ballyhanna Research Project

THE SCIENCE OF A LOST MEDIEVAL GAELIC GRAVEYARD

The Ballyhanna Research Project

Edited by

Catriona J McKenzie, Eileen M Murphy and Colm J Donnelly

TII Heritage 2

First published in 2015 by
Transport Infrastructure Ireland
Parkgate Business Centre, Parkgate Street, Dublin 8, D08 YFF1
Copyright © Transport Infrastructure Ireland and the authors

Library of Congress Cataloguing-in Publication Data are available for this book.
A CIP catalogue record for this book is available from the British Library.

Material from Ordnance Survey Ireland is reproduced with the permission of the Government of Ireland and Ordnance Survey Ireland under permit number EN0045206.

ISBN 978-0-9932315-2-0
ISSN 2009-8480
TII Heritage 2

Copy-editing: Editorial Solutions (Ireland) Ltd
Cover design, typesetting and layout: LSD Ltd
Index: Julitta Clancy
Printed by: W&G Baird Ltd

Front cover—Sixteenth-century woodcut depicting a group of Gaelic Irish soldiers. The title—DRAVN AFTER THE QVICKE—refers to the fact that the anonymous artist had drawn the six men from life (WA 1863.3908 © Ashmolean Museum, University of Oxford).

Back cover—Stylised depiction of a young adult female, buried in a typical extended, supine position with the head to the west (Sapphire Mussen).

CONTENTS

CONTENTS OF CD-ROM

1. Supplementary Texts and Data

Site(s)	Supplementary texts and data	Author(s)
03E1384 Ballyhanna	Ballyhanna tables of burial data	Philip Macdonald & Naomi Carver
03E1384 Ballyhanna	Chapter 8—Supplementary text	Ted McGowan & Tasneem Bashir
03E1384 Ballyhanna	Ballyhanna beads	Ian Riddler
03E1384 Ballyhanna	Ballyhanna small finds	Catherine Johnson
03E1384 Ballyhanna	Ballyhanna medieval pottery	Clare McCutcheon
03E1384 Ballyhanna 04E0012 Magheracar 1 04E0015 Ballynacarrick 1 04E0016 Rathmore & Finner 1 04E0098 Magheracar 2	N15 Chipped and ground stone	Eiméar Nelis

2. Archaeological Excavation Final Reports

Filename	Site description	Director
03E1384 Ballyhanna.pdf	Medieval church and graveyard	Brian Ó Donnchadha
04E0012 Magheracar 1.pdf	Early medieval settlement activity	Brian Ó Donnchadha
04E0015 Ballynacarrick 1.pdf	Prehistoric temporary settlement site	Fintan Walsh
04E0016 Rathmore & Finner 1.pdf	Early modern house	Fintan Walsh
04E0017 Sminver 1.pdf	Burnt mound and holy well	Fintan Walsh
04E0098 Magheracar 2.pdf	Iron Age linear earthwork	Brian Ó Donnchadha & Rob Lynch
A007001 Sminver 2.pdf	Possible megalithic structure	Fintan Walsh

3. Photographic Survey Reports

Filename	Site description	Author(s)
Ballymunterhiggin 1 Photographic Survey.pdf	Holy well	Fintan Walsh
Dunmuckrum 1 Photographic Survey.pdf	Railway bridge	Shane Delaney

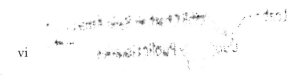

FOREWORD

The discovery in 2003 of a graveyard and the foundations of a small forgotten stone church in Ballyshannon, Co. Donegal, as part of the N15 Bundoran–Ballyshannon Bypass archaeological works, led to the excavation of one of the largest collections of medieval burials ever undertaken on this island; over 1,200 individuals were excavated from the site at Ballyhanna over the winter of 2003–4, representing 1,000 years of burial through the entire Irish medieval period.

It was the recognition of the knowledge potential of the burials that led to the research collaboration that is the Ballyhanna Research Project, which was established in 2005 and owes much to the vision of Project Archaeologist Michael MacDonagh who brought the key stakeholders together. Studies of human remains and burial practice provide great insight into lifestyles, social behaviour, health, diet and disease. The Ballyhanna burials offered the opportunity to explore these issues from the start of the medieval period prior to the Norman invasion through to the Flight of the Earls in the 17th century. Funded and supported by the National Roads Authority (now operating as Transport Infrastructure Ireland since its merger with the Railway Procurement Agency in August 2015) in partnership with Donegal County Council, the Ballyhanna Research Project is a cross-border collaboration linking the distinct academic skills of Queen's University Belfast (QUB) with those of the Institute of Technology, Sligo (ITS), using applied scientific methods to augment the results of the standard visual analysis of the remains. I am delighted to introduce this publication detailing the results of the project. It is an important publication, illustrating fully the value of collaborative research in the field of archaeology and the knowledge potential of the important archaeological remains and sites that have been unearthed throughout the years of significant investment in our strategic road network.

The excavation at Ballyhanna by Irish Archaeological Consultancy Ltd generated huge local interest, in part because it was located within an urban area but primarily because of the huge appetite for knowledge about their heritage shown by the people of Ballyshannon. The excavation was carried out openly, and school and public visits were facilitated and encouraged while the excavation took place. Those buried at Ballyhanna were honoured by the town's religious congregations during moving ceremonies while the site was being excavated and this publication is an important endowment to the people of Ballyshannon acknowledging the role they played in the exciting discovery.

Ballyhanna church and graveyard were located on the banks of the Erne River, close to the location of the historic strategic fording point of Béal Átha Seanaidh, from which the town got its name. In the 1940s the river landscape at Ballyshannon was utterly transformed by the construction of a hydro-electric station; the cutting of a deep river tail-race from the dam down to the sea caused the removal of the ford and the renowned Assaroe Falls further down river. Ballyhanna church now sits close to the N15 Aodh Ruadh Bridge, opened in 2005 as part of the bypass and sharing the name of the High King after whom the Assaroe Falls were once named. The road junction was redesigned during the excavation to avoid the medieval church and a small public park was created around these remains for the people of Ballyshannon and its visitors. It is an important heritage addition to the town and a fitting memorial to those once buried on the banks of the Erne.

Michael Nolan
Chief Executive
Transport Infrastructure Ireland

ACKNOWLEDGEMENTS

The authors and editors would like to express their gratitude to Transport Infrastructure Ireland (TII), formerly the National Roads Authority, and Donegal County Council for their funding of the project and support throughout. In particular, we would like to acknowledge the support of Dáire O'Rourke (†), NRA Head of Archaeology, who sadly passed away during the course of the project, for her approval of the original project proposal. We would like to thank the staff of Irish Archaeological Consultancy Ltd for all their excavation contributions on the N15 bypass especially at Ballyhanna, directed by Brian Ó Donnchadha. Many thanks also to Michael Nolan, Rónán Swan, Tom Carr and Kieran Kelly of the TII for their support throughout. We would like to also acknowledge the support of Aidan O'Doherty, Damian McDermott, Fergus Towey and Richie Bromley of Donegal County Council National Roads Design Office. At the National Museum of Ireland we would like to thank Eamonn Kelly, Nessa O'Connor, Maeve Sikora, Fiona Reilly and Pádraig Clancy for their support and approvals during the term of the project. We would also like to thank the archaeological specialists who provided detailed information on the archaeological finds and samples: Catherine Johnson, Clare McCutcheon, Dr Ian Riddler, Rose M Cleary, Dr Eiméar Nelis and Dr Ellen O'Carroll. We further express our gratitude to the staff at Donegal County Museum, Letterkenny, the McCaffrey family and Eoghan (†) and Mary Coyle, and to the Donegal and Ballyshannon Historical Societies, with special thanks to Anthony Begley for all his assistance and local wisdom. We warmly remember Lucius Emerson (†) for his infectious appreciation of the discovery at Ballyhanna and his knowledgeable contributions on the history of the site and of Ballyshannon.

The contributors from QUB would also like to thank Carmelita Troy of Rubicon Heritage Services Ltd and Kildare County Council for providing information on the medieval skeletal collection from Ardreigh, Co. Kildare. We are grateful to Clare McGranaghan, then of the Centre for Archaeological Fieldwork, QUB, for her help with the initial recording of the inventories for the juvenile skeletons. Thanks are due to Dr Annaleigh Margey of Trinity College Dublin who provided information on historical maps. We would also like to express our gratitude to Dr Evelyn Keaveney, School of Geography, Archaeology and Palaeoecology, QUB, for her advice on dietary interpretations and to Cormac McSparron of the aforementioned School for his guidance on radiocarbon calibration. Thanks are also due to Dr John Dormans and Dr Lauren Tomlinson, Division of Orthopaedic Surgery, The Children's Hospital of Philadelphia; Ms Sarah Ziegler, President of the MHE Research Foundation and Dr John Martin, School of Geography, Archaeology and Palaeoecology, QUB, for information about the cases of multiple osteochondromas. Dr Simon Mays of English Heritage kindly provided second opinions on a number of the juvenile palaeopathologies.

The contributors from the ITS would like to thank Professor Philip Farrell, Ashley Pokallus and Cedric Lemarechal from the University of Wisconsin, Madison. We are also indebted to Dr Mike Taylor, University of Surrey, for his advice on tuberculosis ancient DNA analysis. We are grateful to the technical support staff at ITS, in particular Martin Cronin and James Kelly, and to Jim Foran, Librarian at ITS, Declan Flavin, Finance Officer at ITS, and to Janette Gillen, Business Innovation Centre Manager at ITS. Many thanks also to Donal O'Callaghan of Teckno Surgical and Dr Andrew Macey of Sligo General Hospital for advice on bone sampling.

Artefact and skeletal photographs were taken by Jonathan Hession and Mícheál Cearbhalláin. Illustrations were prepared by Sapphire Mussen and Libby Mulqueeny, School of Geography, Archaeology and Palaeoecology, QUB. Finally, we would like to express our gratitude to Jerry O'Sullivan and Michael Stanley of TII for their advice throughout the publication process and the team under the direction of Editorial Solutions (Ireland) Ltd, who copy-edited, typeset and printed *The Science of a Lost Medieval Gaelic Graveyard: the Ballyhanna Research Project*.

THE N15 BUNDORAN–BALLYSHANNON BYPASS ARCHAEOLOGICAL TEAM

Publication team

Editors: Catriona J McKenzie, Eileen Murphy and Colm Donnelly

Principal authors: Tasneem Bashir, Jeremy Bird, Naomi Carver, Colm Donnelly, Gráinne Leamy, Michael MacDonagh, Philip Macdonald, Deirdre McCarthy, Róisín McCarthy, Ted McGowan, Catriona J McKenzie, Eileen Murphy, Sheila Tierney

Illustrations: Sapphire Mussen and Libby Mulqueeny

Ballyhanna Research Project team

TII: Michael MacDonagh, Gráinne Leamy, Deirdre McCarthy

QUB: Eileen Murphy, Colm Donnelly, Catriona McKenzie, Philip Macdonald, Naomi Carver, Clare Mc Granaghan

ITS: Jeremy Bird, Ted McGowan, Sheila Tierney, Tasneem Bashir, Róisín McCarthy

Irish Archaeological Consultancy Ltd staff

Senior Archaeologist: Shane Delaney

Excavation Directors: Brian Ó Donnchadha, Fintan Walsh, Rob Lynch

Supervisors: Ken Anderson, Nick Fitch, Derek Gallagher, Tom Janes, James Kyle, Marianne Nolan, William O Shea, Paddy Walsh

On-site Osteoarchaeologist: Henny Piezonka

Site Assistants: Faith Bailey, Ellen-Maeve Bergh, Mark Doyle, Kate Ferron, Dylan Foley, Michael Forde, Dominic Gallagher, Liz Gill, Niall Jones, John Kerrigan, Susan Kidner, Lars Krakowicz, Dane Lalonde, Orlaith Lenihan, Sally Lloyd, Susan Lynch, Rory Mac Samhain, Brendan Malone Jnr, Brendan Malone Snr, James McKee, Catriona J McKenzie, C. Mooreshill, Bernard Mullholland, Aodhan Murphy, Edel Murphy, John Murphy, Jean O'Dowd, Tamlyn O'Driscoll, Billy Quinn, Sarah Ranson, Vanessa Salvador, Dan Schneider, Sean Shanahan, Zachary Silke, Kevin Spade, Julian Stroud, Emma Taylor, Bevan Thomas, Katrina Topping, John White, John Winfer

General Operatives: Colm Cronin, Tom Neary

INTRODUCTION
Michael MacDonagh

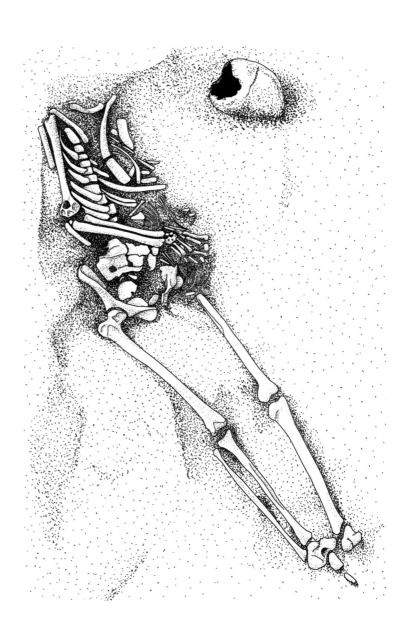

Stylised depiction of a young mother with her newly delivered baby twins carefully placed across her chest and abdomen within the crook of her arm (SK 978, SK 986 and SK 979) (Sapphire Mussen).

They trudged wearily across the ford as their forebears had done for hundreds of years. Their child, born ill, was now borne high over the river and the falls roared. They climbed the river bank to the small burial ground where they placed their offspring in a grave, hard dug and harshly into the remains of those gone before him, and among the dead of the old churchyard they keened their loss. With arms lovingly folded and lightly shrouded, a quartz pebble placed alongside him, he was then covered with soil and the broken bones of others.

The Ballyhanna Research Project (BRP) is a cross-border collaborative research project that was established to investigate a medieval church and burial ground, which was lost from local knowledge for centuries, rediscovered in 2003 and subsequently excavated. One of the primary aims of the project is to show how scientific research may aid our interpretations of archaeology and reveal new insights into past societies. It is about a community who lived in Gaelic Ireland, about their lifestyles, health and diet. The project research tells us of their deaths and of their burial traditions, and through examining all of these aspects, it tells us also about their lives. Most of all it is about the people, a medieval community, who, over the course of a millennium, were laid to rest in a small graveyard by the banks of the River Erne.

The forgotten graveyard, its rediscovery and excavation

In 2003, during the course of pre-construction archaeological works for the 15 km-long N15 Bundoran–Ballyshannon Bypass, a small graveyard and the foundations of a building were discovered in the townland of Ballyhanna[1]. The townland of Ballyhanna is located on the southern bank of the River Erne on the eastern outskirts of Ballyshannon town in south County Donegal (Illus. 1.1). No extant remains of a burial ground were known in this locality prior to the archaeological testing. The burial ground was excavated over the winter months of 2003–4 by Irish Archaeological Consultancy Ltd, under the direction of Brian Ó Donnchadha, and funded by the National Roads Authority through Donegal County Council.

By the end of the six-month excavation in March 2004, the remains of some 1,296 men, women and children had been recovered from the graveyard, making it one of the largest corpora of human remains to have been excavated from a burial ground in Ireland. The first people who were laid to rest at Ballyhanna were buried from the late seventh to early eighth century AD onwards and the burial ground remained in use until the early 17th century (see Appendix 1). The graveyard was small, located at the base of a steep hill in a pocket of soil between the surrounding bedrock—rock which would have prevented lateral expansion of the graveyard over its long period of use. The burials were concentrated to the south and east of the foundations of a building, most likely a small associated church. Upon discovery of the building's foundations, a design change in the junction layout at this location was agreed by the relevant construction partners and this enabled the structure to remain unaffected by the new road design. The foundations of the church were preserved and are now the focal point of a small heritage park which was designed, with input from the local community, to commemorate all those buried at Ballyhanna (see Appendix 2).

---

1   NGR 188105, 360834; height 15 m OD; Excavation Licence No. 03E1384; Excavation Director Brian Ó Donnchadha.

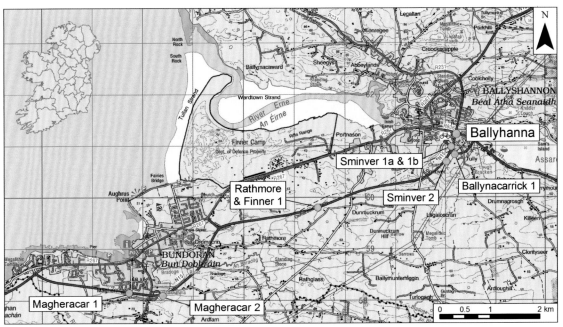

Illus. 1.1—General location map showing the route of the N15 Bundoran–Ballyshannon Bypass (in green) and the location of archaeological sites discovered during pre-construction archaeological works (based on the Ordnance Survey Ireland Discovery Series Map).

Today Ballyhanna sits in the shadow of a landmark structure, the Aodh Ruadh Bridge, which was built over the River Erne in 2005 as part of the N15 Bypass (Illus. 1.2). In medieval times Ballyhanna lay adjacent to an earlier strategic river crossing, the ford of Áth Seanaigh, the most important crossing point along the lower reaches of the Erne (see Text box on page 5). The early history of Ballyshannon is a mixture of myth and legend with all the wonderful and intriguing imagery that belongs to such tales. One such legend suggests that Partholon, eighth in succession from Noah, was the first settler in Ballyshannon around 2700 BC (Begley 2009, 9). Archaeological evidence indicates prehistoric settlement and activity in the general area during the Early Neolithic from around 4000 BC onwards. During the medieval period Ballyshannon was a key stronghold for the Ó Domnaill lineage who ruled Tír Conaill, and one that provided a crossing point between Ulster and Connacht. The River Erne also provided access to the sea, and had rich salmon fisheries in its waters. John O'Donovan translated a 15th-century manuscript titled: *The Banquet of Dun Na N-Gedh and the Battle of Magh Rath: An Ancient Historical Tale,* and in this manuscript the waterfalls at Assaroe are described as:

…the lofty-great, clear-landed, contentious, precipitate, loud-roaring, headstrong, rapid, salmon-ful, sea-monster-ful, varying, in-large-fish-abounding, rapid-flooded, furious-steamed, whirling, in-seal-abounding, royal and prosperous cataract of Eas Ruaidh [Assaroe] (O'Donovan 1842, 105).

Illus. 1.2—The Aodh Ruadh Bridge, which was built over the River Erne in 2005 as part of the N15 Bypass, illuminated at night (Transport Infrastructure Ireland).

The falls were again recorded as a source of wonder by the Dutch traveller Richard Twiss in his book, *A Tour in Ireland in 1775*, in which he described the Assaroe Falls as the 'principal salmon-leap' in the country (Twiss 1776, 90). It was just upstream from these majestic falls, adjacent to the ford of Áth Seanaigh, that the community of Ballyhanna buried their dead over a period of almost 1,000 years. The ford and the renowned Assaroe Falls (see Text box on page 5) are now gone, due to the construction of a hydro–electric power station and dam in the 1940s.

The River Erne at Ballyshannon

The 120 km-long River Erne (Abhainn na hÉirne) rises in County Cavan and flows through Lough Gowna, Lough Oughter and Upper and Lower Lough Erne in County Fermanagh, on through the town of Belleek from which point it falls 46 m over a distance of 7 km to the estuary at Ballyshannon. In the 1940s these falling western reaches of the Erne were transformed by a hydro-electric power station that dramatically changed the river landscape, removing all of its prominent physical features (Illus. 1.3). The works involved in the River Erne Hydro-Electric Scheme included the following: a dam including a fish pass across the River Erne at Cathleen's Falls; a protection embankment on the south bank of the river; a generating station near the downstream toe of the dam at Cathleen's Falls; a tail-race in the bed of the River Erne extending from the site of the power station at Cathleen's Falls to the tidal estuary immediately below the Assaroe Falls (Illus. 1.4); and diversion of the flow of the Erne into this tail-race (Statutory Instrument No. 86/1945: River Erne Hydro-Electric Scheme Approval Order, 1945 [signed into law 27 April 1945]). The power station known as

Illus. 1.3—Hydro-electricity scheme construction works in the late 1940s taken from the station at Cathleen's Falls. The Ballyhanna church site is at the bottom left of the photo marked by the large trees (Liam Thomas, ESB Ballyshannon).

Illus. 1.4—Photograph of Assaroe Falls taken by Robert Welch in the early 20th century (BELUM.Y.W.04.05.2, © National Museums Northern Ireland Collection Ulster Museum).

Illus. 1.5—Aerial photograph of Cathleen's Falls power station and the narrow tail-race at Ballyshannon in 2005. The burial ground at Ballyhanna is marked with an arrow (Ordnance Survey Ireland).

Cathleen's Falls became operational in 1951. Illustration 1.5 is an aerial photograph from 2005 which shows the reservoir and the narrow tail-race that was constructed in the 1950s.

The ford of Áth Seanaidh

The fording point from which Ballyshannon gets its name—Béal Átha Seanaidh—was a key objective in all military incursions into Tír Conaill from the south. According to legend, the ford gets its name from the victim of one such encounter, when in the fifth century AD, Conaill Gulban, the son of Niall Noígiallach, defeated the Ulaidh led by Cana. During the battle, Seannach, son of Cana, was beheaded at the ford (Cana was also killed) and it was thereafter named Áth Seanaigh in his memory (Begley 2009, 14). In 1423 Niall Garbh Ó Domnaill built his castle at the ford on the northern bank of the River Erne, thereby controlling the passageway into Tír Conaill (ibid., 48).

A lost church

There was no trace of the archaeological site at Ballyhanna prior to its discovery in 2003 and it was not marked on any of the early maps of the area. The burial ground had been used for over 1,000 years and it is reasonable to ask how the site, located on the outskirts of a town and next to the high-profile fording point across the River Erne, had become lost from local memory.

In the 1870s the historian Hugh Allingham, a native of Ballyshannon, discovered a reference to a church located in Ballyhanna townland in the parish of Inishmacsaint in an audit of Church lands undertaken by a Crown Commission at Lifford on 12 September 1609:

> They also saie that in the said parish (of Enishmissaugh) [Inishmacsaint] is a chapple of ease, called Ffennoare [Finner] in Macginey, unto which said chapple the viccar of the said parish is to send a curate to saie divine service; and that in the said parish also is another chapple called Ballihanny [Ballyhanna] (Allingham 1879, 74).

Allingham noted that the reference in the audit was 'probably identical with the ruined church at Sminver[2], near to the railway station at Ballyshannon'. He clarified that: 'Though Sminver [church] is not in the townland of Ballyhanna, it is contiguous to it, and some confusion in the boundary lines may have been made when the inquisition was taken' (ibid.). Seventy years later, Father Ó Gallachair, the eminent Clogher historian, resumed Allingham's search for a church at Ballyhanna during the construction works undertaken for the River Erne Hydro-Electric Scheme. Father Ó Gallachair was confident that the ruined church had not been submerged or uncovered during the construction and, as he also noted no physical trace of a church in the townland of Ballyhanna, he agreed with Allingham's theory that the inquisition must have been mistaken in the townland name

---

2   Sminver Church; RMP DG107-058.

(Ó Gallachair 1961, 35). It should be noted that while Ballyhanna lies in the parish of Inishmacsaint, the townland of Sminver lies in Kilbarron parish—this should have cast doubt in the minds of both scholars.

Almost found—19th- and 20th-century discoveries at Ballyhanna

Local historian Anthony Begley has discovered that burials were uncovered on at least three separate occasions over the course of the last 150 years, beneath the roads bordering the site. These finds, however, never led to the discovery of the graveyard (Begley 2009, 470). In the 1870s, during the laying of gas pipes, skeletons were uncovered at the junction of East Port and Station Roads. Skeletons were unearthed once again around 1900 when water pipes were being laid to service the nearby Great Northern Railway Station, as reported locally. Further pipe-laying and road works during the 1950s resulted in the discovery of more human skeletal remains underneath the adjacent roads and, despite being handed into the police authorities, the discovery did not lead to the site becoming recognised, either locally or officially within the archaeological record (ibid., 471). Finally, during the excavations of 2003 and 2004, paving slabs, last laid it is believed in the 1970s, were removed from the footpath to the north of the site directly beneath which lay the remains of human skeletons. It is inconceivable that the skeletons would not have been seen when the footpath was laid but the discovery of human remains, for whatever reason, was never officially registered and the site remained unrecognised. To uncover the mystery of why the graveyard was forgotten in the first place we have to return to 17th-century Ballyhanna.

Ballyhanna after the burials

Ballyhanna probably ceased to be used as a burial ground sometime in the first decades of the 17th century. Throughout the preceding medieval period Ballyhanna was in the parish of Inishmacsaint in the Roman Catholic diocese of Clogher. The diocese was Roman Catholic until AD 1542 when the then Bishop of Clogher, Hugh O'Carolan, renounced his papal appointment, was reappointed as Bishop of Clogher in the Church of Ireland under King Henry VIII and the diocese changed from being Roman Catholic to Church of Ireland. In essence the change did not alter the old Gaelic system of Church administration in Clogher; it is unlikely that the Protestant Bishop of Clogher had genuine power in Gaelic Ulster until after the Nine Years War (1594–1603). In 1605 George Montgomery was appointed Protestant Bishop of Clogher. He had been sent to Ireland to make a survey of the Church lands of Ulster and to provide recommendations to King James I as to how the Roman Catholic Church in Ulster might be transformed into a Protestant establishment (Jefferies 1999, 127). One of the key policies that Montgomery recommended to James I was that all Church lands, and former Church lands, be granted to the bishops of the Church of Ireland (ibid., 128) and his policy, when implemented, effectively ended the old Gaelic system of Church administration.

Following their defeat in the Nine Years War the Gaelic lords of Ulster and their followers fled Ireland for the Continent in 1607. The Ó Domnaill castle and much of the lands surrounding Ballyshannon were granted to Sir Henry Ffolliott, who in 1620 became the first Baron of Ballyshannon (Begley 2009, 85), but the Civil Survey of 1654 records that the land at 'Ballihanna' was still in the hands of the Bishop of Clogher and that it had been rented to 'Martin Arstall Scottish Prottestantt' (Simington 1937, 66). Sir Henry was succeeded by his son Thomas Ffolliott (AD 1613–

96) who, in addition to holding the peerage for Ballyshannon, was also the Governor of Derry. In 1646 grants were provided to Thomas Ffolliott so that the castle at Ballyshannon could be fortified. His son Henry Ffolliott, who was later to become the third Baron of Ballyshannon, held the town of Ballyshannon for William of Orange against Patrick Sarsfield and his Jacobite army in 1689. Henry died in 1716 without surviving issue and the peerage title became extinct (Begley 2009, 86–7).

In 1718 William Conolly—the Ballyshannon-born Speaker of the Irish House of Commons and the reputed richest man in Ireland at the time—purchased the Ffolliott estate for a sum of £52,000 (ibid., 99), and by the 19th century the old graveyard and church site of Ballyhanna had become subsumed within the grounds of Rockville House (Illus. 1.6).

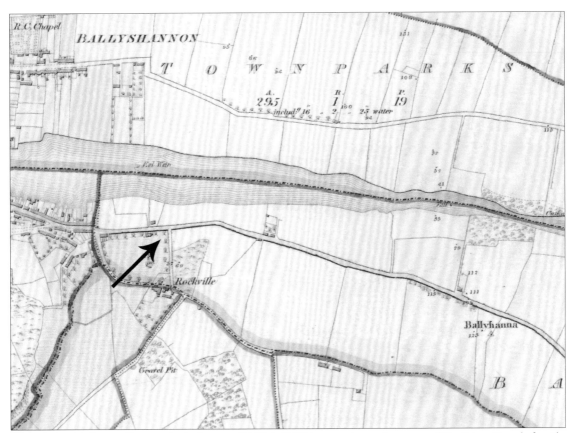

Illus. 1.6—Ordnance Survey six-inch map of 1834–5. This map shows the course of the River Erne before the construction works undertaken as part of the River Erne Hydro-Electric Scheme and the location of Rockville House. The graveyard at Ballyhanna, within the grounds of Rockville House, is marked with an arrow (Ordnance Survey Ireland).

Rockville House is depicted on the first-edition (1834–5) six-inch Ordnance Survey map, but there is no indication of the church on the map, nor on the subsequent 1900 version (Illus. 1.7). Begley (2011, 19) suggests that the family of Dr T W Crawford, surgeon of the Donegal Regiment, were perhaps the first residents of Rockville House. In 1824 Dr Crawford is listed as residing at Main Street, Ballyshannon, however, his daughter, who died in 1833, has 'Rockville' inscribed on her

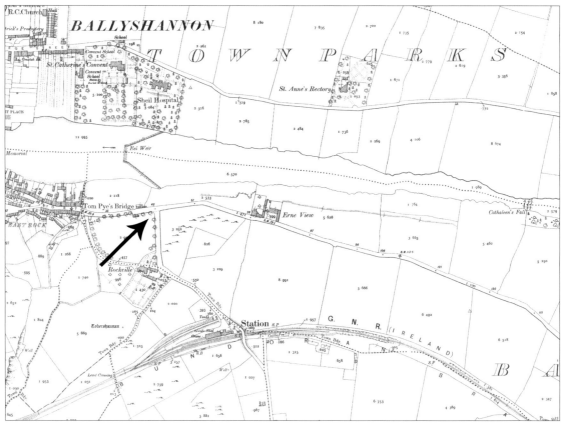

Illus. 1.7—Ordnance Survey 25-inch map of 1900. The burial ground at Ballyhanna is marked with an arrow (Ordnance Survey Ireland).

gravestone suggesting that Rockville House was built between 1824 and 1833 (ibid., 214). The first residents of Rockville would have set about walling their grounds, as was the custom for big houses, creating their own world, secure and separate from that outside the grounds. The old graveyard and ruined church, where people were laid to rest no more than two centuries earlier, would have been incorporated within the new estate.

It is not known for certain whether any trace of the church and burials survived at the time that Martin Arstall was the bishop's tenant at Ballyhanna in the mid 17th century or when Rockville House was built in the 19th century, but the archaeological evidence obtained during the excavation and radiocarbon dating suggests that burial had ended in the graveyard after the first two decades of the 17th century. We do not know if the church was levelled deliberately or if its decline was more gradual but graveyards are seldom lost through progressive degeneration and a measure of deliberate levelling probably played a role in erasing Ballyhanna from local memory, especially given that in the early modern period the destruction of old churches and graveyards was not an uncommon occurrence (see Text box on page 11).

Graveyard discoveries on road developments

The discovery of an unrecorded graveyard at Ballyhanna is only one example of such a site found on recent road projects. Ballykilmore on the N6 Kinnegad–Kilbeggan road scheme, Johnstown on the M4 Kinnegad–Kilcock road scheme and Mullagh on the N5 Longford Bypass are some further examples of formal medieval burial grounds and/or church sites discovered on road schemes. The following text arose from Mullagh in Longford, which was the location of a small, late 14th-century burial ground.

The death of a graveyard

When people read about the excavation of a previously unknown historic burial ground, they often find it difficult to fathom how so central a place in the life of a community could dissolve away into the landscape, lost from local memory until rediscovered, by chance, centuries later. The loss of so many people from the countryside through death and emigration during the Famine and later through urbanisation is most likely the chief cause of such deficits in local folkloric knowledge. Of course, the redistribution of Catholic land confiscated during the plantations of the 16th and 17th centuries will also have had an impact.

In *Historical Notes and Stories of the County Longford*, published in 1886, James P Farrell records the destruction of Kilbreeda graveyard at Corteen in Mullolagher townland, c. 1.5 km south-west of Mullagh. Writing of one of the first members of the Levinge family to live there, Farrell states that he was a man of 'eccentric disposition, violent temper, and uncertain habits'. Kilbreeda graveyard was located at one end of his farm and shortly after taking possession of the lands from the Kennedys of Mullagh House, Mr Levinge forbade interments there. Farrell documents what reputedly followed:

> … the next spring he set horses and plough to work, and, having tilled the graveyard, sowed a large crop of oats in it. In the course of the cultivation he dug up headstones, bones, skulls, and pieces of coffins; but, disregarding the awful sacrilege he was committing—a sacrilege regarded with more than horror by all his Catholic neighbours—he persisted in cultivating the piece of land, until he left it down in grass again, leaving, as the only memento of Kilbreeda Graveyard, a few old stones, which now lie in the ditch that once bounded the cemetery.

Undoubtedly, this was a terrible loss, but more was to follow. His successor 'took another queer notion, which was to level all the existing forts and till their interior level portions'.

Michael Stanley, TII Archaeologist (first printed in *Seanda*, Issue 5, 2010)

Once abandoned, soil was gradually washed down the hillslope by decades of rainfall so that it slowly covered the site. Rubble from the abandoned church and perhaps also stone grave slabs (Illus. 1.8) may have been re-used in the construction of the estate wall, if not also of the house itself—a lintel stone used in the now remodelled old estate wall hints at having come from a grander structure—

Illus. 1.8—Early 19th-century view of Ballyshannon looking north-west along the River Erne to the town (Hall & Hall 1841). This is of a view from the approximate area of the Ballyhanna site.

further reducing any visible markers of the site. If anything was left to see of the site by that time, it would have lain inaccessible within the cocooned grounds of the big house, out of sight. Local memory of the church, and of the tradition of burial at that place, would have then further faded out of mind. This communal memory loss of such an obviously important site would undoubtedly have been compounded by emigration in the centuries after it fell out of use, and in the mid 19th-century famines that impacted greatly on Ballyshannon and the region. It is likely that the last folk memory of the site was swept away at that time, down the Erne and across oceans or into mass Famine graves.

The Ballyhanna Research Project

The BRP was established by the NRA in 2005 following completion of the excavation. The project was a cross-border research collaboration between Queen's University Belfast (QUB) and the Institute of Technology, Sligo (ITS), and was funded through Donegal County Council. The research partners were selected for their expertise in osteoarchaeological research and applied science. The principal aim of the BRP was to examine the human skeletal assemblage using techniques developed in osteoarchaeology, biomolecular science and analytical chemistry to learn about the people buried in the medieval cemetery. It was recognised by the founding project members that this multidisciplinary approach to the study of the human skeletal collection had the potential to reveal exciting new insights into medieval Ballyhanna and, by extension, to add significantly to our knowledge of medieval Gaelic Ulster. The various research elements were explored through the creation of three fully funded doctoral research projects and further sub-projects.

The support of the National Museum of Ireland has been critical to the development and progress of the project. As custodians of our excavated heritage, the National Museum of Ireland is responsible for ensuring that all scientific research undertaken on archaeological material is of importance and will add significantly to our knowledge of the past. When working with human skeletal remains ethical codes of conduct are of particular importance and are strictly adhered to.

The BRP has, from the outset, recognised the importance of making the results of the research accessible to the local community in Ballyshannon and the wider general public through lectures, articles and interviews (see Appendix 3). As part of the archaeological profession it is particularly important to respect local interest and concerns, especially when working with ancestral human remains. The individuals buried at Ballyhanna are very important indeed to the story of medieval Gaelic Ulster, but the site and the people who were buried there are of particular importance to the local community of Ballyshannon. The people of Ballyshannon, through their support, interest and involvement, have greatly contributed to the work which has been undertaken as part of the BRP.

Layout of this publication

The Science of a Lost Medieval Gaelic Graveyard: the Ballyhanna Research Project presents the results of multidisciplinary research undertaken as part of the BRP. This chapter, Chapter 1, has provided an overview of the rediscovery of the Ballyhanna site and has outlined its history since it fell into disuse.

Chapter 2 places the discovery of the Ballyhanna burial ground within its broader historical and archaeological context, weaving the site into the medieval Gaelic story of Ballyshannon. This chapter explores what it would have been like to live in medieval Ballyhanna. The social hierarchy of medieval Donegal is discussed, including the evidence for housing, settlement, trade, economy, diet and warfare.

Chapter 3 explores the archaeology of the Ballyhanna graveyard. An extensive radiocarbon dating programme was undertaken at QUB to assist in unravelling the stratigraphy and chronology of the burial sequence and the results of this are discussed. This chapter will therefore outline the development of the graveyard over the course of the 1,000 years during which people were laid to rest there.

The remains of 869 adults were recovered from Ballyhanna and Chapter 4 explores adult health, disease and trauma within the community. The results of this research provide significant insights into the lifestyles and diet of the medieval Gaelic community.

Chapter 5 details the results of the osteoarchaeological analysis of the juveniles buried at Ballyhanna. A large number of individuals aged less than 18 years were buried in the graveyard, as would be expected for a communal burial ground of the time. The results of this analysis have provided important information concerning child mortality and the health concerns of these medieval children who would have been exposed to life-threatening diseases such as rickets and tuberculosis.

Ballyhanna was used as a place for burial for over 1,000 years and, during this long period of use, the digging of new graves often disturbed older burials. This process caused a large amount of bone to become disarticulated from its original burial context. Chapter 6 provides an insight into the importance of studying disarticulated human remains and highlights two cases studies of pathological bone which are particularly unusual.

The extraction and amplification of ancient human DNA (aDNA) is a relatively new science, fraught with methodological complexities. Chapter 7 outlines the extraction and amplification of aDNA from the Ballyhanna skeletons. The researchers' work, which initially focused on the determination of the sex of the children from Ballyhanna using aDNA, has developed and they explain the importance of aDNA analysis for the detection of genetic conditions and diseases in the past.

Chapter 8 reveals the value of including analytical chemistry in the study of human skeletal remains through the examination of trace elements and stable isotopes. By exploring the chemistry of the bones it is possible to learn about the burial environment and medieval diet.

Finally, Chapter 9 summarises the results of the various strands of research carried out by the BRP and provides an overview of how this work has advanced our knowledge of medieval Ballyhanna and, in particular, its people.

Appendix 1 provides details of all radiocarbon dates obtained from the burials. Appendix 2 provides a review of the conservation of the church foundations and the creation of the Ballyhanna Church Heritage Park. Appendix 3 presents the various means that were used to communicate the results of the research to the local community and to the wider archaeological profession—a commitment that has underpinned the project's foundation and which all involved are proud to have delivered, *The Science of a Lost Medieval Gaelic Graveyard: the Ballyhanna Research Project* being the latest fulfilment of that promise. Appendix 4 provides summary details of other archaeological discoveries made along the route of the N15 Bundoran–Ballyshannon Bypass.

The lead-in to each section of the book features an illustration of human remains. The rationale behind this was to achieve a number of interlinking objectives. First, there was a desire by the team to focus on selected members of the community and allow their bodies—as revealed during the excavation—to tell the modern reader something about their individual lives, their state of health, and how they came to be buried in the graveyard; in essence, the artistic rendition would act as a memorial for a person who has no other means to commemorate their very existence. It was also considered that the use of inked line-drawings as the medium through which this information would be communicated would make a much deeper impact on the reader than the use of photographs; the latter has the potential to elicit only a shallow response from the reader while the impact of the former can have a more profound effect. The line-drawings also provide the modern reader with a reconnect to the medieval tradition—as seen with the early 16th-century graveslabs in St Peter's churchyard in Drogheda and St Brigid's churchyard in the grounds of Beaulieu (Bewley) House, County Louth (Roe 1969; Tait 2002, 32)—of the use of the skeleton as an allegory of death and a reminder to all of the fragility of life. In composite, the illustrations also remind us of our own need as students of the past to find the art in our science.

2

BALLYSHANNON AND BALLYHANNA DURING THE MEDIEVAL PERIOD

Colm J Donnelly

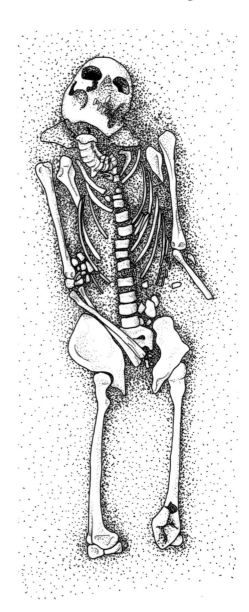

Stylised depiction of a young adult of indeterminable sex, with evidence of degenerative disc disease and trauma of the vertebral column (SK 146) (Sapphire Mussen).

An extensive programme of radiocarbon dating revealed that the earliest interments within the graveyard at Ballyhanna had taken place from the late seventh century to early eighth century AD and that burial had continued at the site until the early 17th century (see Macdonald & Carver, this volume). As such, the skeletons buried within the graveyard belonged to the medieval period and the excavation of this large population from north-west Ireland is of obvious importance to osteoarchaeologists. Contextual information, however, is essential if we are to allow this new data to further our understanding of what life was like for the people who lived here in the medieval period. Who were these people? What was the political landscape in which they lived? How was their society and economy organised? The following chapter seeks to provide answers to questions such as these.

Located on the southern side of the River Erne, the modern townland of Ballyhanna comprises just over 221 acres and is located in the barony of Tirhugh and the Civil Parish of Inishmacsaint (Donnelly 1861, 85). In the medieval period, however, on each side of the Erne waterway was historic Tír Aodha, 'the territory of Hugh', and the origin of the name of the barony—Tirhugh—that encompasses modern south Donegal. The southern section of this territory was Mag nÉne, which extends down to the River Bundrowes and Lough Melvin. The place-names associated with the Ballyshannon region indicate the antiquity of this location as a crossing point over the River Erne; Ballyshannon (Béal Átha Seanaidh) is 'The Mouth of Seannach's Ford', with Seannach, the person in question, a warrior who was slain here by Conaill Gulban, the son of Niall Noígiallach, and the subsequent progenitor of the Cenél Conaill (The People of Conaill), during a battle at the ford between forces from Ulster and those of Connacht (Begley 2009, 14). Another important place-name in our story is Assaroe, which derives from the Irish name Es Áeda Ruaid, which translates as 'Red Hugh's Cataract', with the word cataract in this context referring to a large and powerful waterfall that existed on the River Erne and is marked on the Ordnance Survey first-edition six-inch map sheet from the 1830s. Early Irish legend informs us that the Red Hugh in question was Aodh Ruadh mac Badhuirn who died AD 598 and was the eponymous ancestor of the Cenél nAeda, and who gave his name to the region Tír Aodha (Ó Canann 1986, 24). Aodh was supposed to have drowned at this point in the River Erne and legend had it that he was subsequently buried at Mullaghnashee (Mullach na Sidhe, 'The Summit of the Fairies'), a hill to the north of the town of Ballyshannon where St Anne's Church was constructed in the early 17th century (Father Colmcille 1959, 112; Begley 2009, 129), 'But of the regal grave, nothing now remains to mark the spot where the old king sleeps, the last vestige of the mound on Mullaghnashee having been, it is said, obliterated in 1798, when a star fort was constructed on the hill top, hence the spot is now called *Fort-hill*' (Allingham 1879, 18).

Writing in 1973 Professor Donnchadh Ó Corráin (1973, 64–6) remarked on how in medieval Gaelic society the border between two adjoining territories tended to be the focal point for religious sanctuaries, assembly places, the residences of kings, lords and the learned classes, military mobilisations, commerce, highways and battle sites. This was certainly the case with regards to the Erne waterway and Ballyshannon throughout the period we are concerned with, and all the more accentuated by the fact that this was the location of three fording points across the river. Writing in 1834 during his travels on behalf of the Ordnance Survey in Dublin, the great antiquarian and historian John O'Donovan related how he had visited these fording points during his trip to Ballyshannon: 'These are Ath Culuain, Caol Uisge (Narrow Water) and Ballyshannon. The first retains its name yet and is situated about a mile west of Belleek; the second is now called Coradh Caoil, or the weir of Narrow Water, from a fishing weir placed across the ford. The third is at the bridge of Ballyshannon' (Cunningham 1993, 40–1). That this was a routeway into north-west Ulster in the early medieval period can be judged from entries in the annals such as that recorded for AD 1100 when an army led by Muirchertach Ua Briain was stopped at the ford by the Cenél Conaill (O'Donovan 1856, ii, 965).

Ballyshannon in the early medieval period

Mag nÉne ('The Plain of Ene') was the southern approach to Ballyshannon, and represented a contested landscape located between the River Erne and the River Drowes: 'From Bundrowes to Belleek Bridge and from Lough Melvin to the mouth of the Erne has been known for untold centuries as Mag nÉne or Magh Eine' (Ó Gallachair 1961, 1). At the dawn of the historic period this land was held by the Cenél Cairpre Tuatha Ratha who were located between the Owenmore River in County Sligo and the Erne. It is probable that in the late sixth century the Cenél Cairpre Tuatha Ratha had crossed the Erne into what is now south Donegal and the Barony of Tír Aodha, and would remain to the north of this natural boundary, 'as far north as the church at Ráith Cungi (Racoo, in the modern townland of Ballymagrorty Scotch), until perhaps around 640' (Lacey 2003, 80). During the ninth century, however, the Cenél Conaill had evidently pushed the Cenél Cairpre back southwards across the Erne and into Mag nÉne, the Cenél Conaill then establishing a stronghold at Ard Fothid, probably located at Glasbolie Hill (Ó Canann 1986, 25). Further expansionism by the Cenél Conaill witnessed Mag nÉne become their territory and by the 12th century the Cenél Cairpre Tuath Ratha—now under the leadership of the Ó Flannagáin lineage— had been pushed to the east of Belleek in territory that today is the barony of Magheraboy in modern County Fermanagh, with their main centre at Carrick Lough where they had a fine stone church, constructed around AD 1400, located on a limestone cliff-edge overlooking the lough and its crannog. This evidently was a cause of resentment for the Cenél Cairpre Tuath Ratha, however, and in 1278 their claim to the territory was recorded in the *Register of Clogher*, where Gilbert Ó Flannagáin, their taoiseach (leader), sworn as a witness, stated that Mag nÉne had been part of his lands but that it was occupied by the Ó Domnaills during their conflict with the Anglo-Normans (Nicholls 1971–2, 397). The controversy evidently continued down to the 15th century when a poem by the little-known poet Giolla Íosa Ó Sléibhin asked the rhetorical question of who had the best right to the Assaroe Falls and the Erne estuary. The poet concludes that it rightly belongs to his own patron, Aodh an Einigh Mág Uidhir, tánaiste (heir of the taoiseach) of Fir Manach, 'but he admits that in his own time the area was a hotly disputed battleground between Connacht and Tír Conaill' (Simms 1995, 185). Be that as it may, the area between the Drowes and the Erne would remain in Cenél Conaill hands until the early years of the 17th century (Ó Gallachair 1961, 6).

Until the 13th century the terms Cenél nAeda and Cenél Conaill were interchangeable, since the kings of Cenél nAeda—both Ua Canannáin and Ua Maíl Doraid—were always the overkings of the Cenél Conaill (Ó Canann 1986, 24). The common ancestor of both lineages was Flaithbertach mac Loingsig, King of the Northern Uí Néill and High King of Ireland from AD 728 to 734, and who died in 767. From his two sons—Aodh Muinderg and Murchad—came the two lineages: Aodh Muinderg's great-grandson was Canannáin and Murchad's great-grandson was Máel Doraid. Until the eighth century the Cenél nEógain and the Cenél Conaill exchanged rulership of the Northern Uí Néill, until Aodh of the Cenél nEógain defeated Flaithbertach in 732, 733 and 734, with the latter then retiring to a religious life; Flaithbertach was to be the last of the Cenél Conaill who would be High King of Ireland. His son Aodh Muinderg fought against the Cenél nEógain, as did his grandson Domnall who became King of the Northern Uí Néill but he was defeated in 787 by Máel Dun of the Cenél nEógain. When Máel Dun died in 788, Domnall then took on the kingship again, but was defeated in 789 and from then onwards the Cenél nEógain was the sole lineage that produced kings of the Northern Uí Néill (Hogan 1931–2, 202). Within the Cenél Conaill there would now be difficulties, and by the early ninth century the descendants of the last Cenél Conaill king of Tara, Flaithbertach mac Loingsig, had split into two permanently warring factions. The stronger of the two lineages was the Ua Canannáin who had 22 kings of Tír Conaill between the years 941 and 1250 (Ó Canann 2003, 36–7). It would seem, however, that the division between the two lineages had become reflected on the landscape by the 10th century when a point was reached where they would each have their own designated centres of operation and associated inauguration sites (Illus. 2.1). In the case of the Ua Maíl Doraid this would be at the Leac Uí Mhaíl Doraid, located at a cataract on the River Erne near modern Belleek, and their main centre of operation was within the southern territory of Mag nÉne. The Ua Canannáin had their ceremonial centre at Carraig an Dúnáin, or Doonan Rock, outside modern Donegal town (ibid.), within the northern territory of Mag Sereth, and with their main settlement at Ráith Canannáin; the exact location of this site is now unknown but was 'most likely situated atop one of the many glacial drifts that still overlook the River Eske estuary' (ibid., 52). The middle tuath (political territory)—Es Ruaid, containing Ballyshannon—belonged to the lineage 'who held the overkingship of Cenél Conaill at any given time' (Ó Canann 1986, 37).

English state papers of the early 17th century noted that Tír Aodha was very fertile land, especially around Donegal and Ballyshannon (ibid., 30). Some 1,000 years previously it had evidently been just as fertile if the concentration of ringforts on the landscape is to be used as a gauge. There are approximately 250 ringforts in the modern county of Donegal, but there is a strong concentration in Tír Aodha (Lacey 1995, 7, fig. 1.3). Barrett (1980, 44), for example, identified some 40 ringfort sites to the south of the Erne estuary and River Erne. This corpus includes five examples in the townland of Finner, four examples in Ballymunterhiggin, two in Dunmuckrim, and individual examples in Cherrymount, Drumnagroagh and Raheen (Lacy 1983, 160–87). The last named site, however, is of particular note since the monument does not conform to the typical morphology of a ringfort, and can best be considered as a multivallate earthwork enclosure. Evidently a significant monument, the site overlooks Assaroe Lake and is situated on the roadside of the N3 on the outskirts of Ballyshannon. This road follows the cut of the 19th-century railway line leading into the town and was constructed to replace the old road that was submerged by the hydro-electric scheme in 1946: 'It is situated just above the high water of the Erne Dam but would originally have stood on the high ground just south of the river' (ibid., 187). Now overgrown, our best account of the monument is to be found in Oliver Davies' survey conducted in 1946 (Corlett 2006, 58–9) and which noted that the earthwork crowned a small hill 'and appears to have consisted of five banks and four fosses, with a total diameter of approximately 280 feet', and with a souterrain located immediately inside the innermost bank on the south-west side. A plan and profiles of the complex earthwork and a small D-shaped enclosure were prepared by Davies to accompany his account of the

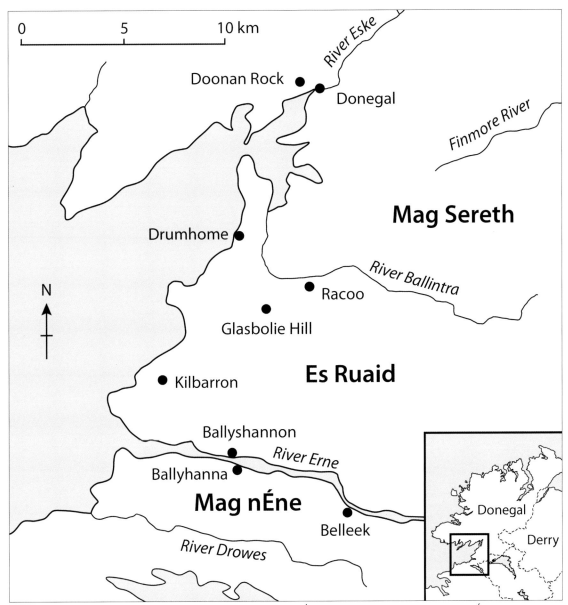

Illus. 2.1—Map of medieval Tír Aodha (Tirhugh) (after Ó Canann 2003, 53, fig. 3, and Ó Canann 2004, 42, fig. 2, redrawn by Libby Mulqueeny, QUB).

monument. The sequence of features can best be recorded on the north, south and west sides of the monument as depicted in Davies' plan, now redrawn and annotated as Illustration 2.2 in the current study. The interior space (a) is surrounded by a double bank (b and d) and berm (c) arrangement, with a second berm (e) defined by an outer ditch (f). This ditch has a further berm (g) or—possibly, given the surviving evidence to the east of the monument—a bank. A second ditch (h) and a final exterior bank (i) make up the remainder of the earthwork sequence which comprises, in total, three banks (b, d and i), three berms (c, e and g) and two ditches (f and h). This is not a typical ringfort, and

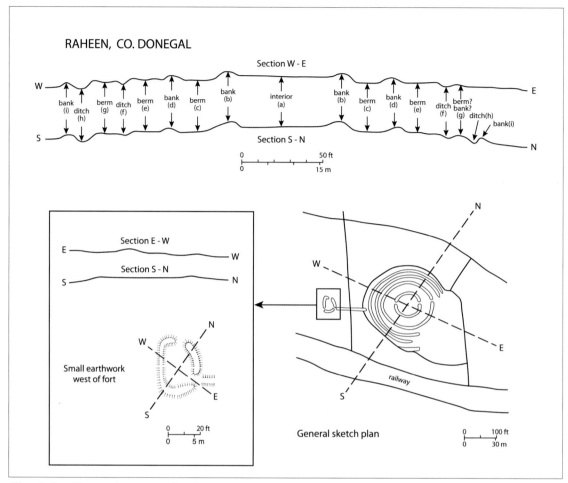

Illus. 2.2—Plan and sections of Raheen Fort, Co. Donegal, based on Oliver Davies' survey of 1946 (after Corlett 2006, fig. 13, redrawn by Libby Mulqueeny, QUB).

it is certainly not a small multivallate ringfort of unknown diameter, as classified by Barrett (1980, 45). It is probable that the name 'raheen' derives from ráithín, 'little fort'. If, however, the stress on the pronunciation were to rest on the '-een' element of the place-name then it is also possible that this fort was named Ráith Éne, 'the fort of Éne' (K Muhr, pers. comm.), perhaps thereby signifying that the site was of prominence in the early medieval political geography of Mag nÉne. It is known that inauguration sites were located close to political boundaries; could this have been an inauguration site associated with the Cenél Cairpre Tuath Ratha? Such knowledge might explain the evident bitterness concerning its loss that existed among their descendants, the Ó Flannagáins of Tuath Ratha, well into the 13th century, as expressed in the *Register of Clogher* (Nicholls 1971–2, 397).

The chief church of the Cenél nAeda dynasts, both Ua Canannáin and Ua Maíl Doraid, was undoubtedly Druim Tuama (Drumhome) which lay close to the Mag Sereth tuath of the Muintir Chanannáin, but its location to the west side of the River Ballintra (which appears to have been the divide between Es Ruaid and Mag Sereth) places it within Es Ruaid, the middle tuath. Given this, it would not be surprising that both of the leading lineages of the Cenél nAeda at this time would have made use of the church, given its location in the tuath that was held by whichever of the two lineages had overlordship of Cenél Conaill. As Ó Canann (1986, 38) has noted, it would not be 'unusual for two families to lay claim to a single church, especially when the two families were from the same dynasty', and he then drew a parallel with the founding of the Cistercian Abbey at Assaroe in 1178 by Ruaidrí Ua Canannáin and the confirmation of that grant by his successor Flaitbheartach Ua Maíl Doraid in 1184 (ibid.). The Cistercians were a Continental religious order whose presence in Ireland is connected with the reform movement within the Church that was being played out in Ireland during the course of the 12th century. This was a process that was underway before the arrival of the first wave of Anglo-Normans in 1169, and the first Cistercian house had been established at Mellifont, Co. Louth, in 1142. In addition to the introduction of new religious orders, however, the reforms also led to the establishment of a diocesan structure based within four archbishoprics (Tuam, Cashel, Dublin and Armagh) and with primacy held by Armagh. Established as a daughter-house of the Cistercian house at Boyle (Father Colmcille 1959, 118), itself settled from Mellifont in 1161, the Order's sources place the foundation date for the abbey at Assaroe as 23 November 1178 by Ruaidrí Ua Canannáin (ibid., 111); the *Annals of the Four Masters,* however, reported the foundation as 1184 and by Ua Canannáin's dynastic rival and successor 'Flaherty O'Muldory, lord of Kinel-Connell, for the good of his soul' (O'Donovan 1856, iii, 63). Whichever may be the case—and, as Father Colmcille (1959, 111) has noted, it is possible that the foundation may have begun in 1178 but was dedicated in 1184—the action resulted in an extensive land grant being made to the new abbey of lands within Mag nÉne between Ballyshannon and Belleek. Such actions should be seen as a means of both or either secular ruler ingratiating themselves with the reforming elements of the Church and thereby receiving clerical support in their political sphere. Such support would be required given that the political spectrum in Ireland had been radically altered with the arrival of the Anglo-Normans; both lineages would have been keen to portray themselves as reformers and to thereby have the Church on their side should any Anglo-Normans attempt to usurp them or infringe on their territory.

Anglo-Norman intervention and the rise of the Ó Domnaill lineage

While Flaitbheartach Ua Maíl Doraid was instrumental in bringing the Cistercians to Assaroe, it should be noted that when he died in 1197 'on Inis Saimer, on the second day of February, after long and patient suffering, in the thirtieth year of his reign, and fifty-ninth of his age', he was buried at the established dynastic religious centre at Drumhome (O'Donovan 1856, iii, 111). After his death, however, Tír Conaill was thrown into political confusion since Flaitbheartach left no heir-apparent. Likewise it would seem the Ua Canannáin lineage was not in a position to exploit this advantage (indeed, they do not feature again as leaders of Tír Conaill until 1247), for we find it is other smaller lineages within the Cenél Conaill who now put forward claimants. The Ua Dochartaigs were the first to advance their cause—a family who are only first mentioned in the annals in 1180 (Mac Giolla Easpaig 1995, 800)—but their claimant Echmarcach was killed in battle in Inishowen against the forces of the Anglo-Norman adventurer John de Courcy a fortnight after Flaitbheartach's death. This period of confusion, however, had ended by 1201 when we learn that Éicnechán Ua Domnaill was engaging in war against the Cenél nEógain (O'Donovan 1856, iii, 123).

The Ua Domnaill surname is first reported in the *Annals of the Four Masters* under the year 1010 (O'Donovan 1856, ii, 763); the lineage's name was the Clann Dalaigh, from Dalach who had died in 868, and it was from his grandson Domnaill that they derived their hereditary surname (O'Donovan 1862, xxx). They originated out of the rulers of the Cenél Lugdach in northern Tír Conaill, based at Lough Gartan in north Donegal, with their inauguration site at Kilmacrennan, and came to prominence about 1200 under Éicnechán, who ruled from 1200 to 1207. At a crucial time in the mid 13th century in Tír Conaill the Ua Domnaill (or, more appropriately, Ó Domnaill, the Classical Modern Irish form that is in use from the 13th century onwards) dynasty were particularly fortunate to have three effective leaders who held back the tide of Anglo-Norman intervention—Máel Sechlainn (1241–7), Gofraid (1248–58) and Domnall Oć (1258–81) (McGettigan 2005, 476). Their early association with Ballyshannon is suggested by the Ó Domnaill genealogies. The *Craebhscaoileadh Cloinne Dálaigh* relates how Éicnechán, the first Ó Domnaill lord of Tír Conaill, was succeeded by his son Domnall Mór, who ruled from 1207 to 1241 and who in turn had five sons; the first of these sons to rule after his father was 'Maelsechlainn [Máel Sechlainn] of Bellashanny' who ruled from 1241 to 1247 (Walsh & O Lochlainn 1957, 159). The same text further informs us that Domnall Mór had 'joined an order of grey friars at Assaroe 1241' (ibid., 159). The fact that the ruler of the Cenél Conaill would opt to end his days with the Cistercian community on the northern shore of the Erne estuary speaks volumes concerning the importance placed by the Ó Domnaill lineage by the mid 13th century on Tír Aodha in general and on the Ballyshannon region in particular. This can surely be viewed as an effort to consolidate their control of their territory by placing themselves at the heart of the lands held previously by the Ó Cannanáin and Ó Maíl Doraid lineages, with all three tuatha within Tír Aodha—Mag nÉne, Mag Sereth, and Es Ruaid—now under Ó Domnaill control and divided up into estates that were given out to their lucht tighe (supporting lineages) and learned classes.

The meeting of Brian Ó Néill, Fedlimid Ó Conchobhair and Tadg Ó Briain at Cáeluisce (the 'narrow water', on the River Erne) in 1258, and the making of Domnall Oć Ó Domnaill as king of the Cenél Conaill at that time was probably an event that was played out at the Leac Uí Mháíl Doraid, and indicates that the Ó Domnaill lineage may have inaugurated their kings at the old Uí Maíl Doraid centre of power when they took over Tír Conaill in the 13th century (Ó Canann 2003, 46). It also helps explain why the River Erne and its estuary proved such an enticing target for the Anglo-Normans in the 1240s. Not only did this offer fords that might be used to cross into Gaelic controlled Tír Conaill, but the capture of this region would enable the caput of their enemies to be taken under their control, much as John de Courcy had achieved in 1177 with his rapid advance and capture of Downpatrick from the Ulaid king, Ruaidrí Mac Duinn Sléibe. By extension, this in turn may also explain the presence of the Ó Domnaill rulers in this landscape since they needed to be a visible and strong presence to deter any such Anglo-Norman advancement. Indeed, it was in resisting an Anglo-Norman force that Máel Sechlainn was killed in 1247. The Anglo-Norman interest in pushing into Tír Conaill had commenced in 1212 with the construction of a castle at Cáeluisce near Belleek, but this was destroyed in the following year and it would not be for another 35 years that a concerted effort would be made by the Anglo-Normans to make a further attempt to invade Tír Aodha when Maurice FitzGerald (1194–1257), second Lord of Offaly and former Justiciar of Ireland, was given a speculative grant to Tír Conaill by Hugh de Lacy II. In essence this was a go-ahead for FitzGerald to carve out a lordship for himself in the Gaelic territory. Initial success in 1247 at the battle at Áth Seanaigh (in which Máel Sechlainn died) led to the construction of a new castle and the construction of a second castle at Cáeluisce followed in 1252. Attempts have been made to identify where these castles at Cáeluisce may have been located but Father Ó Gallachair (1966, 106), in his study of the location of the fortifications along the River Erne, noted that Cáeluisce did not seem to be a specific place per se, but rather the name for a district along the route of the waterway. As such, the Anglo-Norman castles could be located anywhere along this stretch of the river.

It was in the aftermath of Máel Sechlainn's death that the Ó Canannáin lineage made a brief—and final—comeback as lords of Tír Conaill. Sidelined between 1188 and 1247, FitzGerald now seems to have placed them back in power, perhaps as puppet-rulers: 'The country was then plundered and desolated by them [the English], and they left the chieftainship of the Kinel-Connell to Rory O'Canannan on this occasion' (O'Donovan 1856, iii, 323). If so, it was a short-lived arrangement since later in 1247 the Anglo-Normans returned to Ballyshannon with a force under the command of FitzGerald's son but, met by Ó Canannáin, they failed to advance any further. What is of note, however, is the fact that the Anglo-Normans had attacked 'at the desire of Godfrey O'Donnell' (ibid., 327) and that this must have marked some form of rapprochement between the Anglo-Normans and the Ó Domnaills, for in the following year, 1248, we read that FitzGerald was back harrying in Tír Conaill and that he 'banished Rory O'Canannan into Tyrone, and left the lordship of Kinel-Connell to Godfrey, the son of Donnell O'Donnell' (ibid., 329); a subsequent counter-attack by Ó Canannáin with the assistance of the Ó Neills failed and Ruaidrí was killed. His successor, Niall, seems to have gained the lordship over Ó Domnaill in 1249 but he too was subsequently killed in 1250 when, as a prisoner, he tried to escape from FitzGerald (ibid., 341); this action represented a final end to the lineage's political power and 'after that date the family of Ó Canannáin does not merit one single mention in any of the annals' (Mac Giolla Easpaig 1995, 796). Anglo-Norman efforts to force their way into Tír Aodha, however, did not come to an end until FitzGerald was killed in battle at Drumcliffe in 1257 (Ó Gallachair 1961, 6). As Katharine Simms (1987, 121) noted, the battle of 1247 was of significance since 'Mac Somurli, king of Argyle' is reported as having also been killed during the fighting; this is the first hint that we have from the sources for Gaelic lords obtaining martial help from Scotland, a major development in the war against the Anglo-Normans and one that the Ó Domnaills would subsequently exploit through marriage alliances that would bring lineages of heavily armoured warriors—the galloglass—from the western highlands and islands of Scotland to the assistance of the Tír Conaill lords. This placed a brake on further Anglo-Norman intrusion into their territories, and in Tír Conaill these galloglass would be represented by the Mac Suibhne lineages.

Medieval Tír Aodha

The Anglo-Normans remained potent, but a series of events in the first half of the 14th century conspired to undermine their position. These comprised the Bruce Wars (1315–18), which coincided with a great pan-European famine, the assassination in 1333 of William de Burgh, the fourth Earl of Ulster, and the arrival of the Black Death in 1348. Consequently, by the end of the century a new political equilibrium had been reached; Anglo-Norman (or, more appropriately, Anglo-Irish) control contracted to their heartlands around Dublin—the Pale—augmented by outlying lordships in the south of the island which were ruled by major Anglo-Irish magnates such as the earls of Kildare, Ormond and Desmond. Elsewhere, the political landscape was dominated by the Gaelic lords, and this would remain the case until the mid 16th century. Within these Gaelic regions of late medieval Ireland, political power was held by autonomous lineages, each of which was ruled by a lord who controlled the geographical territory and its people, with the overall strength of a lineage largely dependent upon the abilities of the lord, and the following and support commanded by him within his own lineage. Succession for the lordship within a lineage came from within the derbfine group, comprising the male descendants from within four generations of the previous lord, and the most suitable candidate with the largest following became the new elected lord of the lineage (O'Dowd 1986, 123; Nicholls 2003, 29). In 1333 the *Annals of Ulster* inform us that Áed Ó Domnaill died and was buried in the monastery of Assaroe, and that his son Conchobar assumed his place, but 'a dispute afterwards arose between this Conor and Art, his brother, concerning the lordship; and Art was soon killed by Conor in combat'. The reason for violent episodes such as this was the nature of the succession process itself. A successful lineage would multiply and distinct family units would emerge. However, this created tension within the derbfine for those families who had moved to the outer margin of eligibility. If they did not secure the lordship then they ran the risk of falling out of the succession and, as a consequence, they would drop down the social order, thereby incurring economic and social losses (Hogan 1931–2, 249). The dynastic struggles among the members of the derbfine could be vicious, but it should be remembered that it was among the upper echelons of society that such political assassinations took place, as indeed was the case across much of contemporary medieval Europe. As Hogan (ibid., 251) noted, the succession disputes within the aristocratic dynasties might be damaging, and the 'chief sufferers in all this were the dynasts themselves' who lived dangerous lives and often met violent deaths (ibid.), but 'behind the dynastic turmoil, which looms so largely in the annals, the people, clergy, and lower ranks of the nobility lived unchronicled but comparatively peaceful lives'. This violence was largely played out among the elite of Gaelic society but it was not about killing on a grand scale; for example, Ireland was spared the political turmoil—and associated violence—of the degree experienced by England during the 15th-century Wars of the Roses (1455–87). In addition, while Gaelic lords might hold their power by the sword, warfare was a small-scale activity and the objective was not to exterminate an enemy population and seize their lands but to force the submission of the lord of that territory in order that they—and the people who lived there—might then provide their new overlord with tributes and services. We see the political framework behind this situation in documents such as the Ceart Ui Neill, where Ó Neill lays claim to the tribute and services of all the other major lordships in Ulster, including the Ó Domnaill lineage (Ó Doibhlin 1998, 30). How enforceable this claim might be would vary over time, but in general it should be viewed as an aspiration. To make it reality would require the prosecution of a successful campaign in the Ó Domnaill territory and then it would only be binding for as long as the Ó Domnaill lordship remained in a weakened condition. The objective was to destroy crops, steal livestock and burn houses thereby forcing a submission; the Church, however, frowned heavily on attacks on women, children and clerics (Simms 1975–6, 100).

Within this political context the land under the control of the lord was normally divided up for different uses. FitzPatrick (2004, 196) has noted that there were five distinct categories of landholding within the Gaelic lordships. These are (1) the estates of the various branches of the ruling family; (2) the demesne estate attached to the lord himself, generally situated around his principal residence;

(3) the estates that formed the mensal lands that provisioned the lord's household; (4) the estates of the main freeholders; and (5) Church lands free from the lord's exactions. In medieval Gaelic society the land was divided into units on which tax could be assessed and levied by an overlord (McErlean 1983, 328). The largest of these land units was the ballybetagh (*baile biatach*, settlement of the food providers) which would be held by a kin-group or lineage. Further subdivision would see the ballybetagh divided into four quarters (*ceathramha*), with each quarter divided into four balliboes (*baile bo*, cowland). The balliboes, therefore, were the smallest territorial unit within Gaelic society. While the Plantation period witnessed the destruction of many of the ballybetaghs, their constituent elements—the balliboes—were used as the building blocks for the creation of the new Planter estates. As a consequence, the balliboes have survived to modern times in the form of our townlands.

The mensal lands of the Ó Domnaill lineage were situated in Tír Aodha (Simms 1995, 190), by far the best land in Tír Conaill (Ó Canann 1986, 30), and it was here that the lucht tighe or household families were located, as well as the learned classes—the poets, brehons (lawyers), physicians, historians and musicians—who were given grants of land in return for their professional services (Simms 1995, 195) on land that had formerly been held by both the Ua Canannáin and Ua Maíl Doraid lineages (Ó Canann 1986, 39). These included the Ó Cléirigh (historians) who held land in Kilbarron, Kildony, Creevy and Drumacrin, the Mac an Bhaird (poets) at Ballymacward and Lettermacaward, and the Ó hUiginn (also poets) at Ballymunterhiggin. That there was a strong medical tradition in Ireland is clear, with hereditary families associated with local magnates; in the case of the Ó Domnaill lineage their family of medics were the Mac Duinnshléibhe. It is evident that the medical families were well versed in European medical theories, as witnessed by the translation into Irish of medical texts from the Continent and England (Malcolm 2005, 324), but how far down the social classes these doctors practised is a moot point and it is probable that folk-medicine was practised among the poorer elements of Gaelic society. As we have seen, the Ua Maíl Doraid lineage ceased to be a ruling dynasty after 1197 and it would seem that they provided no opposition to their new Ó Domnaill rulers; indeed, it would seem that they were actually incorporated into the new order, becoming part of the Ó Domnaill lucht tighe and the guardians of the important dynastic church at Drumhome (Ó Gallachair 1960, 271). Another earlier lineage who also did not disappear were the Ó Gallachairs, hitherto relations and supporters of both the Ua Canannáin and Ua Maíl Doraid lineages, who may have transferred their claim on the Cenél Conaill throne in return for the responsibility of the inauguration of the kings of the region (Ó Canann 2004, 40). It would seem that they too now made the transition across to the new rulers of Tír Conaill and became a central supporting lineage to the Ó Domnaill lordship.

Forts, castles and ecclesiastical foundations

There are few physical remnants associated with the medieval period in the modern landscape around Ballyshannon, but we do know the general location of the castle, and a few stretches of walls remain upstanding at Assaroe Abbey. If, however, we want to gain greater insight into the region during this time our best evidence is to be found in historic English cartographic sources. Three historic maps, in particular, are worthy of individual comment for what they show relating to the Erne estuary. The first of these is the untitled map from c. 1591 by Brown and Baptiste (Illus. 2.3)

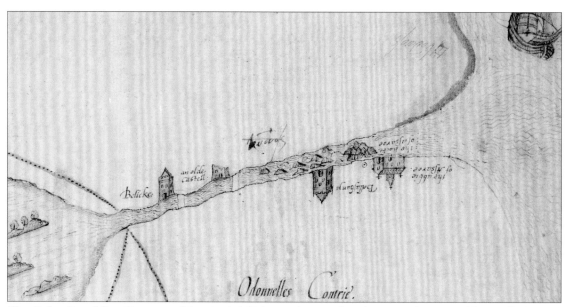

Illus. 2.3—Detail from Browne and Baptiste's 1591 map, showing their depiction of Assaroe Abbey, Ballyshannon Castle, an unnamed old castle and the castle at Belleek (© The National Archives, ref. MPF1/81).

which shows the abbey at Assaroe, the Rock of Assaroe, Ballyshannon Castle, an unnamed old castle, and the castle at Belleek. The second map is a pictorial view of the Battle of the Erne Fords on 10 October 1593 (Illus. 2.4 and 2.5) between an English force led by Henry Bagnal and Hugh O'Neill, second Earl of Tyrone, against the Maguires who were defending the ford at Beál Ath Culuain (Belacooloon). The work is that of John Thomas, an English soldier-artist responsible for this image and another that depicts the siege of Enniskillen Castle in 1594. It is an accomplished view, if lacking perspective, and shows the castles at Belleek and Ballyshannon and the abbey at Assaroe. The third map is the splendid 'A true description of the Norwest partes of Irelande' from c. 1600 (Illus. 2.6), the work 'collected and observed by Captain John Baxter. Finished by Baptista Boazio'. This view shows the Erne estuary and—as we shall see—a host of detail for the Ballyshannon area.

As we have seen earlier in this chapter, the foundation of a Cistercian house at Assaroe occurred in the late 12th century, and within the Cistercian Order this abbey was known as Samaria, an evident adaptation of Saimer, the Irish name for the River Erne, with the island on the Erne waterway at Ballyshannon named Inis Saimer (Illus. 2.7). The latter name is applied to the abbey in the annals although it is located about a mile to the west and, while it is possible that some form of religious retreat or older monastic establishment existed on the island (Father Colmcille 1959, 112), this has no definitive supporting evidence in our historical sources or archaeological record, other than statements such as that relating to Áed Ó Domnaill, who had ruled from 1281 to 1333 and who 'died, victorious over the world and the devil, in the habit of a monk, on the island of Inis-Saimer, and was interred with great honour and solemnity in the monastery of Assaroe' (O'Donovan 1856, iii, 553). It is clear in this entry that the author has made a distinction between Inis Saimer, where Ó Domnaill died, and Assaroe, the monastery where Ó Domnaill was buried. This association between the Ó Domnaill lords and Assaroe Abbey as a suitable place where they might retire to die reached back to 1241 when Domnall Mór (ruler from 1208 to 1241) 'died in the monastic habit, victorious

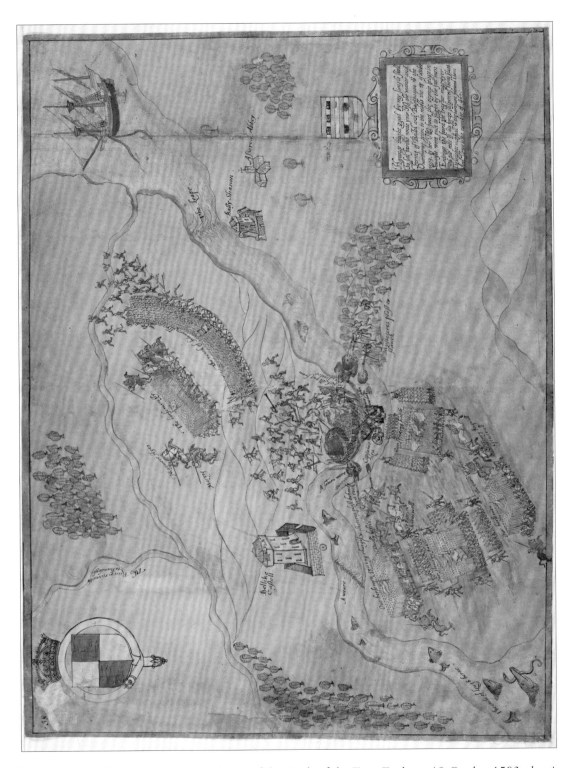

Illus. 2.4—John Thomas' 1593 pictorial map of the Battle of the Erne Fords on 10 October 1593, showing the castles at Belleek and Ballyshannon (© The British Library Board, ref. Cotton MS Augustus I.ii.38).

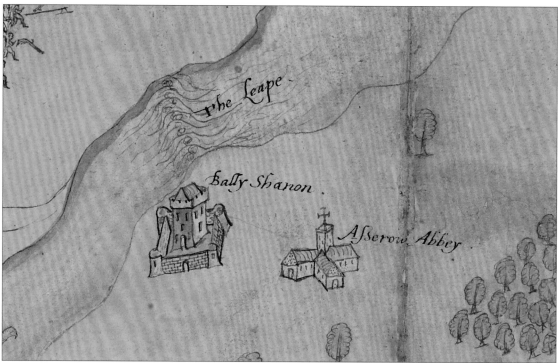

Illus. 2.5—Detail from John Thomas' 1593 pictorial map of the Battle of the Erne Fords on 10 October 1593, showing the Ó Domnaill tower house at Ballyshannon and Assaroe Abbey (© The British Library Board, ref. Cotton MS Augustus I.ii.38).

over the world and the devil, and was interred with honour and respect in the monastery of Assaroe, in the harvest time' (ibid., 303). The practice of allowing a benefactor to take on the monastic habit in their old age was common among the Irish Cistercians and was known as 'ad succurrendum' (towards salvation), when they were allowed to join the house as a member, usually in return for providing a charitable donation to the monastery in question. The last such recorded example for Assaroe Abbey was Toirdhealbhach an Fhíona (of the Wine) Ó Domnaill, who died there in 1423 (Father Colmcille 1959, 113–14).

The castle at Ballyshannon was constructed in 1423 by Toirdhealbhach's son and successor Niall Garbh, but for 200 years prior to this it would seem that one of the primary centres for the Ó Domnaill lordship was at Ráith or Dún Murbhaigh, 'The Fort of the Sea Strip' (Ó Gallachair 1958, 65). O'Donovan considered that this may have been a reference to Murvagh in the barony of Tirhugh about one mile to the west of Ballyshannon (O'Donovan 1856, iii, 417) or that it may be Murvagh in the parish of Drumhome, about three miles south-west of Donegal town (ibid., 578–9), but it is a site that is mentioned on a number of occasions in the annals. In 1272 Muiris MacDonagh 'died in Ó Donnell's garrison [longphort, or stronghold] at Murvagh' (ibid., 417), while in 1342 Conchobar Ó Domnaill, ruler from 1333 to 1342, was killed by his brother Niall (who ruled between 1342 to 1348) after the latter had 'attacked him by night in his own fortress [longphort] at Murbhach' (ibid., 579). In 1419 a force was led by Brian Ó Conchobhair Sligigh in alliance with the English and the Ó Neills into Tír Aodha destroying the 'grass, corn and buildings' from Donegal to Ballyshannon;

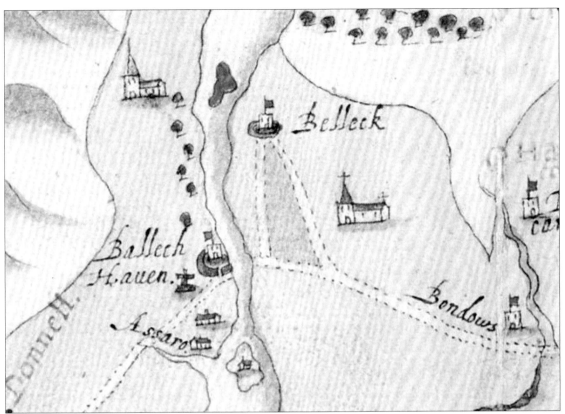

Illus. 2.6—Detail from 'A true description of the Norwest partes of Irelande' from c. 1600, the work 'collected and observed by Captain John Baxter. Finished by Baptista Boazio', showing the Erne estuary (© National Maritime Museum, Greenwich, London, ref. MS P/49 (7)).

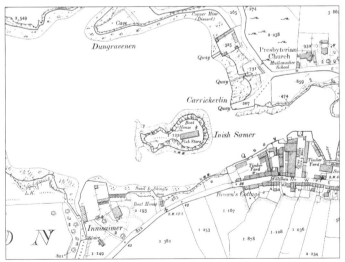

Illus. 2.7—Detail from Ordnance Survey second edition (1900) 25-inch map sheet of Ballyshannon, showing 'Inish Samer' and Dungravenen promontory fort (Ordnance Survey Ireland).

they also 'burned Murvagh, Ó Donnell's fortress [longphort]' (ibid., iv, 839). The longphort within these references to the Ó Domnaill fortress is a term that is used in the annals from 1200 to 1400 to distinguish a class of high-status sites separate from crannogs (artificial islands) and castles. O'Conor (1998, 84–5) has noted that the available evidence suggests that longphorts tended to be located on dry land rather than on islands, although there are exceptions to this, such as the Ó Flaithbeartaig longphort at Iniscreamha which was located on an island in Lough Corrib, Co. Galway, and comprised a massive circular, mortared masonry fortification surrounded by a rock-cut ditch and constructed sometime in the 11th or 12th century (FitzPatrick 2009, 276).

Father Ó Gallachair considered where the Ó Domnaill fortress might be on the modern landscape, using the contents of a bardic poem in his research. Composed by Gofraidh Fionn Ó Dálaigh, one of the leading poets of the Mac Carthaigh Mór lineage of Desmond, the poem celebrates Conchobar Ó Domnaill, who—as we have noted—was murdered in 1342 by his brother Niall at his 'fortress [longphort] at Murbhach' (O'Donovan 1856, iii, 579). Translated and published by McKenna (1919, 4–5), the poem begins by taking its audience on a journey to Tír Conaill, 'the land of the prince I admire', to 'green Magh n-Eine of the fair bright slopes', to 'Eas Ruaidh' with its boats and waters rich in trout and salmon, and to Siodh Aodha. In the poet's mind-journey evidently Mag nÉne, Assaroe and Mullaghnashee are all worthy of being name-checked, and the clear implication is that Murbhach is located in the Erne valley as well: 'In that land established is my friend Conchobhar, in his round castle his wise-guided folk, the native warriors of Conall' (ibid.). McKenna opted to translate the poet's description of Ó Domnaill's *cathair chorr* as 'round castle', but a more appropriate translation—'round fort'—is supplied by Ó Gallachair (1958, 66). O'Donovan (1856, iii, 579), in a footnote associated with the death of Conchobhar, had stated that 'Roderic O'Flaherty' had added in a margin of a copy of the *Annals of the Four Masters* in Trinity College Dublin that Conchobhar's murder had happened in his house in 'Findrois'. McKenna was evidently aware of this footnote and in his introduction to the poem he stated that Conchobhar 'was attacked in his house at Findros' which he equated to The Rosses in west Donegal. This is an unlikely location for Conchobhar's house, however, given that Ó Dálaigh has concentrated his efforts in mapping out a landscape in his poem which is clearly in the vicinity of modern Ballyshannon, and not in west Donegal. As Ó Gallachair (1958, 68) noted: 'Apparently Findrois was another name for Murvagh, cf the place-name, Finner, part of which is situated in Murvagh today, on the Erne estuary'. The place-name evidence therefore points to Murvagh as having been in the Ballyshannon region, but it is at this point that we have to ask ourselves a question: where is Inis Saimer in Ó Dálaigh's poem? Should such a famed site—the location of Partholon's home in the Book of Invasions—not be the very stuff that the poet would incorporate into his work? For Ó Gallachair, the answer is simple: the reason why there is no mention of Inis Saimer is because Ó Domnaill's longphort at Murvagh is Inis Saimer! He further amplifies this argument by noting that

> …the placename Murvagh lives on today in a strip of land along the left bank of the Erne estuary in the townlands of Finner and Dunmuckrin … Murvagh or Magh Murbhaigh [the plain of the sea-strip] was then evidently the name of the northern edge of Mag nÉne along the tidal waters of the Erne, right up to the Falls of Assaroe. Here then was the celebrated flat plain of Murvagh with its famed fort, Rath Murbhaigh, on adjacent Inis Saimer (ibid., 67).

A mid 13th-century poem by Giolla Brighde Mac Con Midhe in praise of Gofraid Ó Domnaill, who died in 1258, mentions that he had a fortress on Inis Saimer (O'Conor 1998, 82). Ó Gallachair (1958, 67) proceeds to note that the old fortress on Inis Saimer may have been superseded by the new castle nearby in 1423, but that it was not abandoned; it would seem that it became occupied by the Ó Gallachairs. With their overlord now ensconced in his new tower house perhaps it may have been considered appropriate that this supporting lineage, as members of the *lucht tighe* who held military responsibilities, would base themselves within the walls of the old fort nearby. It was here that Domnall Ó Domnaill, brother of Maghnus (who ruled from 1537 to 1563), was invited and subsequently murdered by Eóghan Ó Gallachair in 1546 (O'Donovan 1856, v, 1495). In addition, in July 1597 during the Nine Years' War the English landed their stores on the island, suggesting that some form of building or fortified structure existed there. This was during their failed attempt under the command of Sir Conyers Clifford to capture Ballyshannon Castle (ibid., vi, 2035). Baxter and Boazio's map of c. 1600 certainly depicts what looks to be a house on the island. The island saw action again during the war when in March 1602 it and the castle were both captured by the English under Captain Edward Digges and their ally Naill Garbh Ó Domnaill (ibid., 2329).

The report commissioned in 1946 by the Office of Public Works to document those monuments and buildings to be affected by the Erne Hydro-Electric Scheme included a section written about Inis Saimer, the contents of which suggest that some form of basic archaeological investigation had been undertaken at the site:

> Digging with a trowel on the north slope … revealed some large bones (probably ox), scraps of iron, glass, brick, mortar and a gun-flint. At the south-west corner of the fish store trowel digging revealed small fragments of charcoal, some bones and teeth which were obviously older than the bones mentioned above, and two sherds of pottery. These sherds are of thick black ware, with stab decoration (comb?). One, a rim sherd, is decorated on the rim. Mr O Davies, who was present, is of the opinion that the sherds show Neolithic B tendencies, but in our opinion they are of the same type as the sherds from a crannog at Ballydoolough, Co. Fermanagh, on exhibition in the Crannog Room, The National Museum (Corlett 2006, 54).

Among the artefacts revealed during this investigation it is the identification of the two sherds of pottery as being probably medieval Ulster coarse pottery that is of significance. This is a hand-built (as opposed to wheel-thrown), unglazed ceramic tradition that was in use across Ulster from the mid 13th century through to the 17th century (McSparron 2011, 117). The presence of the pottery on the island certainly indicates some sort of human presence there during this period, but it would be unreasonable to suggest that these two sherds are proof positive that this was the high-status site of Dún Murbhaigh! In addition, we can note at this point that the annals have already indicated to us that Inis Saimer was in occupation at this time, either as some form of religious retreat associated with Assaroe Abbey, or as a secondary fort for the Ó Gallachairs once the new castle of Ballyshannon had been constructed in 1423.

Ó Gallachair (1958, 67) had also noted that the area today called Murvagh may be the 'last remnant of the ancient Magh Murbhaigh', which may have been a more extensive area. As such, while the fort may indeed have been located on Inis Saimer, it may equally have been located somewhere else within this greater area. Two possible locations present themselves for consideration. The first of these is the promontory fort of Dungravenen (see Illus. 2.7) in the townland of Townparks, on the north side of the Erne estuary and overlooking Inis Saimer (Lacy 1983, 227–9). The date of this monument remains unknown; its origins may belong to late prehistory or the first millennium AD, with the presence of a souterrain (artificial cave) suggestive of an early medieval date, but it is possible that it may have continued in use through to the medieval period. Certainly there is a suggestion that something of substance was present here in the early 15th century; in 1419 Brian

Ó Conchobhair Sligigh launched an attack into Tír Aodha and his forces burnt the 'fort of Dún Cremhanain', which Ó Gallachair (1961, 7) noted was 'the promontory fort of Dungrevenan, off the Mall, over the Erne estuary'. The second possibility is that Dún Murbhaigh now lies under the Market Yard in Ballyshannon and that its site was re-used in 1423 for the location of the new tower house. As we have seen, the cashel at Iniscreamha on Lough Corrib was surrounded by a deep rock-cut ditch. Similar ditches associated with tower houses are known through excavations at Parke's Castle, Co. Leitrim (Foley & Donnelly 2012), and Castle Derg, Co. Tyrone (Newman 1992), while Richard Bartlett's view of Dungannon Castle in 1602 shows the castle surrounded by rock-cut ditches (Andrews 2008, 107). While it may be the case that at each of these sites the ditches represent efforts by their builders to provide additional defensive strength to the castle, and call to mind the 'great ramparts and ditches' referred to by Richard Stanihurst as being present at other Gaelic castles of the late medieval period (Lennon 1981, 147), it could also be the case that these ditches pre-dated the construction of the tower houses and represent features associated with an earlier longphort, marking both the continuity of high-status occupation but also the transition from longphort to castle that occurred among the Gaelic elite during the period after 1400. We might seek support for such a position from the depiction included in the Baxter and Boazio map of c. 1600 which shows the castles at both Belleek and Ballyshannon surrounded by what appear to be circular ditched enclosures. Evidently care needs to be taken, however, in reaching such a conclusion, given that the depiction of both castles from John Thomas' pictorial map of 1593 shows them surrounded not by ditches, but by masonry bawns.

Ballyshannon Castle

Following his successful raid in 1419 Brian Ó Conchobhair Sligigh constructed a castle at Bundrowes the next year. Given the threat from his neighbour it is not surprising to learn that Niall Garbh Ó Domnaill constructed his new castle at Ballyshannon as a means of guarding this fording point across the Erne (Simms 1996, 112). Castles evidently had a role to play within this contested landscape, not only providing the various lineages with a means of controlling the landscape, but also providing security to their occupants—such as the learned lineage of the Ó Cléirigh in Kilbarron Castle—at a time when there was no central government and the primary form of warfare was raid and counter-raid. This dominance of castles is visually depicted on Baxter and Boazio's map of north-west Ireland c. 1600, which depicts a landscape that is studded by castles. Niall Garbh's castle at Ballyshannon was located where the Market Yard is today, and by the late 19th century it was reported that

> … nothing now remains but a portion of one of the walls (about 10 feet high and 5 feet thick), part of which is incorporated with a grain store, and part with a butter shed on the north side of the market yard. The castle buildings doubtless occupied the whole or greater part of the ground now used for market purposes, and probably extended some way further up the river bank … . The castle park (a name still preserved in some old leases of adjacent premises) extended almost, if not entirely to the summit of the hill northward of the castle (Allingham 1879, 31).

Lacy (1983, 384) was of the opinion that the sections of the castle that survived into the late 19th century 'were probably part of the 17th-century building', and—unless this was one of the building's end-walls, which would be the thinnest wall in a tower house—the thickness of the wall at five feet (1.5 m) is indeed narrow if it were the side-wall of a castle.

Fortunately, however, the Tudor soldier John Thomas took effort in illustrating both this castle and its neighbour at Belleek in his view of the battle at the Erne Fords in 1593 and his depictions of the two buildings—both now demolished—can help provide us with some insights into their morphology (see Illus. 2.4). If the castle that was constructed at Ballyshannon by the Ó Domnaills in 1423 is the same building that was depicted by John Thomas in his map—and there is no reason to think that this might not be so—then it was evidently the case that both it and the castle at Belleek were tower houses. The date when this genre of castellated architecture commenced in Ireland is c. 1400 and perhaps as many as 3,000 of these small castles had been constructed throughout the island—by both Anglo-Irish and Gaelic lineages—by the end of the 16th century. Belleek Castle stands within a stone bawn with no evident internal buildings and with a plain arched gateway leading into the interior. The building is slender, with the entrance located in the side-wall at ground level, and stands at least three storeys in height, with narrow opes. Two of these opes are present in the end-wall at ground level while another example is shown in the side-wall at this level. There is what looks to be a mezzanine level ope at the far end of the side-wall between ground and first floor levels and this may represent the location of the internal staircase at this corner of the building. There are further opes in each wall at first floor level and two opes in each wall-face at second floor level. The parapet overhangs slightly and is crenellated, and there is a gabled pitched roof, seemingly covered in a solid material which might be shingles or slate.

Thomas's depiction of the castle at Ballyshannon is smaller in scale but evident effort has been made to neatly delineate the architectural features associated with the building and, because of this, it is possible to identify subtle differences with the castle at Belleek. The bawn at Ballyshannon, for example, has an arched gateway leading into the interior, but Thomas has depicted circular flanking towers at each of the corners of this enclosure. The tower house is three storeys in height but this is perhaps not to be taken prescriptively since the opes are large, and effort may have been made only to indicate to the viewer that the building had narrow loops. More evident, however, is the level of detail that he has taken in his depiction of the upper parts of the building, with its overhanging parapet and pitched roof, although—unlike Belleek—a buff colour is used for the roof, perhaps intimating that the building was under thatch. It is the location of the entrance at ground floor level, however, that indicates Thomas' attention to detail, for he clearly has attempted to indicate a difference between the two buildings. At Ballyshannon the entrance is at ground level in the building's end-wall. This is different from his illustrations of the tower houses at both Belleek and Enniskillen where the entrances are depicted in the buildings' side-walls. While the entrance in a side-wall is known elsewhere in Gaelic Ireland (most notably Rockfleet Castle, Co. Mayo), the more usual arrangement was for the entranceway to be located—as depicted at Ballyshannon—in the end-wall.

Ballyhanna Castle

The tower house at Ballyshannon was not, however, the only masonry castle in the Erne valley. There was also Ballyhanna Castle, now submerged as a result of the 1946 River Erne Hydro-Electric Scheme under the waters of Assaroe Lake (Illus. 2.8 and 2.9). Fortunately, however, the building was surveyed by Oliver Davies prior to this event and two photographs and a plan of the castle from this work are provided by Corlett (2006, 64–5). These images demonstrate that the building was devoid of architectural features that might help provide a

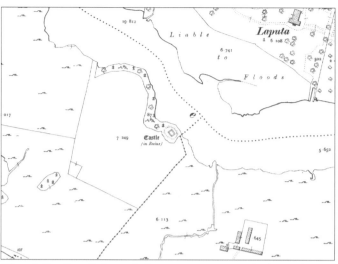

Illus. 2.8—Detail from Ordnance Survey second edition (1900) 25-inch map sheet of Ballyhanna Castle, now submerged beneath Assaroe Lake (Ordnance Survey Ireland).

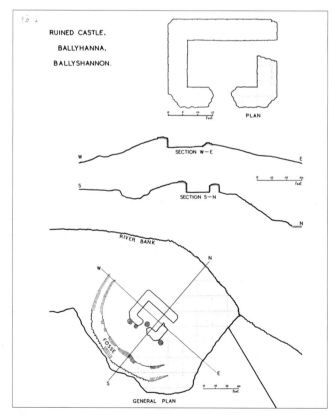

Illus. 2.9—Plan and sections of Ballyhanna Castle, Co. Donegal, undertaken during Oliver Davies' survey of 1946 (reproduced in Corlett 2006, fig. 23).

date for its construction, save that it was rectangular and blockish in form, standing about 1.8 m high, with external measurements showing a building with walls 11.12 m long (east to west) by 8.86 m wide (north to south) and 2 m thick. 'It stands on a mound which is surrounded, on the landward side, by a fosse which is partly cut through rock … . The castle was dug into the mound, so that the ground level inside the wall is now roughly five feet below the level of the top of the mound just outside the wall' (ibid., 63). The survey highlighted the opening to the east side of the building to be the location of the doorway, and noted that there was 'no trace of any other opening'. The accompanying plan, however, depicts a large opening on the southern side-wall, about 2 m in width, but it is not explained why it was considered that this was not an entry into the building.

The map compiled by Brown and Baptiste in 1591 (see Illus. 2.3) highlighted 'an olde castell' on the southern bank of the Erne, set between the castle at 'Belicke', depicted as a tower with crenellated roofline and pitched roof and also on this side of the river, and a similarly depicted tower at Ballyshannon on the opposite shoreline beside 'the abbie of Assaroe'. Was this 'olde castell' the castle at Ballyhanna? Hugh Allingham, writing in 1879, clearly thought that this was the case:

> Besides the ford of Athseanaigh, there were other fords on the river which were occasionally used. One of these was about half a mile west of Belleek, the ford of Ath-cul-uain. There was another fortress, the walls of which are still standing on the south bank of the river, at Cherrymount. This "keep" was built on the summit of an artificially constructed mound, so that the soldiers in charge might have better command of the river below (Allingham 1879, 31).

The author then adds in a footnote on the same page that this fortress 'seems to have fallen into disuse before the time of Queen Elizabeth, as in an old map of that period, preserved in the Public Record Office, London, this building is marked as "an olde castell" and is represented as a ruin ...'.

Assaroe Abbey

A final building that is depicted by John Thomas and that requires consideration is Assaroe Abbey. As we have seen, this Cistercian foundation was established in the late 12th century but little of its original fabric remains upstanding, except for some sections of walls belonging to the abbey church (Lacy 1983, 327). A review of the historical evidence for the nature of the site is included by Stalley (1987, 242) who notes that the abbey survived as a religious community to about 1607. The best description of the complex comes from an English inquisition of 1588–9 which noted that there was a church with steeple, shingled and thatched, a ruined dormitory, three other stone buildings, and four cottages (Gwynn & Hadcock 1970, 127). In addition, the presence of vaulting in the building is suggested by an account of 1776 which stated that 'some of the gilding in the vault of the cloister is still visible' (Lockwood 1901, 180). The abbey would seem to have replaced Drumhome as the principal burial ground among the elite within Cenél Conaill society from the mid 13th century onwards when Ó Domnaill taoiseachs, including Domnall Mór (1241) and Áed (1333), were buried there. In 1377 the abbey was burnt, although no explanation is provided in the *Annals of the Four Masters* as to how or why this event happened; it may have been as part of a raid or perhaps accidental. Given its location in the southern part of Tír Aodha close to a fording point over the Erne, however, the abbey did evidently get caught up in dynastic confrontations, and this would seem to have been particularly the case in the last decades of the 14th century. Some form of Ó Domnaill military camp seems to have been present in 1380, while an attack by Ó Conchobhair forces on an Ó Domnaill camp near Assaroe is noted in 1388. Then, 10 years later, Tír Aodha and the abbey were raided by the Ó Neills who 'plundered the monastery of all its treasure' (O'Donovan 1856, iv, 757).

John Thomas has depicted the abbey as a rather long, thin building with a transept to one side and a crossing tower, crowned by a cross (see Illus. 2.5). The entrance is in the nave and the south transept also has what appears to be an entrance; the roof of the building is of similar buff colour to that at the tower house at Ballyshannon, perhaps indicating that both lay under thatch roofs.

One is minded here of the plans and appearance of friary churches such as Donegal, Killydonnell, Rathmullen—all in County Donegal—or Creevelea in County Leitrim, rather than the more heavy, austere architecture one would expect to see at a Cistercian foundation of the late 12th century, such as Jerpoint, Co. Kilkenny, Inch, Co. Down, or Mellifont, Co. Louth. Indeed, the location of the cloister is something one would expect to see on the southern side of the church at a Cistercian foundation; the location of the cloister to the north of the church—which seems to be what Thomas is showing, hidden behind the church—is more indicative of the ground plan expected at a friary. This might lead us to question whether Thomas had actually seen the abbey or whether he was depicting what he believed the building to look like, based perhaps on his knowledge of friaries that he had actually visited. Given the level of detail that the soldier-artist included in his depictions of other historic buildings in the region—Enniskillen Castle, Belleek Castle, and Ballyshannon Castle—on balance we should probably conclude that what he drew was indeed what he had seen. This in turn, however, generates another set of questions: was the Cistercian abbey rebuilt in the aftermath of the fire in 1377 or the raid of 1398 and, if this happened, was it reconstructed using the late medieval Irish Gothic architectural style found at the Gaelic friaries being constructed during this era, and hence the similarity in appearance depicted by Thomas? As we have seen, the historical evidence associated with the abbey is limited with most available sources dating to the late 16th century, but lack of textual evidence should not be used as negative evidence in considering this issue. While 'many moulded fragments of late 12th/early 13th century date are scattered throughout the cemetery' (Lacy 1983, 327), the presence of a dressed stone piece—seemingly part of the tracery associated with a Late Gothic window and roughly depicted among a collection of sketches of such elements that accompanied his article on the monument—certainly led Lockwood (1901, 180) to conclude that 'there must have been some work introduced to the building of a later date'.

Ballyshannon, Tír Conaill and the wider medieval world

The depiction of Ballyshannon Castle prepared by John Thomas for his map of 1593 shows the building to have been a tower house, and part of a building series that commenced in Ireland c. 1400 (see Illus. 2.4 and 2.5). The historical date for the construction of the castle at Ballyshannon is 1423 and this, therefore, places the building at the start of a major construction phenomenon across the island that would continue into the 17th century. What is significant here, however, is the fact that by the start of the third decade of the 15th century, the concept of the tower house as a lordly residence had been taken up by the Gaelic lords in the north-west. The implication of this is two-fold: first, the Ó Domnaill lineage was willing to accept new ideas and implement them and, second, they were not divorced from what was happening elsewhere on the island. Likewise, any assumption that the Gaelic territories of north-west Ulster were backward places on Europe's western fringe does not stand up to scrutiny. The artefact collection from the great monastic settlement on Lough Erne at Devenish, for example, retrieved during the excavation of the east range of St Mary's Priory, included imported south-west French pottery of 13th- to 14th-century date, green and yellow Beauvais jugs from northern France, south Netherland maiolica and a Spanish costrel of early 16th-century date (Waterman 1979, 47)—all indicative of Continental connections associated with the monastery's location on the routeway to the famous pilgrimage site at Lough Derg. Pilgrimage, however, was a two-way experience and many members of the local Gaelic elite journeyed to the great religious centres of Europe and beyond. For example, Aodh an Einigh Mág Uidhir, tánaiste to Tomás Mór Mág Uidhir, made pilgrimages to Compostella in Spain, Rome, and the Holy Land, dying on his return to Ireland in 1428 (Livingstone 1969, 30); while Murtough Ó Flannagáin, lord of Tuath Ratha, went on pilgrimage to Rome in 1450, where he and Nicolas Ó Flannagáin, parson of Devenish, both died; this seems to have been part of a general group of the Mág Uidhir and Ó Flannagáin lineages who went on pilgrimage to Rome that year (O'Donovan 1856, v, 968). Other more secular journeys were also made, such as when the grand old warlord Aodh Ruadh Ó Domnaill visited James IV of Scotland in 1495 at the age of 68 years. His son Aodh Dubh undertook a two-year pilgrimage to Rome from 1510 to 1512, during which he spent some eight months at the court of Henry VIII and received a knighthood, also visiting James IV in 1513 (McGettigan 2005, 477). Such connections also enabled the Ó Domnaills to keep abreast of new developments in military matters, as exemplified by the capture of Sligo Castle from the Ó Conchobhairs by Maghnus Ó Domnaill (who ruled from 1537 to 1563), an action that was facilitated through his friendship with a French knight who had been on pilgrimage at Lough Derg in 1516 and who had 'on his arrival, and at his departure' visited Ó Domnaill

> …from whom he received great honours, gifts, and presents; and they formed a great intimacy and friendship with each other; and the knight, upon learning that the castle of Sligo was defended against O'Donnell, promised to send him a ship with great guns; and the knight, too, performed that promise, for the ship arrived in the harbour of Killybegs. She was steered directly westwards to Sligo; and O'Donnell and his army marched by land, so that they met from sea and land at the town. They battered the town very much before they obtained possession of it, and O'Donnell gave protection to the warders (O'Donovan 1856, v, 1335).

As Bradshaw (1979, 29) has noted, the motivation for this action was probably to control the strategic route between Connacht and Ulster, extend the Ó Domnaill overlordship into north Connacht, and control the fishing dues associated with the town. The fishing industry was of great importance since it enabled Gaelic lords to obtain iron goods, salt, cloth and arms from foreign fishermen who paid for fishing and landing rights in return for the processing of the herring catch in bay and havens along the coastline. This was particularly the case by the 16th century when the herring fishing industry became concentrated in the seas off Donegal (O'Neill 1987, 33, 91, 131). The extent of this industry was such that a Tudor English official, writing in 1561, reported that Maghnus Ó Domnaill was the 'best lord of fish in Ireland and he exchangeth fish always with foreign merchants for wine, by which [he] is called in other countries, the king of fish' (Brewer & Bullen 1867, 308). 'It does appear, however, that in the 15th and 16th centuries a cheap, low quality wine became more readily available in Gaelic areas as Spanish and English merchants developed a pattern of trade in which wine, beer and bales of cloth were exchanged for salt meat, hides and fish' (Simms 1978, 87). A hint at how Toirdhealbhach an Fhíona (of the Wine) Ó Domnaill may have received this sobriquet can be found in a permit from during his rule and dating to 1402–3 that enabled merchants from Dublin to bring six tuns of wine to Assaroe in that year (O'Neill 1987, 56), while an almost incidental insight into the nature of this trading activity at Ballyshannon is highlighted in the *Annals of Connaught* and the *Annals of the Four Masters* in the year 1420 which recounted how Niall Garbh Ó Domnaill escaped death by jumping into the harbour beyond the Assaroe Falls (i.e. Ballyshannon) during an attack by Ó Conchobhair forces, and getting on board a 'trading ship which lay there'. The implication is that foreign ships were able to put-in at the Erne estuary.

There is a depiction of a large brown cross located on a patch of green close to the road leading away from the castle at 'Ballechhauen' and past the abbey at 'Assaro' in Baxter and Boazio's map of c. 1600 (see Illus. 2.6). Brown and Baptiste's map of 1591, depicting the Gaelic town of Cavan comes to mind, where a large cross is depicted at the centre of the settlement there, and one which must be a market cross, a central feature of any medieval town. This was a meeting place within the market area, a symbol of the prosperity of an urban settlement, and a common feature of the urban landscape across medieval Ireland and Britain. The potential exists that Baxter and Boazio depicted a cross at Ballyshannon to indicate that this too was a significant economic centre by the end of the 16th century. Any such interpretation, however, must take into account that two similar brown crosses are depicted on the map elsewhere in the Donegal landscape. The first is shown close to a large church on a hilltop outside Castlefinn, and the second on the mainland beside St Patrick's Purgatory at Lough Derg. As such, it is possible that the cartographers may have been using the brown crosses as symbols to identify sites of religious significance—and hence a cross is located close to Assaroe—but if that is the case then it was not a symbol being used to pinpoint each and every religious establishment since, for example, no such cross is used in the vicinity of Donegal town where a major Franciscan house was located. Leaving this aside, the evidence suggests that Ballyshannon was indeed an established economic centre by the end of the 16th century. The fact that King James I granted a 21-year lease of the 'customs and subsidies, as well small as great, of all merchandise brought into the ports of Dirry [Derry] and Ballishannon, and exported out of the same' on 11 November 1603 would indicate that Ballyshannon was a recognised market port in the first years of the 17th century, and before the establishment of the new towns associated with the Plantation era (Anon. 1966, 14). As an evident centre of economic importance, however, what might the settlement at Ballyshannon have looked like in the late medieval period? From the details contained in the pictorial maps of the English cartographer Richard Bartlett from c. 1602 we can hazard a guess. First, we can envisage that there was some form of nucleated village—if not town—in and around the port and castle. This is what we see in Bartlett's depiction of Dungannon Castle in Tyrone (National Library of Ireland, Ms2656, v), where the Ó Neill tower house stands within a rock-cut ditched enclosure which has a lower ward containing nine small houses, and we can envisage something similar for the environs of the Ó Domnaill castle at Ballyshannon. The dangers of living close to a trading harbour, however, are highlighted in the *Annals of Ulster* where it is reported that in 1478: 'A great plague came in a ship to the harbour of Es-ruadh [Assaroe] and that plague spread throughout Tír Conaill and in Fermanagh and in the province in general. And many losses were caused to them, and Mac-an-baird of Tír Conaill, namely, Godfrey, died of it'.

Life on the erenagh estate at Ballyhanna

While Assaroe had become a principal burial place for the elite within Tír Aodha, we can imagine that the lower levels of medieval Gaelic society in the Ballyshannon region were buried in the graveyards associated with chapels such as those at Finner, Ballyhanna and Sminver. Ballyhanna was

Church land owned by the Bishop of Clogher but he—like other bishops in Gaelic regions—did not manage this land himself. This was the work of the erenagh (*airchinneach*) lineages, the lead-tenants on an estate that was used to support a parish church and its associated priest. The erenagh farmed this land with their sub-tenants and agricultural workers, maintained the church buildings, provided hospitality for travellers, and entertained the bishop during his visitations, with the outlay for all of these activities covered by the revenue generated by the estate. Finally, at a time before the establishment of seminaries, the erenagh was also responsible for the education of the clergy (Ó Doiblin & Hamill 1992, 53); the men of the erenagh lineages tended to be well-educated and frequently pursued a career in the Church, often becoming clergy within the local parishes. The erenagh's position was hereditary, with the same maxims in place as would be found among a secular lineage. When an erenagh died the land reverted back to the bishop until a new erenagh was appointed, and when an erenagh lineage became extinct then the bishop selected a new lineage to hold the position. This new lineage would then select a leader who in turn would be approved in his position by the bishop (Ó Gallachair 1961, 27). The leader of the erenagh lineage was elected by the males within the lineage's derbfine, and had to be approved by their overlord, the bishop. And like any tenant-lord relationship, misconduct could mean the erenagh was deprived of his land by his bishop (Nicholls 1971–2, 371). 'The erenagh then was an important personage on the local scene, really a local territorial lord' (Ó Gallachair 1961, 27).

The 'McGockqin', the erenagh lineage associated with Ballyhanna, was reported in the Crown Commission's Inquisition at Lifford on 12 September 1609 into the Church land in the 'Countye of Donegall'. In the text it is stated that they held one half-quarter of land called 'BallymcGockquin whereof McGockquin is herenagh', with a fishing weir for eels, a watermill, and the 'moytie of a salmon leape called O'Skullion', for all of which they paid an annual rent of three shillings and four pence to the Bishop of Clogher. Ó Gallachair (1960, 278) considered the lineage name recorded by the commissioners as 'probably an attempt at [i.e. to anglicise] Mac Gabhann, still very common in this district under various English forms, like McGowan, Goan and Coan', while elsewhere he also noted that the name could also be found as Coane and Keown (Ó Gallachair 1961, 28), but that the lineage may have originated within the Cenél Conaill, perhaps as 'the Magumháin, Meagudháin or Mac Gudhain' (ibid., 30). Ó Gallachair (ibid., 35) was of the opinion that they may have also been erenaghs at the chapel-of-ease at Finner, given that the hill towards the Ballyshannon side of the churchyard was called 'Knockmakigan, probably from another corruption of the difficult erenagh name and meaning "McGockquin's Hill"'.

At the time of his research Ó Gallachair (ibid.) was unaware of the existence of the church at Ballyhanna, noting that 'the modern townland of Ballyhanny … shows no ruins there of an old church at all, to identify with this medieval chapel'. Following Allingham's line of thought, Ó Gallachair concluded that the church in question must have been the old chapel at Sminver, itself now in a sorry state and almost completely forgotten. The site is listed in the *Archaeological Survey of County Donegal* as having been rubble-built but surviving only to its lower wall courses which were some 1 m in thickness. The building measured 19 m by 9 m internally but there were no architectural features visible and the entire building was covered in vegetation and fallen masonry (Lacy 1983, 349). A further religious element of this landscape was the holy well of Tobershannon which was located between the church at Sminver and the lost chapel at Ballyhanna. This well was excavated in 2001 and was revealed as a sub-circular D-shaped feature surrounded by large stones placed around the mouth of a natural spring, with a spread of round stones surrounding the well. Writing in 1936 on the holy wells in the county, Ó Muirgheasa (1936, 144) had stated that 'no stations at present. Only unbaptised children now buried in the graveyard'. Given that Tobershannon is not located within a graveyard and that the graveyard at Ballyhanna was a lost element of the landscape, it can be suggested that this is a reference to the old church and graveyard at Sminver and that it had become used as a *cillín* in the early modern period. Ó Gallachair (1961, 35) went on to support his view that the historical references to Ballyhanna actually belonged to Sminver by stating that 'Sminver was also called Fallychocaen, a corruption of BallyMcGockquin, which the jurors call Ballyhanny'. While evidently the archaeological evidence now disproves this hypothesis, a significant point remains within his statement. If Sminver were called Fallychocaen, and this was indeed a corruption of Ballymacgockquin, then it could suggest that the McGockquins were not only an erenagh family in charge of the chapels at Finner and Ballyhanna, but that they had also acted, in essence, as erenaghs, or some form of estate managers, for the monks at Assaroe at Sminver. In essence, the chapels and associated Church land at Ballyhanna and Finner belonged to the bishop while the chapel at Sminver belonged to the monks, but all three estates were managed for their ecclesiastical lords by the same local erenagh family.

Economy

The Crown Commission's Inquisition of 1609 also revealed some important information relating to the economic life within the erenagh estate at Ballyhanna. It is recorded that there was a fishing weir for eels; this is Corry McGinty, located 'a quarter of a mile upstream of Ballyshannon Bridge' (Went 1945, 217), and is the eel weir marked on the first-edition Ordnance Survey six-inch map sheet in the River Erne to the immediate north of the location of Ballyhanna chapel on the southern bank of the river. While Went was oblivious to the origin of the weir's name, Ó Gallachair (1961, 28) notes that this was 'obviously the modern corruption (only one of many) of the Cora (eel-weir) of McGockquin, the surname of the old erenagh sept here'. The McGockquin erenaghs also had 'the moytie of a salmon leepe called O'Skullion', which Ó Gallachair (ibid.) successfully demonstrated was a horrendous 17th-century anglicisation of the Irish place-name Eas Chaitlín, Cathleen's Falls, now the location of a hydro-electric power station. In addition to these fishing interests, the erenagh also had a mill on the 'Brook of Bellashanny', now a small stream called The Tobies. Famines are a feature of Gaelic Ireland as reported in the annals, with particularly bad periods experienced in the 1310s, when famine occurred for four years in a row, the 1440s, with three years in a row, and the 1460s, with four years marked out in that decade (Nicholls 1993, 410). In 1497, for example, it was reported that 'among the Gaels a small beart of oats containing ten meadars was purchased for an in-calf [i.e. pregnant] cow; and beef was sold for a mark; and a milch [milking] cow for two in-calf cows and a shilling more' (O'Donovan 1856, iv, 1238). Accounts such as this should therefore indicate to us how important cereals were as a component of the Gaelic diet and, as O'Dowd (1986, 130) has noted, the inclusion of cereals among the rents-in-kind paid to overlords indicates that 'a good deal of cultivation [was] taking place in Gaelic Ireland'; the account of Hugh O'Neill's rents compiled by Sir Toby Caulfield in 1610, for example, noted that the earl had been entitled to oats and oatmeal (Russell & Prendergast 1874, 534–6). This finds resonance in the dues from the Ó Diobhlin lineage reported in the Ceart Uí Neill, a late 15th- or 16th-century text that set out the rights and entitlements of the Ó Neills from their subservient lineages: 'twenty wholemeal loaves in the spring from each half quarter (of land), and a meadar of butter with each loaf: and four pecks of malt in the spring, or a barrel from each half quarter, and a meadar of butter per week' (Ó Diobhlin 1998, 60). Likewise, Sir John Davies' summary of the contents of a similar document for the Mág Uidhir lords of Fir Manach, now lost, lists meal as one of the foodstuffs paid in rent to their overlord by those who resided on his mensal lands (Simms 2009, 97–8).

Given all this, a mill would have been an essential element in the working life of a rural community. Evidence of such activity in the local landscape was reported in the late 19th century by Hugh Allingham who noted that a

…remembrance of the industries of our ancestors is preserved in the names Carricknaronia and Lugalustran, both names referring to the preparation and manufacture of corn into meal. On the shore below Wardtown [Ballymacaward] are a series of sandstone rocks, their name, Carrick-na-mbrointe, ie the rock of the mill stones, shows that it was here the querns or ancient Irish hand-mills of the district were obtained. Not long ago the upper stone of a quern was found in the vicinity of these rocks, and as it is only partially shaped, it is evident that it must have been cut where it was quarried, and left by its maker in an unfinished state … Lugalustran [Legaloscran], ie the hollow of the burnt corn, is a place not far from the "Rock". It was here that corn used to be burned in the ear to prepare it for the querns. This process of removing the husks continued in operation in some parts of the country a century ago, and was prohibited by parliament (Allingham 1879, 113).

The mill at Ballyhanna is mentioned in the 1609 inquisition but where would it have been located? Presumably it was on The Tobies, and in the same spot as shown in the 1654 Down Survey map as being the location of the mill at that time. In addition to oatmeal and fish, the other staple element in the diet of the people in Ballyhanna would have been dairy produce and meat. In 1397 the Catalan Raymond, viscount of Perelhos, visited Niall Mór Ó Neill during his journey to Lough Derg on pilgrimage. In his account of what he witnessed in Tír Eóghain the aristocratic traveller noted that the lower classes within Gaelic society ate meat and drank water (Haren & de Pontfarcy 1988, 109) and that 'they have plenty of butter, for oxen and cows provide all their meat' (ibid., 110–11).

Housing

Andrews (2001, 176) has noted that over 200 houses are depicted in the maps from c. 1602 undertaken by the English cartographer Richard Bartlett during the last stage of the Nine Years' War but only one cornfield is shown, beside the Gaelic Confederate fort at Inishloughan (National Library of Ireland, Ms2656, vi). Presumably other cornfields existed but had been destroyed by the English as part of their general 'scorched earth' policy in Ulster (O'Donovan 1856, vi, 2428), or the planting of the crop had been heavily disrupted by the ongoing conflict. Either way, as Andrews noted, there had to have been corn grown to provide the thatched roofs for the houses shown elsewhere in Bartlett's maps! But what types of housing might we expect the people of Ballyhanna to have been residing within? The houses that Bartlett depicted have been studied by Andrews (2008, 54) for the information that they can tell us about their form, construction and materials:

> Most cabins have plastered or whitewashed walls one storey high, capped by roofs of yellow thatch. Otherwise, some roofs are hipped, others gabled; some houses have a chimney, more often centrally placed (presumably indicating an internal cross-wall or partition) than in the gable. Others evidently consumed their own smoke.

The variation in form can best be witnessed in his map of Mountnorris Fort (National Library of Ireland, Ms2656, ii), where Bartlett has depicted houses with front elevations that comprise a door set to one side of a window, or a door flanked on either side by windows. It is unlikely that there would have been a village within the erenagh estate at Ballyhanna, and the landscape would have been dispersedly populated with rural dwellers, a view that is supported by Bartlett's maps where we see houses in the countryside both isolated (ibid., xi) and in small clusters of two and three buildings (ibid., ix).

What are also of note, however, are the contents of a survey of the parishes of the diocese of Derry undertaken in the first decade of the 17th century. The original text of this survey was written for Bishop George Montgomery in 1607, before the Flight of the Earls in that same year, and—by extension—before 'any progress had been made at anglicising and protestantising the church. Hence it reveals a great deal of the personnel and structures of the Catholic church in the Diocese of Derry before the Plantation' (Jefferies 1996–7, 46, 74). While his efforts as a missionary for the new Protestant religion in Ulster were poor, Bishop Montgomery proved much more successful in securing some 61,000 acres of former Church and erenagh land for the new Church of Ireland (Hill 1877, 210; Jefferies 1999, 129). The 1607 survey belongs to the early stages of Montgomery's work on this front, and most of the properties detailed in the text were erenagh estates. The importance of salmon and eel fishing becomes apparent in the documents, as does mills and milling and other structures, such as at Aghadowey where there was 'a timber bridge … near the erenagh's house' (Jefferies 1996–7, 58). What is also evident, however, is the presence of stone houses on Church land, with 26 examples reported at 13 different estates, often in multiple numbers, as at Clonmany where there were: 'Six stone houses; three roofed and three unroofed. Two good roofed castles. A bridge in a convenient position in the same place is intact' (ibid., 65).

The 1607 text certainly suggests that stone buildings were a significant element in the architectural tradition to be found at the Church estates in the diocese of Derry in the period before the Plantation, but whether this was also the case on neighbouring secular estates must remain a moot issue. Given, however, the status—and associated economic control—that erenaghs held as the representatives of ecclesiastical lords it is possible that a similar situation existed on their estates across Gaelic Ulster. These stone houses, however, were probably the homes of vicars, rectors and erenaghs rather than those of the ordinary people working on an estate, but is it possible to identify any such building on the McGockquin land at Ballyhanna? Returning to Clonmany, we should note that the entry lists 'two good roofed castles' on this erenagh estate. We have already seen that there was a castle in Ballyhanna, albeit one that was submerged under the waters of the Erne Hydro-Electric Scheme's Assaroe Lake in 1946. Ballyhanna Castle does not betray any evidence to suggest that it was a tower house; its ruins are devoid of architectural features and it is blockhouse-like in plan (Corlett 2006,

63). It remains, however, best described as a castle and, while it is possible that this may have been an outpost for the Ó Domnaills on the southern side of the river, it is equally possible that this was the home of the McGockwins as a strong erenagh family, and one that mirrors the situation with the Ó Cléirigh lineage of professional historians who had their own castle at Kilbarron to protect them during raids and counter-raids. The Brown and Baptiste map of 1591 (see Illus. 2.3) depicts an 'olde castell' on the southern bank of the river between Belleek and Ballyshannon which—as we have discussed—Allingham (1879, 31) believed to be the castle at Ballyhanna. Evidently it was in a ruinous condition even before the Nine Years' War, as the map detail would suggest, but this might also explain why it was not considered worthy of mention by the incoming commissioners who were assessing the property of the McGockquins in 1609.

The end of Ballyhanna church and graveyard

The Dissolution of the Monasteries in 1539 made no impact in Gaelic Ulster and monastic life continued in Assaroe until 1607, or possibly 1606, when the abbot, Eugene O'Gallagher, and a monk, Bernard O'Trevir were murdered by the English close to the abbey. This was around the time of the Flight of the Earls in 1607, when the former protectors of the monastic orders within the Gaelic lordships had been forced to flee to the Continent (Father Colmcille 1959, 124–5). The strategic importance of Ballyshannon, however, was well recognised by the English, and much of the area was granted to one of their soldiers, Sir Henry Ffolliott, including, by a deed dated 20 May 1608, the dissolved abbey at Assaroe; the Cistercians, however, remained active in the vicinity as a dispersed community and the last abbot of Assaroe was Thomas Quinn who died 30 May 1669 and was buried in the graveyard of the abandoned abbey (ibid., 129). With the exception of four balliboes formerly held by the Ó Cléirigh lineage and which were granted to Trinity College Dublin, Ffolliott bought up the interests of the other Englishmen in the area 'so that he became landlord of Mag nÉne (except for the College lands) and of both banks of the Erne, with the salmon and eel fisheries as well' (Ó Gallachair 1961, 8). Ó Gallachair proceeds to note, however, that the Church land at Finner and Ballyhanna were granted to the Church of Ireland and remained outside Sir Henry's grasp.

The Civil Survey of 1654 counts the 'halfe a Quarter of Land called Ballihanna' within the Church land owned by the Bishop of Clogher in the parish of 'Enismcsainte', leased to 'Martin Arstall Scottish Prottestantt' and comprising 58 acres, 'with a small Sallmon ffishing belonging to itt'. As we have seen, the land units used in medieval Donegal comprised the ballybetagh, divided into four quarters, with four balliboes in each quarter. The evidence from the Civil Survey for Ballyhanna indicates that the erenagh estate here comprised a half-quarter, which presumably can be equated to two balliboes. At the time of the commissioner's writing, the land was held by the heirs of Martin Arstall through a lease for a 60-year period that commenced in 1638 for the sum of £12 per year and it is noted that it was 'yet to expire fortey fowre years', which would be around 1682 (Simington 1937, 66). The contemporary Down Survey barony map (Illus. 2.10) provides additional detail to our understanding of what existed in the Ballyshannon area during the Cromwellian era. The centrepiece feature of the settlement is the depiction of Ffolliott's large gabled house with chimney stacks; now demolished, we might envisage that this building was perhaps similar to some of the more grandiose

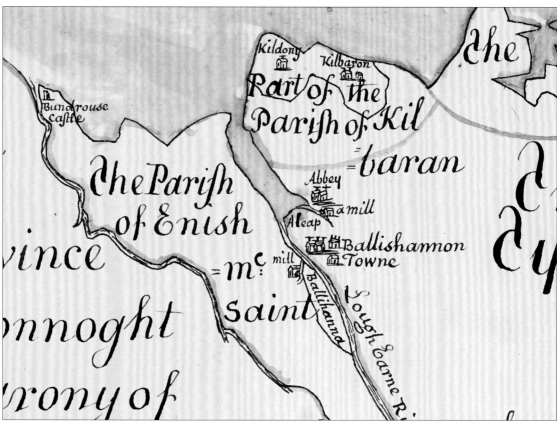

Illus. 2.10—Detail from the mid-17th-century Down Survey barony map highlighting the settlement at Ballyshannon and Ballyhanna (courtesy of the Deputy Keeper of the Records, Public Record Office of Northern Ireland, ref. D597/3/1).

constructions erected in Ulster during the early 17th century, such as at Castle Caulfield in County Tyrone. The house is set amid five other buildings, three of which appear to have chimneystacks, the 'Abbey', and a watermill. When we move to the southern bank of the river the cartographers have deliberately defined the territory of 'Ballihanna' with a boundary, perhaps to denote that this was the property of the Bishop of Clogher. At the western end of the property effort has been made to show an inlet for a stream running into the Erne, with a watermill located on the west bank of this waterway; this is presumably The Tobies stream and the location of the earlier medieval mill as noted in the inquisition of 1609 (Ó Gallachair 1961, 28). A consideration of the archaeological evidence obtained during the excavation programme at Ballyhanna (see Macdonald and Carver, this volume) suggests that burial in the graveyard had ceased by the early decades of the 17th century. There is no church depicted in 'Ballihanna' on the mid 17th-century Down Survey barony map and this might suggest the building had been demolished by that time. Alternatively, if the church was particularly ruinous then perhaps its significance may have been lessened to the Cromwellian cartographers and they may have decided not to include it as a notable feature on the landscape. In short, we do not know if the church was levelled deliberately in the early decades of the 17th century or whether it had been left to fall more gradually into ruin, but graveyards are seldom 'lost' through progressive degeneration and a measure of deliberate levelling more than probably played a role in Ballyhanna having become forgotten from local memory.

It would appear, however, that at some point the land at Ballyhanna was sold off by the Church of Ireland into the ownership of the Conolly family. The Griffith Valuation of 1858 states that its landlord is Thomas Conolly, with the plot (3A) in the townland containing the church site under the lease of Mary O'Neill, widow of Captain Charles O'Neill of Rockville House. Thomas Conolly was a descendant of William Conolly (1662–1729), a native of Ballyshannon who had risen from his humble beginnings to become reputedly the richest man in early 18th-century Ireland and Speaker of the Irish House of Commons. In 1718 he purchased the Ffolliott estate (Walsh 2010, 65) but whether it was the case that Ballyhanna had been purchased by the Ffolliotts from the Bishop of Clogher prior to 1718—and thus had become part of the portfolio purchased by Conolly in that year—or whether it was subsequently purchased by Conolly after 1718 as a separate transaction must remain unknown. It is possible, however, that William Conolly's direct ancestry may have had some bearing on the issue, for his mother Jane was a member of the Coan family in Ballyshannon and—as we have seen—Ó Gallachair (1960, 278) believed the 'McGockwin' erenagh lineage at Ballyhanna to be an attempted anglicisation of Mac Gabhann, 'still very common in this district under various English forms, like McGowan, Goan and Coan', and that 'the last prominent Catholic member of this family that we can trace was the Ballyshannon merchant, Thady Coan, who lived in Carrickboy, in this parish, died and was buried in Abbey Assaroe in 1723' (ibid., 281). It would seem that Thady Coan was Jane Conolly's brother and that members of the family—including Thady's son Terence— acted as land agents for her son William on his Ballyshannon estate (Walsh 2010, 13). Given their influence as land agents to their relative Conolly, however, it would seem unlikely that the Coans would have been responsible for, or indeed have overseen, the destruction of the old church and graveyard at Ballyhanna. As such, it can be suggested that the abandonment had come about during the 17th century when the land was under the control of a tenant of the Bishop of Clogher, but within perhaps as little as three or four generations after the inquisition of 1609, and certainly within 110 years of that event, a descendant of the old erenagh family of Ballyhanna—William Conolly— had become the wealthiest and one of the most powerful men in Ireland and, through that wealth, the old ancestral land of his mother's people came back into their descendants' possession.

Conclusion

As we shall see in the following chapter, the archaeological evidence suggests that Ballyhanna had its origins in the early medieval period as a small monastic site which continued in use through the later medieval era as a religious centre for an erenagh estate, before its abandonment in the early decades of the 17th century. The current chapter has sought to provide a political, social and economic overview for the site over this period of nearly 1,000 years. It has charted how the Ballyhanna landscape formed part of the tuath of Mag nÉne, held by the Cenél Cairpre Tuatha Ratha at the dawn of the historic period, before becoming the central territory of the Ua Maíl Doraid lineage, through to the 1200s when the Ó Domnaills first established themselves at Ath

Seanaigh as the new rulers of Tír Conaill. On first impressions, Ballyhanna may appear as a rather unremarkable place in the overall story of medieval Ireland, but as this chapter has demonstrated, this small ecclesiastic centre was actually situated close to the very heart of political power in the north-west during this long era. As we survey the skeletons of the dead from this small graveyard one cannot help but wonder what these men, women and children made of the world they lived in.

3

ARCHAEOLOGICAL EXCAVATIONS AT BALLYHANNA GRAVEYARD—CHRONOLOGY, DEVELOPMENT AND CONTEXT

Philip Macdonald & Naomi Carver

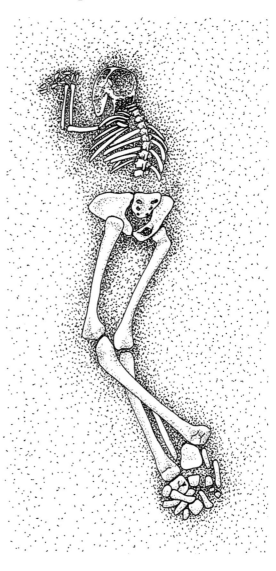

Stylised depiction of a young adult male, who was one of six individuals at Ballyhanna buried in a prone position (SK 484) (Sapphire Mussen).

The excavated part of the graveyard at Ballyhanna was located in the north-east corner of a field bordered by East Port Road and Station Road (an area referred to here as the main area of excavation). The field had been used in recent years for the growing of silage, but had once formed part of the small park associated with Rockville House (Ó Donnchadha 2006, 3). A cottage stood immediately to the west of the site, as depicted in the first-edition Ordnance Survey six-inch map sheet of 1834–5 (see Illus. 1.6), but it was demolished during the 1970s. The site was situated in a relatively flat area at the base of a steep hill overlooking the River Erne, whose southern bank, prior to the channelisation and narrowing of the river associated with the River Erne Hydro-Electric Scheme, was located only 50 m to the north across a narrow flood plain. Significantly, the site was also located in close proximity to the historic ford of Áth Seanaigh, which formed the main crossing point on the river at Ballyshannon throughout the medieval period when the graveyard at Ballyhanna was used. Archaeological investigation in the field in which the graveyard was located revealed an undated shallow ditch upon the crest of the hill, approximately 100 m to the south of the graveyard, which might be associated with the ornamental tree-ring depicted on the first-edition Ordnance Survey map of 1834–5 (see Illus. 1.6). No other archaeological remains were discovered in the field although a number of burials were subsequently excavated in four outlying service trenches which crossed the junction of East Port Road and Station Road immediately to the north and east of the main excavation area.

The analysis of the graveyard presented in this chapter is restricted to the main excavation area. Those burials excavated in the outlying service trenches, under the adjacent roads were in an extremely poor state of preservation having been compacted under road traffic for many years and, as a consequence, could not meaningfully be included in the consideration of the graveyard's chronology, development and context.[3]

The excavation of the topsoil and other superficial deposits (C 1; depth 0.10 m) at the site was initially undertaken using a mechanical excavator and was completed by hand, exposing the uppermost burials, the remains of a rectangular building subsequently identified as a medieval church and a couple of other associated features. The burials were excavated by hand using the standard context recording method. With the exception of a narrow *sondage*, the foundations and internal deposits within the church were only exposed and not investigated since it had been decided by the road design team that the structure would be preserved *in situ*. Excavation demonstrated that the quantity of burials within the main excavation area was significant and much truncation and disturbance of earlier skeletons had occurred during the digging of grave cuts for later burials (see R McCarthy, this volume). Few of the skeletons were complete as a result of this superimposition. In addition, the integrity of the skeletal remains located close to the edge of the field had often been further compromised by the roots of adjacent trees that lined the field boundary. The superimposition of burials often made the recognition of individual grave cuts and fills problematic for the excavators and so the mixed graveyard soil was largely excavated as a single unit (C 2). When elements of graves

---

3   For the purposes of the current analysis the excavation grid that had been used was divided into 4 m grid squares. The excavation grid was not established on True North and has been rotated on all of the published plans here so as to meaningfully represent both burial orientation and the direction of superimposition of stratigraphically related burials. Unfortunately, whilst being internally consistent, the original site survey of surrounding features was not detailed enough to enable the grid to be precisely aligned to True North. Consequently, there is an estimated, but consistent, five degree margin of error in all of the quoted alignments and angles.

cut into the natural subsoil were recognised, these, and their fills, were awarded separate context numbers; however, the majority of the skeletons could not be associated with either individual grave cuts or fills.

The natural subsoils at the site consisted of a yellow and brown clay (C 29) and a gravel-rich clay (C 22), which were both of glacial origin, as well as a fine yellow sand (C 3) that the excavator plausibly identified as a naturally formed estuarine or riverine deposit located 'at the base of the hill' (Ó Donnchadha 2006, 9). The interpretation of this latter deposit as 'natural' is problematic, however, and has a significant bearing upon an understanding of the graveyard's chronology and development. Several finds were recovered from the sand, including a sherd of everted-rim ware pottery, three iron nails (Small Find Nos 3:1–3), an L-shaped, rectangular-sectioned fragment of iron (Small Find No. 3:2) and a squared spatulate-headed, copper-alloy stick-pin (Small Find No. C3:4) that can confidently be dated, by analogy with examples from Waterford and Dublin, from the mid 12th to the mid 13th century AD (Scully 1997, 438–48, table 15.1; O Rahilly 1998, 29; see Small Finds Report included in the accompanying CD-ROM). Considered by the excavator to be part of the 'natural geology' of the site (Ó Donnchadha 2006, 9), the true relationship between the sand deposit (C 3) and the burial activity at Ballyhanna is uncertain. Given the date of the artefacts recovered from the sand it is reasonable to conclude that it was deposited during the medieval period at a point in time when the graveyard had already been in use for several centuries. If the finds were genuinely recovered from the deposit of sand, then rather than representing the 'natural geology' upon which the archaeologically significant elements of the site's stratigraphic sequence were superimposed, the sand represents an episode, or episodes, of inundation of the churchyard (ibid.). The location of the sand layer in the western part of the main excavation area may have masked the full extent and western boundary of the graveyard.

The boundaries of the graveyard

Estimating the original size and shape of the graveyard is difficult because only its southern edge was identifiable during the excavation. The extent of the area containing burials that was exposed in the main area of excavation was approximately 30 m (east–west) by 18.5 m (north–south). The burials uncovered in the service trenches under the adjacent roads indicate, however, that burial activity at Ballyhanna extended for at least 8 m to the north and 6 m to the east of the main excavation area. Consequently, the graveyard at Ballyhanna was at least 36 m (east–west) by 26.5 m (north–south) in size, with the medieval church being located on the western edge of this area of known burial activity (Illus. 3.1). The locations of skeletons discovered in the area during various works in the 19th and 20th centuries as noted by Begley (2009, 470–1) are too imprecisely recorded to enable them to be used to assess whether the graveyard at Ballyhanna was larger still.

The southern edge of the area of burial activity uncovered during the excavations coincided with the base of the steep hill that slopes upwards to the south. No remains of a formal boundary survived though, presumably, the edge of the graveyard was, when in use, defined by an earthen bank or hedge that was removed upon the abandonment of the site and its return to agricultural use. This southern edge of burial activity was located 9 m to the south of the ruined church and formed a slightly curved line, suggesting that the graveyard may originally have been curvilinear in shape.

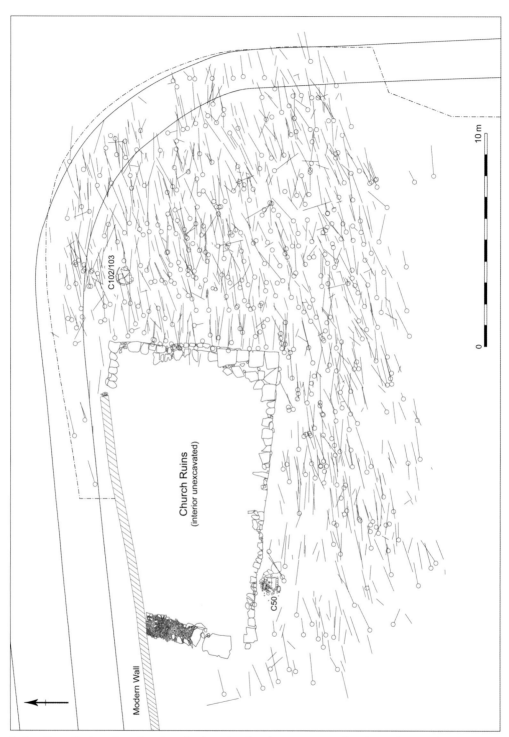

Illus. 3.1—Overall site plan showing the burials, church ruins, stone-lined circular pit (C 102/103) and 'quadrangular' reliquary shrine (C 50) (Prepared by Sapphire Mussen and based on the original site plan by Irish Archaeological Consultancy Ltd).

Only two burials lay beyond this line. The skeletons of a young adult female (SK 217) and a young adult male (SK 216) were located, 1.5 m and 2.2 m respectively, beyond the edge of burial activity within Grid Square Fvi. It is unlikely that the burial ground extended further to the south onto the lower slope of the hill—no disarticulated bone was found to the south of the area of known burial, and presumably the relatively thin depth of the soil in this area prohibited expansion of the graveyard in this direction. While it might be argued that cultivation in this area may have destroyed the *in situ* burials, this would not have removed the resulting disarticulated bones from the soil. In addition, one might also expect that this destructive process would in turn have resulted in a significant increase in the amount of disarticulated bone occurring in the southernmost part of the graveyard as a result of hill-wash. Analysis of the disarticulated bone indicates, however, that it was not concentrated just at the foot of the slope, but rather had a wide distribution which mirrored the density of burial across the whole of the graveyard (C J McKenzie, pers. comm.).

Although the main area of excavation extended a significant distance westwards beyond the church building, no burials were recovered from this area (see Illus. 3.1). While it is possible that burials did not extend far west of the church, the excavator suggested that the area to the west of the church may have been truncated during the construction of the 19th-century cottage that had formerly stood adjacent to the site (Ó Donnchadha 2006, 49). The ground surface gently falls away in a westerly direction and, consequently, any constructional terrace that may have existed would most likely have resulted in the creation of a scarped slope at its eastern edge. As the excavation revealed no such feature, however, this explanation for the general absence of burials to the west of the church is questionable. An alternative reason for the lack of burials is suggested by the deposit of sand, noted above, that apparently extended over much of the western part of the site (C 3). This sand represented an episode, or possibly several episodes, of flooding which is dated by the recovery of a stick-pin (Small Find No. C3:4) to around the mid 12th to mid 13th century AD. As a deposit, it is possible that the sand may have covered and effectively masked the western part of the graveyard. Perhaps after the inundation event, or events, burial was concentrated in the slightly higher areas to the south and east of the church which were less prone to flooding. Such an explanation would explain why no burials were uncovered any significant distance beyond the western end of the church.

In addition to the burials themselves, which are discussed below, the excavated portion of the graveyard at Ballyhanna contained three features: the foundations of a medieval church, a stone-lined circular pit (C 102/103) and a quadrangular reliquary shrine (C 50) (see Illus. 3.1).

The church

The foundations and part of the lowest masonry course of a rectangular building were uncovered in the north-western part of the site (Illus. 3.2). Most of the northern and western walls of the building had been removed, but enough remained extant to indicate that the structure had a simple, rectangular form with external dimensions of 14.2 m by 8.0 m and that its shorter, presumably gable, walls had been at least one metre thick. The longitudinal axis of the building was aligned approximately east–west. Given its medieval date (see below), dimensions, orientation and association with a burial ground, the building can be confidently identified as the remains of a church. This building is almost certainly the remains of the chapel-of-ease of 'Ballihanny' first recorded in the early

17th-century Plantation inquisition (Allingham 1879, 74; Anon. 1966, 384, no. XXXI–22; see MacDonagh, this volume).

As it was decided very early during the excavation at Ballyhanna that the church building would be preserved, the interior of the church was only partially investigated in a narrow *sondage* towards the eastern end of the structure. This revealed a layer, 0.64 m deep, of probable stone masonry fragments in a sandy clay soil matrix (C 82/84) that overlay a mortar-rich deposit of dark brown sandy clay (C 83; depth 0.30 m). Although such deposits could have been the result of

Illus. 3.2—Foundation of the medieval stone church discovered during excavation (Transport Infrastructure Ireland).

the gradual collapse of the building, there was an absence of any building rubble or dressed stone which had obviously been cleared from the site. Whether this indicates that the church collapsed and its rubble was subsequently removed, or that it was deliberately knocked down and the fallen masonry carried away, cannot be known for certain. These deposits overlay a thin, cemented layer of black silt (C 87; depth 0.07 m) that probably formed a bed for a robbed-out floor and, which in turn, overlay a hard-core of small and medium-sized stones (C 88; depth 0.50 m). Excavation was not continued beneath the hard-core deposit.

The exposed foundations of the building consisted of an irregular, drystone wall (C 17) set in a narrow foundation trench (C 76; width 0.40 to 0.50 m) and backfilled with a loose deposit of sandy clay (C 77). A single course of large, roughly dressed stones survived in the south-eastern corner of the building. No trace of lime mortar was observed in the wall, but the demolition layer in the church was mortar rich and it is unlikely that this relatively large structure was a drystone construction. The rectangular form of the building indicates that the church was a relatively simple single-celled building (i.e. Rodwell 1989, 67, fig. 22.1). No evidence was observed to suggest that the building was the product of more than a single phase of construction; however, given the restricted scale of its excavation, the interpretive weight that can be placed upon this negative evidence is limited.

One of the burials (SK 787) that was definitely stratified beneath the church foundations was sampled for radiocarbon dating (UBA-14972) and provides a *terminus post quem* (from the Latin *terminus post quem non licet*, meaning 'limit after which one may not go') of between AD 1263 and 1381 (see Appendix 1). This suggests that the excavated church post-dates at least the middle of the 13th century—an observation which is consistent with the 13th-century date suggested by Clare McCutcheon for the fragment of a cross-inscribed strap handle from a possible 'everted-rim/ crannog type' cooking pot (Illus. 3.3) which was recovered from the cemented deposit of black silt (C 87) that probably formed a bed for the robbed-out floor of the church.

Given that the programme of radiocarbon dating indicates that burial at Ballyhanna began, at the

Illus. 3.3—Fragment of a cross-inscribed strap handle from a possible everted-rim/crannog-type cooking pot recovered from the cemented deposit of black silt (C 87) that probably formed a bed for the robbed-out floor of the church (Jonathan Hession).

latest, by the second half of the eighth century AD (see below), it is unlikely that the exposed walls represent the earliest church at the site. Western Ulster is a region in which mortared stone churches apparently remained in the minority until at least AD 1200 (Ó Carragáin 2010, 15, 110, figs 1 and 119). Consequently, any earlier church at Ballyhanna was probably built from organic materials such as turf, wattle and timber. The location of an earlier medieval or early medieval church within the graveyard at Ballyhanna is uncertain as no trace of such a structure was recognised during the course of the excavation. Unfortunately, the constructional techniques likely to have been used for building early wooden churches would rarely leave an identifiable archaeological signature (ibid., 19–22). Assuming, however, that no significant level of burial activity took place inside an earlier church present at Ballyhanna, then the widespread distribution across the site of radiocarbon-dated burials which either exclusively pre-date AD 1000 (see Illus. 3.6) or fall exclusively between AD 950 and AD 1300 (see Illus. 3.7), suggests that any earlier church was not located within that portion of the graveyard excavated in 2003 and 2004. It is a strong possibility that any earlier church, if one had existed, would be located in the position where the stone church was subsequently built.

The stone-lined circular pit

Located a couple of metres to the east of the north-eastern corner of the church was a feature consisting of a circular pit (C 103; diameter 0.90 m, depth 0.45 m) dug into the natural subsoil and lined with flat stones (C 102; see Illus. 3.1). It was filled with a charcoal-rich deposit (C 100) and was apparently sealed by a flat cap stone (C 101) placed across its top. While the amount of charcoal present in the fill of the pit might suggest this was some form of hearth, there was nothing to suggest that either the stone lining contained evidence of *in situ* burning or that the surrounding subsoil had been heat modified (Ó Donnchadha 2006, 23). That the feature pre-dated the commencement of burial activity, or at the latest occurred at a relatively early date within the burial sequence at Ballyhanna, is suggested by the observation that it did not cut through any burials and that six skeletons physically overlay it, and therefore must post-date it (i.e. SK 576, SK 592, SK 598, SK 1095, SK 1212 and SK 1217). All six of these skeletons were stratified above a burial (SK 1242) that returned a date of between AD 670 and 772 (UBA-11453; see Appendix 1). It is not possible to ascertain whether the pit had an industrial or domestic function. No evidence for an associated superstructure was observed, although if it had once existed it would probably have been destroyed by the subsequent burial activity.

The reliquary shrine

The third structure within the graveyard was a partially disturbed, box-like structure (C 50) that was located immediately adjacent to the southern wall of the church (Illus. 3.4). This feature consisted of a series of broken slabs arranged to form the base and three near-vertical sides of a shallow box (0.75 m by 0.55 m and c. 0.25 m deep), which was aligned east–west, partly set into the natural subsoil and apparently left open to the west. Seventy-six pieces of white quartz stone and unworked rock crystal, and six beach-rolled pebbles were found within the feature, which was filled with a loose deposit of sandy clay (C 52) that was in turn overlain by a flat slab which the excavator considered to be a displaced cap stone. The box-like

Illus. 3.4—The quadrangular reliquary shrine (C 50) following excavation (Photo by Irish Archaeological Consultancy Ltd, annotation by Libby Mulqueeny).

form of the structure, its east–west orientation, and the large number of quartz stones, rock crystals and rounded pebbles contained within it suggest that it represents the remains of a quadrangular reliquary shrine.

Five comparable features, all occurring on early ecclesiastical sites in the south-west of Ireland, have previously been excavated. Two of these were located on the monastic island of Illaunloughan, Co. Kerry—one in a secondary position upon a small, raised platform which also supported an example of a tent-shaped gable-shrine (Marshall & Walsh 2005, 64–6, 171, fig. 49) and the other to the south of the island's drystone oratory (ibid., 160–1). A third excavated example was located on Church Island, near Valentia, Co. Kerry (O'Kelly 1958, 87–90, fig. 6, pl. II.c), whilst the fourth was positioned adjacent to the front of the oratory at Reask, Co. Kerry (Fanning 1981, 84–6, fig. 7, pl. IIIb). The final excavated example, a larger and more elaborate structure, was positioned over a grave whose lintels exhibited wear patterns consistent with devotional activity at Caherlehillan, Co. Kerry (O'Sullivan & Sheehan 1996, 265; Sheehan 2009, 199). In addition to the excavated examples, comparable features are also known from the Skellig Michael hermitage (Horn et al. 1990, 50, fig. 43; Marshall & Walsh 2005, 64) and Kildreenagh, Cool East, Co. Kerry (Ó Carragáin 2003, 143, fig. 9.6). These quadrangular shrines have a relatively simple form made up of vertical sides and a paved floor, however, the Church Island, Reask and Caherlehillan shrines were also furnished with corner posts or pillar stones (O'Kelly 1958, 87–9, fig. 6; Fanning 1981, 84; Sheehan 2009, 199). Excavation demonstrated that both of the Illaunloughan quadrangular shrines contained a large number of quartz stones, but no human bone. The Church Island shrine also contained a mass of quartz pebbles and a single fragment of human bone, whilst the Caherlehillan shrine was empty, save for its earthen core. Although no quartz stones were recovered from the heavily truncated example from Reask, phosphate analysis suggested that the feature had contained reinterred human bone (Fanning 1981, 85). The available dating evidence suggests that the quadrangular shrines date to the early medieval period. The corner-post shrine at Caherlehillan was probably the last structural addition to a site that was abandoned during the eighth century AD (Sheehan 2009, 199–200) and the two quadrangular shrines from Illaunloughan are confidently attributed to the eighth- to ninth-century AD phase of the site's sequence (Marshall & Walsh 2005, 160–1, 171). Whilst no direct dating evidence was recovered for either the Church Island or Reask shrines, the former is on a site that was established, at the latest, by the mid seventh to mid eighth century (Edwards 1990, 117), whilst the Reask shrine appeared to be a focus for the earliest burials at the site suggesting it also had a similar date (Fanning 1981, 152).

The original form of the quadrangular reliquary shrines is uncertain because all of the known examples have been truncated or otherwise disturbed. Fanning (ibid., 85) considered them to be directly analogous to the better-known examples of tent-shaped reliquary structures that are variously called gable, house or slab shrines and which are known from a number of early ecclesiastical sites along the west coast of Ireland (for a recent survey of the type see Marshall & Walsh 2005, 55–8). Alternatively, Marshall and Walsh (ibid., 66) have plausibly suggested that the pillar stones located in the corners of the examples from Reask and Caherlehillan indicate that the quadrangular shrines might be better considered as a crude variant of the corner-post shrines of northern Britain (Thomas 1971, 150–9; O'Sullivan & Sheehan 1996, 265), which are dated on art-historical grounds to the eighth and ninth centuries AD (Thomas 1998, 94–5). Sheehan (2009, 199–200) has recently argued that the Caherlehillan shrine never contained translated relics and simply functioned as a marker for a founder's grave that directly formed a focus for devotion. The results of the phosphate analysis undertaken at Reask suggest, however, that this interpretation should not be applied uncritically to all quadrangular shrines. If genuine, the absence of translated remains in the Caherlehillan shrine may be a consequence of the relatively short duration of the site's use after the shrine was built.

Regardless of the precise character of its original form, the Ballyhanna shrine and most of the other quadrangular shrines can be confidently interpreted as being reliquary shrines that held the translated bones, and possibly associative relics, of saints. Although direct dating evidence for the structures is poor, the excavation of the examples from Illaunloughan, Caherlehillan and Reask suggest that most, if not all, of the Irish examples date to the early medieval period. The virtual absence of references to the translation of relics in the *Annals of Ulster* before AD 700 suggests that the majority of Irish reliquary shrines are unlikely to pre-date the eighth century AD (Ó Carragáin 2010, 67). The example from Ballyhanna is the most northerly of the known Irish reliquary shrines, but its location is consistent with their distribution along the west coast of Ireland. The recognition of a reliquary shrine in the graveyard at Ballyhanna suggests that at some point during the early medieval period a corporeal relic cult of at least one saint had become established at the site. Although no bones that could represent the exhumed remains of a saint were recovered from the feature, given the disturbed state of the shrine, this absence should not be considered interpretively significant. As the reliquary shrine was not stratified over any burials it is likely that it was built relatively early in the sequence of activity at the site. It is notable that given the density of burial activity at Ballyhanna, the shrine was not disturbed by any later burials (see Illus. 3.1) suggesting that the shrine continued to be respected, and presumably venerated, throughout the medieval period.

The burials

The majority of the burials[4] within the graveyard at Ballyhanna were interred in shallow, simple earth-dug graves; the bodies being aligned approximately west–east in an extended, supine position with the head to the west and the arms by the side of the body with the hands either at the sides or placed over the pelvis. While the intensity of burial at Ballyhanna resulted in many burials being disturbed, the complete plans of a small number of grave cuts associated with adult burials were recorded. These were mostly sub-rectangular in shape with rounded ends or corners (e.g. C 10, C 33, C 35, C 39, C 48, C 53, C 55, C 59, C 63, C 65, C 71 and C 89), but there were also a number with a distinctly tapered form (e.g. C 27, C 40 and C 94). The extant grave cuts of neonate, infant and younger child burials, however, were all ovoid in plan (e.g. C 48, C 61 and C 78).

Chronology and spatial arrangement

The 72 radiocarbon dates derived from skeletons excavated at Ballyhanna (Illus. 3.5) indicate that the earliest burials occurred at the site in the late seventh to early eighth century AD and that burial at a consistent rate had commenced by the second half of the eighth century AD until at least the first quarter of the 17th century. There is, however, an under-representation of dates that

---

4   A summary of all burial data is provided in a table in the accompanying CD-ROM.

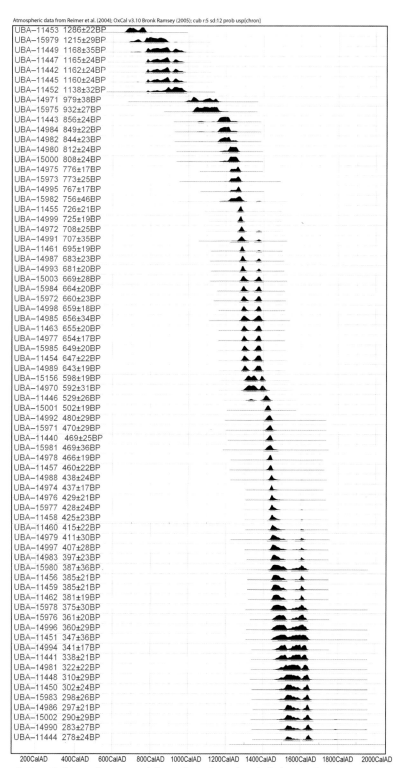

Atmospheric data from Reimer et al. (2004); OxCal v3.10 Bronk Ramsey (2005); cub r:5 sd:12 prob usp[chron]

UBA−11453	1286±22BP
UBA−15979	1215±29BP
UBA−11449	1168±35BP
UBA−11447	1165±24BP
UBA−11442	1162±24BP
UBA−11445	1160±24BP
UBA−11452	1138±32BP
UBA−14971	979±38BP
UBA−15975	932±27BP
UBA−11443	856±24BP
UBA−14984	849±22BP
UBA−14982	844±23BP
UBA−14980	812±24BP
UBA−15000	808±24BP
UBA−14975	776±17BP
UBA−15973	773±25BP
UBA−14995	767±17BP
UBA−15982	756±46BP
UBA−11455	726±21BP
UBA−14999	725±19BP
UBA−14972	708±25BP
UBA−14991	707±35BP
UBA−11461	695±19BP
UBA−14987	683±23BP
UBA−14993	681±20BP
UBA−15003	669±28BP
UBA−15984	664±20BP
UBA−15972	660±23BP
UBA−14998	659±18BP
UBA−14985	656±34BP
UBA−11463	655±20BP
UBA−14977	654±17BP
UBA−15985	649±20BP
UBA−11454	647±22BP
UBA−14989	643±19BP
UBA−15156	598±19BP
UBA−14970	592±31BP
UBA−11446	529±26BP
UBA−15001	502±19BP
UBA−14992	480±29BP
UBA−15971	470±29BP
UBA−11440	469±25BP
UBA−15981	469±36BP
UBA−14978	466±19BP
UBA−11457	460±22BP
UBA−14988	438±24BP
UBA−14974	437±17BP
UBA−14976	429±21BP
UBA−15977	428±24BP
UBA−11458	425±23BP
UBA−11460	415±22BP
UBA−14979	411±30BP
UBA−14997	407±28BP
UBA−14983	397±23BP
UBA−15980	387±36BP
UBA−11456	385±21BP
UBA−11459	385±21BP
UBA−11462	381±19BP
UBA−15978	375±30BP
UBA−15976	361±20BP
UBA−14996	360±29BP
UBA−11451	347±36BP
UBA−14994	341±17BP
UBA−11441	338±21BP
UBA−14981	322±22BP
UBA−11448	310±29BP
UBA−11450	302±24BP
UBA−15983	298±26BP
UBA−14986	297±21BP
UBA−15002	290±29BP
UBA−14990	283±27BP
UBA−11444	278±24BP

200CalAD 400CalAD 600CalAD 800CalAD 1000CalAD 1200CalAD 1400CalAD 1600CalAD 1800CalAD 2000CalAD

Illus. 3.5—Calibrated ranges of the radiocarbon-dated skeletons (Cormac McSparron).

fall between the beginning of the 11th century AD and the second half of the 12th century AD—a period which is represented by the dates of only two male young adults (SK 555; UBA-14971 and SK 571; UBA-15975), located in Grid Squares Aiii and Eiv. This anomaly in the regularity of the sequence of radiocarbon dates is not the product of a variation in the calibration curve (C McSparron, pers. comm.) and therefore probably reflects, if not an actual period of abandonment of the site, then certainly a marked decline in the use of the excavated part of the graveyard for the purposes of burial. It is notable that this period of reduced use of the graveyard partly coincides with the mid 12th- to mid 13th-century date range proposed above for the flooding of the graveyard as represented by the deposit of riverine or estuarine sand (C 3).

The radiocarbon-dated skeletons were sub-divided into four successive, and partly overlapping, chronological groups (pre-AD 1000; AD 950–1300; AD 1250–1500; and post-AD 1450) and their distribution by grid square was plotted (Illus. 3.6–3.9). Those skeletons whose dates did not fall exclusively within a single chronological group, when calibrated and expressed at two sigma, were excluded from this part of the analysis. As the spatial distribution of radiocarbon-dated skeletons across the site is broadly consistent with the overall distribution of skeletons (compare Illus. 3.10 and Illus. 3.11), it is reasonable to conclude that any chronological variations in the distribution of burials that can be identified are meaningful and that variations in the distribution plots of the four chronological groups reflect genuine changes in the use of the graveyard over time. Although only seven skeletons fall into the pre-AD 1000 chronological group of dated burials (Illus. 3.6), their placement broadly reflects the overall distribution of burials (see Illus. 3.1), although it is notable that only one of the skeletons is located in the western half of the main excavation area. This latter observation is consistent with the possibility, suggested above, that an inundation of sand (C 3) may have covered the western part of the site. The 11 burials that make up the second chronological group (AD 950–1300) were distributed throughout most of the main excavation area, however, only one was located in the easternmost third of the site (Illus. 3.7). With such a small sample size certainty is not possible, but the general absence of burials in the east of the main excavation area suggests that, during the period AD 950–1300, the size of the area actively used for burial may have contracted to around the immediate vicinity of the later church. Given that the apparent hiatus or reduction in the rate of burial during the 11th and 12th centuries AD falls within this period, a concomitant reduction in the size of the graveyard would not be unexpected. Skeletons within the third chronological group (AD 1250–1500) were distributed throughout that part of the main excavation area in which burials were uncovered (Illus. 3.8). However, the distribution of the last chronological group (post-AD 1450) was exclusively restricted to the eastern half of the main excavation area (Illus. 3.9), suggesting that the area to the south of the church fell out of favour for burial before the middle of the 15th century.

The radiocarbon dating of the burial assemblage suggests that burial ceased at Ballyhanna in the first half of the 17th century, consistent with the historical record as the lands changed ownership at this time (see MacDonagh, this volume). Clay smoking pipes are an artefact type that proliferated in Ireland in this century with the introduction of tobacco from the Americas. The absence of any clay pipe fragments from either the graveyard soil (C 2) or any other deposit associated with the burials, and the recovery of only two undated stem fragments from the topsoil (Small Find Nos C1:2–3), suggests that both burial activity and regular use of the churchyard must have ceased in the first couple of decades of the 17th century (Norton & Lane 2007, 435–7).

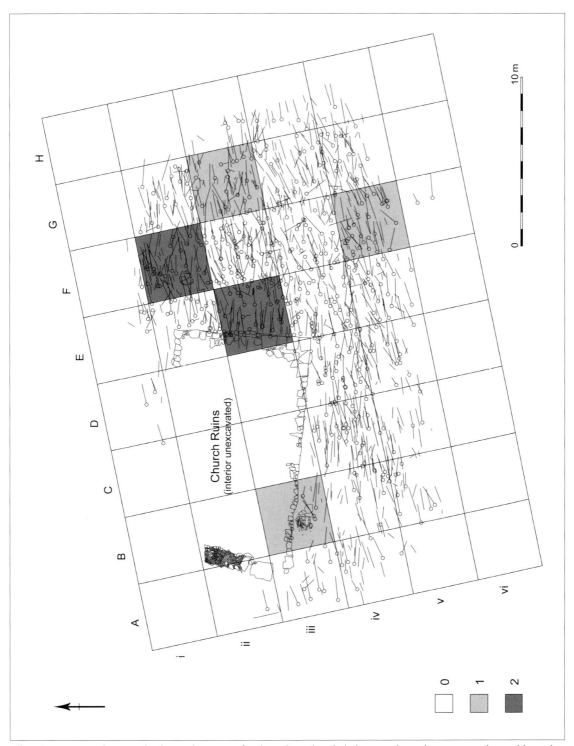

Illus. 3.6—Distribution plot by grid square of radiocarbon-dated skeletons whose date range, when calibrated at two sigma, falls exclusively before AD 1000 (Prepared by Sapphire Mussen and based on the original site plan by Irish Archaeological Consultancy Ltd).

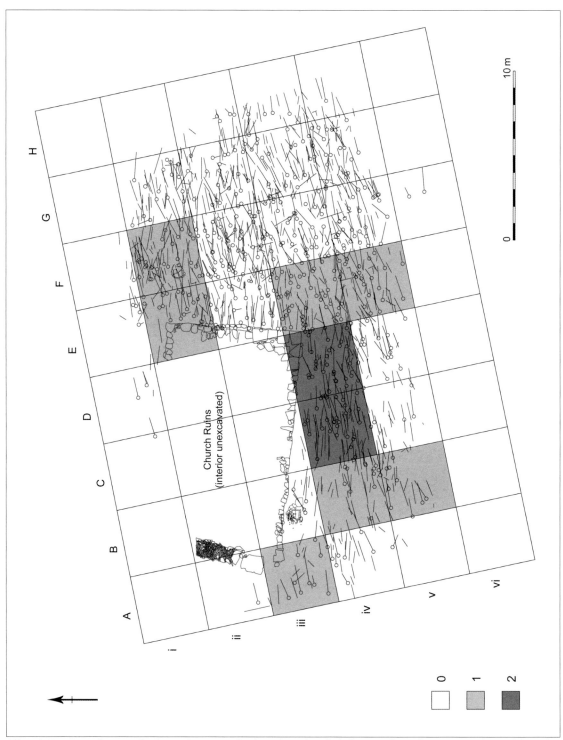

Illus. 3.7—Distribution plot by grid square of radiocarbon-dated skeletons whose date range, when calibrated at two sigma, falls exclusively between AD 950 and AD 1300 (Prepared by Sapphire Mussen and based on the original site plan by Irish Archaeological Consultancy Ltd).

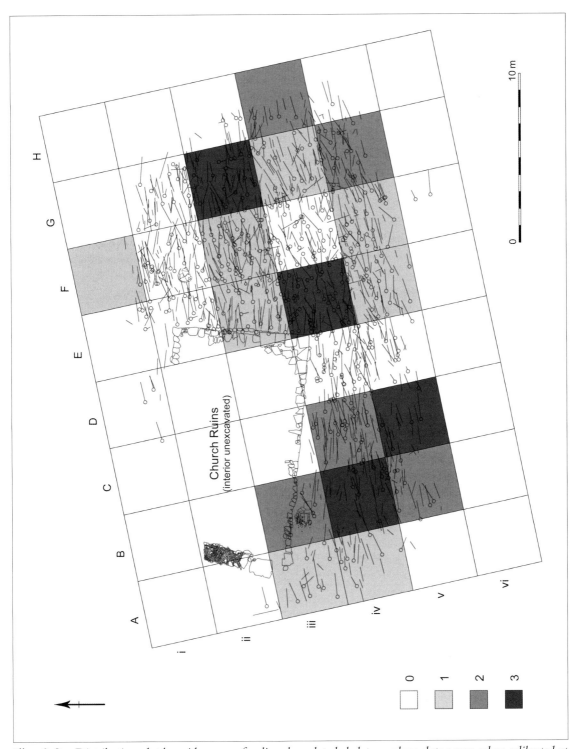

Illus. 3.8—Distribution plot by grid square of radiocarbon-dated skeletons whose date range, when calibrated at two sigma, falls exclusively between AD 1250 and AD 1500 (Prepared by Sapphire Mussen and based on the original site plan by Irish Archaeological Consultancy Ltd).

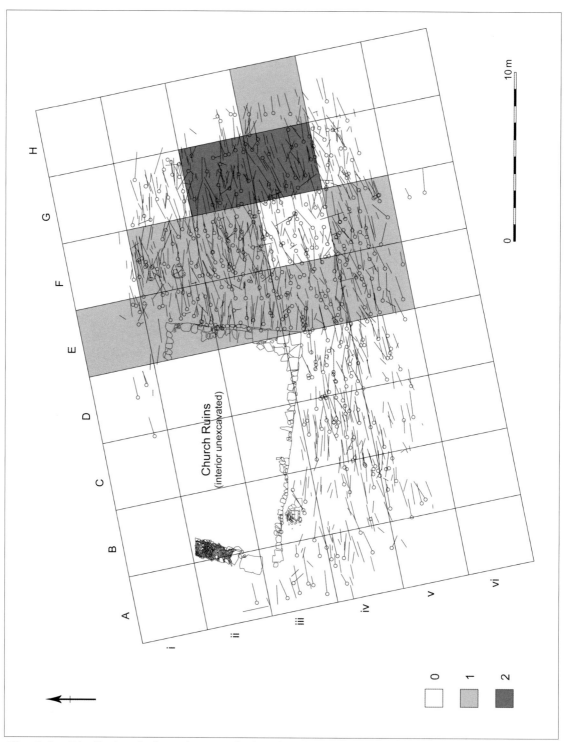

Illus. 3.9—Distribution plot by grid square of radiocarbon-dated skeletons whose date range, when calibrated at two sigma, falls exclusively after AD 1450 (Prepared by Sapphire Mussen and based on the original site plan by Irish Archaeological Consultancy Ltd).

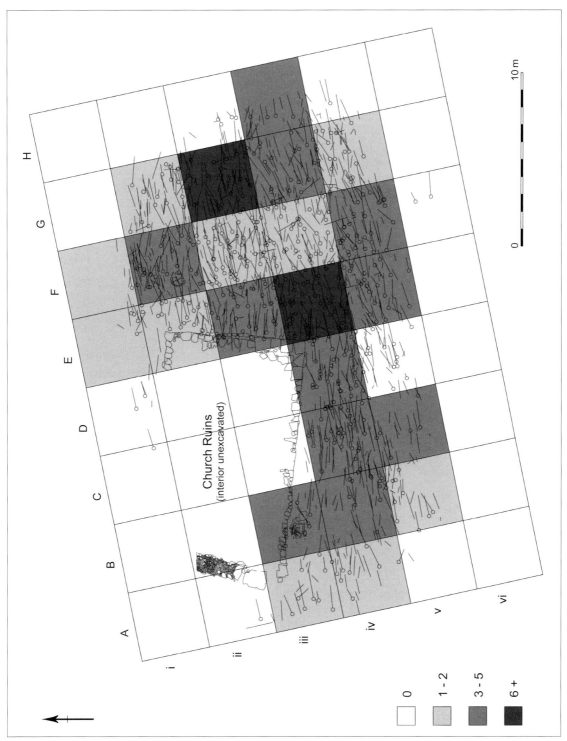

Illus. 3.10—Distribution plot by grid square of all radiocarbon-dated skeletons (Prepared by Sapphire Mussen and based on the original site plan by Irish Archaeological Consultancy Ltd).

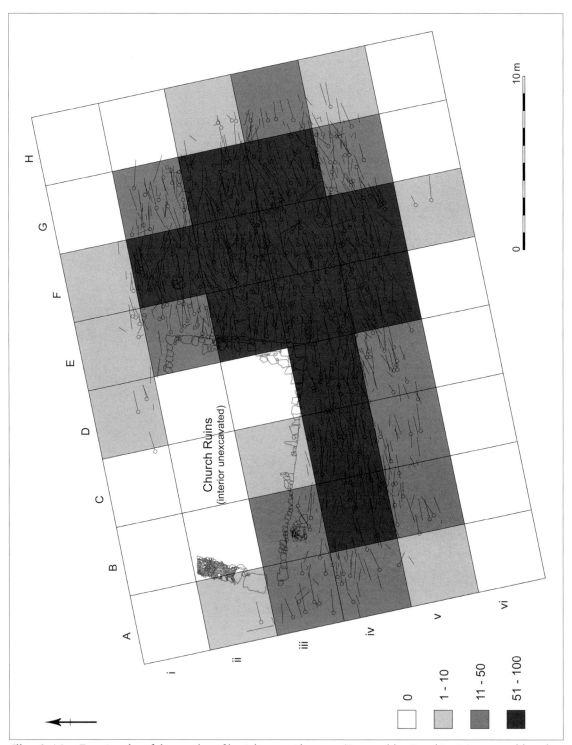

Illus. 3.11—Density plot of the number of burials per grid square (Prepared by Sapphire Mussen and based on the original site plan by Irish Archaeological Consultancy Ltd).

Graveyard management

Analysis of the rose diagram plan (see Text box on page 66) shows that a marked, and relatively consistent, bipolar pattern of superimposition existed across the site. This indicates that, rather than occurring at random within the graveyard, burial mostly occurred in alternating eastward- and westward-running rows across the excavated portion of the site. Given that west–east burial alignment was normal, such an arrangement would mean that for the eastward-running rows the head of each new burial was located at the foot of the previous burial, and for the westward-running rows the feet of each new burial was located adjacent to the head of the previous burial. This methodology for identifying the pattern of cemetery development has only been applied to one other site—that of the medieval graveyard of Ardreigh, Co. Kildare. At Ardreigh there was also a bipolar pattern of superimposition, but one which was arranged north–south and trending slightly to the east, indicating that burial occurred in alternating northward- and southward-running rows of burials interred 'shoulder-to-shoulder' that developed away from the medieval church and towards the east over time (Opie 2009, 400–3, figs 18.2 and 18.3). At Ballyhanna no exclusively northward or southward trend within the east–west bipolar pattern exists. Presumably this reflects the long duration of burial activity at the site and the possibility that, over the centuries, rows of burials have been interred within the same area repeatedly. This would explain why no obvious east–west aligned rows of burial can be seen in the overall site plan (see Illus. 3.1). Although Daniell (1997, 146) considered that north–south aligned rows of burials laid out 'shoulder-to-shoulder' was likely to be the medieval norm, a comparable arrangement of organising successive burials in 'strings' or rows, albeit only running eastwards, has been recognised at Clonmacnoise, Co. Offaly, beneath the site of the Cross of the Scriptures (Manning 2005, 54).

No evidence for the use of long-term grave-markers, such as inscribed stones or settings for wooden crosses was recognised during the excavation, although, given the disturbed conditions on site, evidence for these would have been difficult to recognise. It is likely that the location for digging each grave was made with reference to the unsettled mound of earth that would have fairly accurately shown the position of the previous burial.

The quadrangular reliquary shrine (C 50), located adjacent to the southern wall of the church, did not form a specific focus for burial. Although it should be noted that any early burials located to the north of the shrine have been either sealed or truncated by the unexcavated church, it is notable that there was neither a cluster of burials around the shrine, nor did burial activity radiate out from the feature. The probable reason for this has been noted by Ó Carragáin (2010, 82–5) who has observed that by the eighth century AD a sophisticated model of Christian burial had developed in Ireland, which involved both rituals to consecrate graveyards and the concept of saying Masses for the dead, meaning that proximity of burial to 'holy' human remains (i.e. saintly people) had become of relatively little importance. That said, the shrine would still have probably formed a focus for other activities important to the local community, such as oath-taking and rituals for the sick and dying (ibid.), and the fact that it was not compromised by subsequent burial suggests that it continued to be respected, if not actively venerated, throughout the medieval period.

Interpreting graveyard management at Ballyhanna—the use of rose diagrams

An innovative methodology has been developed by the authors to consider the way in which burial activity within the graveyard at Ballyhanna was both managed and developed over time. This analysis has been achieved by recording the direction of superimposition of stratigraphically related burials (see spreadsheet included on accompanying CD-ROM). The direction of superimposition was defined as the angle, relative to True North, of a line drawn from the centre of the earlier skeleton (that is a point just above the pelvis) to the centre of the later skeleton (Illus. 3.12). In those cases where the centre of a skeleton was missing this point's original position was estimated.

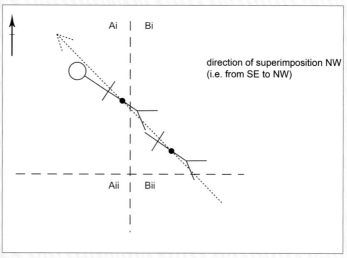

Illus. 3.12—Diagram showing how the direction of superimposition of two stratigraphically related burials was calculated. Note that the majority of the relationship is located within Grid Square Bi (Sapphire Mussen).

The data generated by this analysis has been used to produce a site plan consisting of rose diagrams for each grid square (Illus. 3.13). A rose diagram is a histogram that is drawn in a circle. They are a particularly useful tool for representing information that has a directional component—in this case the direction of superimposition of burials across the site. The separate sectors of a rose diagram consist of equal angles but differ in how far they extend from the circle's centre—the length of the individual sectors being proportional to the number of occurrences in that range or direction. In this case the occurrences being represented are the number of stratigraphic relationships between burials aligned per 45° sector of the compass. It must be borne in mind when interpreting the plan that, rather than reflecting the alignment of individual burials, the rose diagrams depict the direction of the stratigraphic relationships between successive burials (where this direction can be established with an estimated 90% level of confidence). Consequently, the individual rose diagrams depict the directions in which burial activity spread through time in each of the site's grid squares.

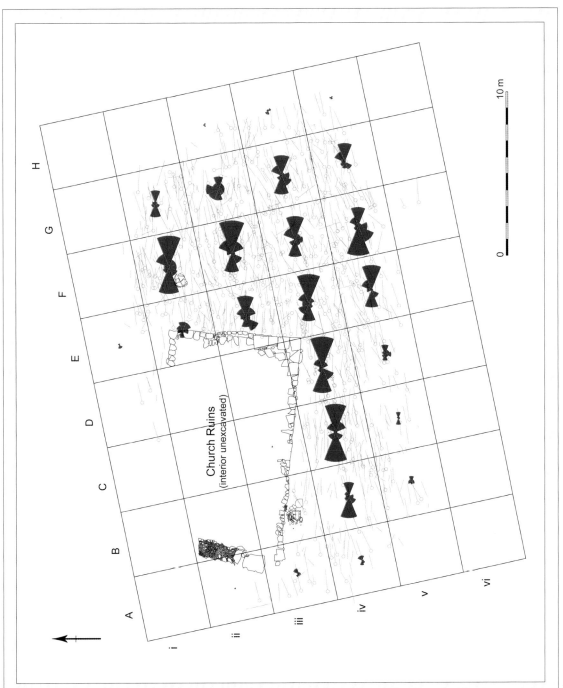

Illus. 3.13—Overall site plan with superimposed rose diagrams showing the direction of superimposition of stratigraphically related burials within each grid square, where this can be assessed with an estimated 90% level of confidence (Prepared by Sapphire Mussen and based on the original site plan by Irish Archaeological Consultancy Ltd).

Age and sex profile

In terms of the age-at-death and sex of the skeletons, there was little evidence of meaningful patterning in the distribution of burials. Osteoarchaeological analysis identified a total of 869 adult skeletons, of which 322 were male and 333 were female (see McKenzie, this volume)—these sexed burials were evenly distributed across the main excavation area (Illus. 3.14). The sex of the remaining 214 adult skeletons could not be identified, either because they were too incomplete or because they displayed no significant sexually dimorphic characteristics. A total number of 427 juvenile burials were excavated, consisting of 47 foetuses or neonates (under one month), 22 infants (one to 12 months), 198 younger children (one to six years), 91 older children (six to 12 years) and 69 adolescents (12 to 18 years) (see Murphy, this volume). Burials of individuals of all ages are fairly evenly distributed throughout the graveyard (Illus. 3.15), however, it is notable that the burials of foetuses, neonates and infants are largely, although not exclusively, restricted to the area east of the church. The significance of this pattern is uncertain. Although analysis of the radiocarbon-dated skeletons indicates that those directly dated burials which post-dated AD 1450 were also restricted to the eastern half of the main excavation area (see above; Illus. 3.9), this coincidence does not signify that all of the neonate and infant burials at Ballyhanna were equally late in date. For example, one of the infant skeletons sampled for radiocarbon dating (SK 1100) produced a date of AD 1271–1381 (UBA-11461), whilst another (SK 474) was stratified below a skeleton (SK 541) dated to AD 1410–40 (UBA-15001) and a fourth infant (SK 1022) was stratified below a skeleton (SK 824) dated to AD 1409–50 (UBA-14992). It is possible that variations in environmental burial conditions, caused by the different natural subsoils present across the site, resulted in preferential survival of bone in the eastern half of the main excavation area. Any such variations would be more marked in the survival rates of the smaller and less robust bones of foetuses, neonates and infants.

Grave orientation

Rose diagrams showing the alignment of skeletons within each grid square, where these can be assessed with an estimated 90% level of confidence, have been superimposed upon the site plan (Illus. 3.16; see Text box on p. 66). Following Christian tradition, the majority of the skeletons had an approximate west–east orientation with the head positioned to the west (of the 810 burials, for which the alignment can be measured with an estimated 90% level of confidence, the alignment of 697 (86%) fell between 241° and 300°). The reasons given in medieval texts for the adoption of the west–east alignment (with the head to the west) by the Christian Church are listed by Rahtz (1978, 4). It is notable that at Ballyhanna, although both the church and the majority of the burials are orientated approximately west–east, the church is aligned in a slightly more southerly direction than the majority of the burials. This slight, but marked, difference in alignment suggests that, in general, graves were not aligned with reference to the church. Given the wide range of recorded alignments of the skeletons that are classified here as being approximately west–east, it is possible that the position of the sun rise, which at Ballyhanna varies between approximately 47° and 133° degrees throughout the year, was used as a reference for the alignment of graves rather than the church building.

Although a wide range of other burial alignments are represented at Ballyhanna, the most common of these atypical alignments are reversed burials (i.e. east–west with the head to the east)

Illus. 3.14—Plan of all adult burials showing distribution of male, female and adult skeletons of indeterminable sex (Prepared by Sapphire Mussen and based on the original site plan by Irish Archaeological Consultancy Ltd).

Illus. 3.15—Plan of all burials showing distribution by age of all juvenile skeletons (Prepared by Sapphire Mussen and based on the original site plan by Irish Archaeological Consultancy Ltd).

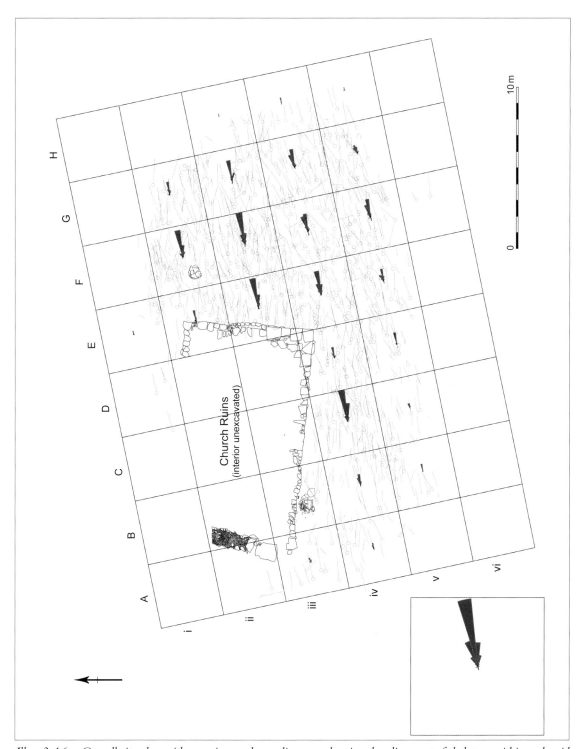

Illus. 3.16—Overall site plan with superimposed rose diagrams showing the alignment of skeletons within each grid square, where this can be assessed with an estimated 90% level of confidence (Prepared by Sapphire Mussen and based on the original site plan by Irish Archaeological Consultancy Ltd).

and those burials aligned either south–north (head to the south) or north–south (head to the north).

Thirty-five (approximately 4%) of the skeletons had a reversed alignment, that is they were buried east–west with their head to the east (for details see table included in the accompanying CD-ROM). Osteoarchaeological analysis indicates that children, adolescents and also adults of both sexes were buried in this reversed position. Within the main area of excavation, the distribution of the reversed burials is predominantly easterly—all but two of the reversed burials (SK 132 and SK 341) were located to the east of the church. Only one of the burials with a reversed, east–west burial alignment (SK 121) was sampled for radiocarbon dating and it returned a date of between AD 1434 and 1619 (UBA-14997; see Appendix 1). This relatively late date is consistent with the evidence provided by those other reversed burials that were stratigraphically related to skeletons that had been sampled for radiocarbon dating. One of these burials (SK 1000) was stratified above a skeleton (SK 882) that was dated to AD 1488–1648 (UBA-11448) indicating that the practice of reversed burial extended until at least the final quarter of the 15th century. Further evidence suggesting that the occurrence of reversed burials might be a relatively late phenomenon is provided by the observation that of the eight reversed burials (SK 260, SK 651, SK 891, SK 963, SK 997, SK 1050, SK 1142 and SK 1146) which were stratified beneath skeletons sampled for radiocarbon dating, the earliest returned date range (UBA-14988; AD 1425–78) only provided a 15th-century *terminus ante quem*. Although the radiocarbon dating evidence is not detailed enough to be certain, it suggests the possibility that the practice of reversed burial at Ballyhanna was restricted to the late medieval period.

It is uncertain whether the occurrence of burials with a reversed alignment reflects a deliberate burial rite. The tradition that reversed burials are those of priests who will be resurrected facing their congregation during the Day of Judgement dates to the early 17th century and cannot be used to explain late medieval, or earlier, occurrences of east–west aligned burials (Rahtz 1978, 4–5; Daniell 1997, 149). It has plausibly been suggested that the alignment of many reversed burials may simply have been the result of a mistake arising from the use of heavier cloth for burial shrouds (Stones 1989, 115). If such an interpretation was applied to the examples from Ballyhanna then the apparent increased incidence of reversed alignment during the late medieval period might reflect a shift to using heavier cloth for burial shrouds.

Ten of the skeletons were aligned south–north (head to the south), while seven were aligned in the opposite, north–south direction (for details see tables included in the accompanying CD-ROM). Although the number of south–north and north–south burials is small, they include both adults (n=4) and children (n=6) of various ages and must represent intentional deviations from the use of the normal west–east burial alignment. Where the sex of the adult skeletons was identifiable, the south–north aligned burials were all female (SK 432, SK 495 and SK 882), however, both male (SK 606 and SK 799) and female (SK 677) skeletons were aligned north–south. Given the small number of burials, the apparent female exclusivity of the south–north burials cannot be considered statistically significant. As with the reversed burials, the distribution of the south–north and north–south aligned burials is easterly—all of the examples being located to the east of the church. Radiocarbon dating suggests that these burials were predominantly, if not exclusively, medieval in date. Three of the south–north burials (SK 432, SK 495 and SK 882) were sampled for radiocarbon dating and returned dates of AD 1160–1254 (UBA-14982), AD 1499–1791 (UBA-14990) and AD 1488–1648 (UBA-11448) respectively, whilst one (SK 1091) was stratified above a burial (SK 1242) that produced a date of AD 670–772 (UBA-11453), and another (SK 146) was stratified between two skeletons (SK 528 and SK 121) that returned dates of AD 1186–1270 (UBA-15000) and AD 1434–1619 (UBA-14997) respectively. None of the north–south burials were directly sampled for radiocarbon dating, but one (SK 799) was stratified below a burial (SK 858) that was dated to AD 1494–1661 (UBA-15002), whilst another (SK 994) was stratified above a burial (SK 1030) that returned a date of AD 1287–1391 (UBA-14989). These radiocarbon dates are consistent with, but not definitive proof of, the south–north and north–south burial rite being a later medieval, rather than early medieval, practice at Ballyhanna.

Coffins

There was no evidence for either stone-lined or timber-lined graves—none of the surviving grave cuts were rectangular or significantly larger than the skeleton they contained. Similarly, there was no definitive evidence to suggest the use of coffins at Ballyhanna. Rodwell (1989, 164) notes that a nailed coffin cannot be made with less than 12 nails, although it is possible to construct a fully-jointed coffin with only two to three nails which would be necessary to secure the lid and strengthen any defective joints. Although four burials (SK 104, SK 110, SK 126 and SK 1117) were apparently associated with single nails (Small Find Nos 28:1, 104:1, 110:1 and 1117:2), these may all have been residually deposited in the grave fills. Catherine Johnson has suggested that a fragment of a rectangular-sectioned strip of iron (Small Find No. 732:1) that was recovered from the fill associated with the disturbed skeleton of a female adult (SK 732A) may have been part of a coffin fitting (see Small Finds Report in the accompanying CD-ROM), but this identification remains conjectural.

Shrouds and dress activities

Little evidence was recovered to indicate whether the bodies interred at Ballyhanna were buried in shrouds or clothed. The excavators explicitly recorded on only four occasions that the hunched posture or position of the arms of four skeletons (SK 62, SK 137, SK 287 and SK 688) suggested that they were interred in shrouds which were either tightly bound across the chest or gathered at the head. All four of these skeletons were of adults, one of indeterminate sex (SK 62), one probably female (SK 137) and two definitely female (SK 287 and SK 688), however, with such a small sample it is not possible to assess whether this apparent age and sex bias is significant. None of the skeletons were directly sampled for radiocarbon dating, but one (SK 287) was stratified below a burial (SK 1C) that returned a date of between AD 1284 and 1391 (UBA-11454; see Appendix 1). Despite the lack of direct evidence, it is likely that the majority of individuals buried at Ballyhanna were interred in a shroud or a winding sheet. As pins were almost certainly not used as the principal means of securing shrouds, but rather as temporary ties employed during the stitching of the shroud (Gilchrist & Sloane 2005, 110), the lack of pins recovered during the excavation does not indicate that shrouds were not used at Ballyhanna. Only one burial, that of a neonate (44 lunar weeks) (SK 100), was associated with what might be identified as shroud pins (Small Find Nos C100:1–3). The three pins, all manufactured from a finely drawn copper-alloy wire, were associated with the skull of the infant. Two were found under the back of the cranium, with one on each side of the skull, whilst the third was found under the base of the skull. Their position suggested to the excavator that they were possibly part of a head-dress, but it is impossible to verify whether they were dress accessories or used for gathering a shroud. The infant skeleton was stratified above a skeleton (SK 484) that was dated (UBA-15982) to between AD 1182 and 1379 (see Appendix 1). Although the use of 'shroud pins' was once considered to be a Tudor introduction in the 16th century, this radiocarbon date is also consistent with the early 12th-century date at which pins are now known to first be associated with burials in Britain (ibid., 110).

None of the dress accessories recovered during the course of the excavation can be confidently associated with burial clothing. Although examples of stick-pins directly associated with burials are known (e.g. Cleary 1996, 97), as noted above, the stick-pin from Ballyhanna (Small Find No. C3:4) was recovered from a deposit of estuarine or riverine sand (C 3) and not a burial context. The possible copper-alloy pin fragment (Small Find No. 312:1) was found in the fill of a deposit overlying a heavily disturbed skeleton of an adult of undetermined sex (SK 312) and cannot be directly associated with the body, whilst the iron dress pin (Small Find No. C2:11) was recovered from the general graveyard soil (C 2) and may represent a casual loss. A possible annular buckle or brooch frame (Small Find No. C106:1) was recorded as found with the burial of a probable female adult (SK 106), buts its precise association is not clear. Finally, the copper-alloy button back (Small Find No. C80:2), recovered from a non-archaeological context (C 80), is of a 19th- or 20th-century type (Peacock 1978, fig. 19.5) which post-dates the cessation of burial activity at the site.

Grave goods and associated finds

As with the dress accessories, it is difficult to identify with certainty examples of grave goods being deliberately interred with individual burials as part of a funerary rite, although two of four hammered silver pennies (Small Find No. C2:80-83) discovered on the site were associated with individuals (SK 483 and SK 932) (Illus. 3.17). For the other two coins it is impossible to know whether they were originally associated with specific burials, or simply represent casual losses within the graveyard. The *Fasciculus Morum,* a 14th-century preacher's manual, contains dire examples warning of the consequences of deliberately including coins within a burial (Daniell 1997, 150). This reflection of the Christian authorities' horror with a burial rite that had apparently pagan origins, combined with the lack of recorded examples of the practice in Ireland, suggests that the coins recovered during the excavation at Ballyhanna may not have been intentionally deposited as grave goods. It is possible that in the cases of SK 483 and SK 932 they had been located within the clothing of the individuals and were accidentally included in the burials. Collectively, the coins range in date from the final quarter of the 13th century to the first quarter of the 15th century, but they may have remained in circulation for several decades prior to their deposition or loss (R Heslip, pers. comm.). Iron tools may have been associated with two burials, although neither of the artefacts can be closely dated. An incomplete, whittle-tanged knife (Small Find No. C652:1) was recovered from under the pelvis of a possible female adolescent (SK 652) that was directly stratified above a skeleton (SK 809) radiocarbon dated (UBA-14993) to between AD 1275 and 1385 (see Appendix 1). It is not certain whether the knife was genuinely associated with the burial and, given its incomplete condition, it must be considered doubtful whether it was intentionally deposited as a grave good. A small awl or punch with a rectangular-sectioned arm (Small Find No. C380:1) was found associated with the skeleton of a probable male adult (SK 380), but given the level of disturbance to the burial ground it is also possible that it simply represents the casual loss of a tool

Illus. 3.17—Four silver hammered pennies ranging in date from the final quarter of the 13th century to the first quarter of the 15th century (Jonathan Hession).

within the graveyard. However, in France, tools were occasionally buried with the deceased as a sign of their trade and, although the practice does not seem to have occurred in England (ibid., 165), two 12th- to 13th-century burials from Waterford were associated with a copper-alloy point and an iron awl or punch (Hurley & McCutcheon 1997, 209) indicating that the inclusion of metal-working or leather-working tools as a grave good is not unknown in a medieval Irish context. More convincing evidence for the deliberate interment of grave goods at Ballyhanna is provided by the recovery of glass beads (Small Find Nos 2:72, 2:73, 2:74a and 2:74b) from a position suggesting that they were placed around the neck of an adult female burial (SK 495) which was radiocarbon dated to between AD 1499 and 1791 (UBA-14990; see Appendix 1). Ian Riddler (see report in accompanying CD-ROM) notes one example, from Cork, of rosary beads being recovered from a late medieval Irish burial (Hurley 1995, 115, fig. 24.5). Although it is likely that the beads represent the remains of a rosary that was interred with the woman, a large number of unassociated fragments of crania and mandible were also recovered from around the skull of this burial and it remains a possibility that the beads may have been originally associated with an earlier burial that was disturbed when the grave for the adult female (SK 495) was dug; that one of the beads (Small Find No. 2:74b) was fragmented indicates at least some level of disturbance. The most convincing evidence for the inclusion of an artefact with a burial is provided by an iron arrow-head (Illus. 3.18; Small Find No. C208:1) that was recovered from the rib cage of the skeleton of a young adult male (SK 208). It is possible that the arrow-head was left in the body after its use in a fatal attack on the young man, although it should be noted that no osteoarchaeological evidence for its passage through the body was identified and its inclusion in the grave either accidentally or as part of a funerary rite cannot be excluded as a possibility (see McKenzie, this volume). The arrow-head has been identified by Andrew Halpin as an Anglo-Norman type of late 12th- or 13th-century date, and its presence at Ballyhanna reflects the occasionally violent consequences for the local population of living close

Illus. 3.18—Iron arrow-head of Anglo-Norman type dating from the late 12th or 13th century associated with SK 208, a young adult male (Jonathan Hession).

to the strategically important ford of Áth Seanaigh which formed one of the few routes for the Connacht-based Anglo-Normans into Tír Conaill and north-west Gaelic Ulster (see Donnelly, this volume).

Evidence for metal-working

In addition to the artefacts already discussed, a small number of other metal finds were recovered during the course of the excavations, including a fragment of a small copper-alloy bell (Illus. 3.19; Small Find No. 2:84) recovered from the graveyard soil (C 2). Bells of this open-mouthed clapper form are not uncommon finds on the sites of religious houses in Britain and have been plausibly identified as liturgical bells used at Mass when the host was elevated (Biddle & Hinton 1990, 725–7, nos 2270, 2270A–E and 2271; Egan 2005, 212, no. 1175). Comparable cast copper-alloy bells with iron clappers, however, have also occasionally been identified as both medieval and early modern bells worn by sheep and horses (Bailey 2008, 66, figs 6 and 8; Minter 2009). Given that the bell was recovered from a graveyard associated with a medieval church, its identification as an altar or sacring bell can be considered as probably correct. The ringing of a bell at the blessing of the sacred elements of the Mass is a practice first recorded, in a British context at least, in the 12th or early 13th century (Jennings 1989, 9; Biddle & Hinton 1990, 725). Catherine Johnson has speculated that the bell may have been a mis-casting based on its broken condition (see Small Finds

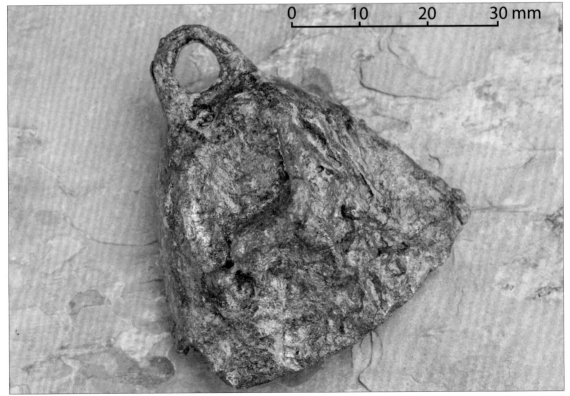

Illus. 3.19—Fragmentary copper-alloy open-mouthed clapper bell recovered from the graveyard soil (C2) (Jonathan Hession).

Report in the accompanying CD-ROM). The presence of ferrous corrosion on its internal surface suggests, however, that it had been fitted with an iron clapper. If so, it may not have been a miscasting, as a clapper is unlikely to have been fitted to such. That a probable altar bell from Abbots Lane, Southwark (Egan 2005, 212, no. 1175), also has a comparable, slightly tapering break which extended from the mouth to just below the crown of the bell suggests that such fractures were not uncommon in bells of this type. Consequently, it is reasonable to suggest that the example from Ballyhanna may have been accidently broken and then casually discarded in the churchyard—the bell's deformation and poor condition being the result of episodic disturbance and redeposition during the digging of graves.

Six pieces of spheroid hammerscale were recovered from the grave fills associated with five skeletons (SK 702, SK 744, SK 1029, SK 1082 and SK 1115). These burials were all located within three adjacent grid squares to the east of the church (Fiv, Gii and Giii), however, it is uncertain if this concentration in their distribution is significant. Hammerscale is difficult to identify and, as the soil samples taken from the site were not systematically analysed for ferrous metal-working residues, both the scale and distribution of iron-working activity represented by the six identified examples is uncertain. Spheroid hammerscale forms as a result of the solidification of small droplets of liquid slag expelled from iron during hot working (Starley 1995, 1). Therefore, the recovery of spheroid slag particles is suggestive of either the primary smithing of a bloom into a billet or bar, or general smithing activity in the immediate vicinity of the site. The relatively small number of recovered examples suggests, however, that the spheroids may have been residually deposited within the grave fills. Consequently, the metal-working activity signified by these finds could as easily pre-date the graveyard by several centuries as be contemporary with the burial activity.

Unconventional burials

In addition to those burials which were not interred with the conventional west–east alignment (see above), a number of other examples of unusual burial rites were identified during the excavation at Ballyhanna. With the exception of a small number of female adult skeletons (e.g. SK 277 and SK 978) that were interred with neonates located within, or on, their pelvic area and presumably represent the remains of women and their babies who died during, or shortly after, the birthing process (see Murphy, this volume), only one example of a double burial (SK 289 and SK 290) was recognised. Given both the difficulties in recognising individual grave cuts and the significant degree of superimposition of burials at Ballyhanna, however, it is possible that other multiple burials were not recognised during the course of the excavation. The skeletons of two adults, one identified as definitely male (SK 290) and the other as probably male (SK 289), were interred in a single grave. Both skeletons were aligned west–east (with head to the west) and were buried in near supine positions with flexed legs. That the leg bones of the definite male (SK 290) lay over those of the probable male (SK 289) indicates that the probable male, who was located on the northern side of the grave, was interred first. Osteoarchaeological analysis indicated that two separate sharp force trauma injuries to the right femur and right patella, consistent with being attacked by a sword, had occurred to the probable male at around the time of his death (see McKenzie, this volume), but no comparable injuries were present on the other skeleton and the reasons for the two bodies being buried in the same grave are uncertain.

Six skeletons (SK 179A, SK 484, SK 561, SK 651, SK 932 and SK 1146) were buried in a prone position—that is, with the body laid face down. Four of the skeletons buried in a prone position were identified as male adults (SK 179A, SK 484, SK 561 and SK 651), while the other two were female adults (SK 932, SK 1146). The prone burials were not clustered in any one part of the main excavation area. One of the male skeletons (SK 484) provided a date of between AD 1182 and 1379 (UBA-15982), whilst the female example (SK 1146) was stratified between two skeletons (SK 1135 and SK 931) that returned dates of AD 1273–1386 (UBA-14987) and AD 1515–1661 (UBA-14986) respectively. Citing an account of the works of Abbot Suger at St Denis, France, Gilchrist and Sloane (2005, 154) have plausibly suggested that the burial of a person prone may have been a penitential act intended to expiate the sins of either the deceased or other family members. Given that the bodies were presumably buried wrapped in a shroud, it is possible that some may have been accidentally interred in a prone position, but the position of one of the prone skeletons (SK 484) was almost certainly not the result of an accident as its left arm was bent over the head in a manner which those interring the body could hardly have failed to notice. Rather than necessarily reflecting a careless or disrespectful attitude on behalf of the burial party, it is perhaps possible that individuals buried in such unusual postures may have died in a fire, as a result of hypothermia or been buried in *rigor mortis* (Cross & Bruce 1989, 141).

There are only a few other examples of bodies buried in unusual postures. Excluding a number of preterm, neonate and infant burials, three individuals were buried in a crouched position (SK 182, SK 524 and SK 543). SK 182 was a female adult, buried lying on her right side, facing south with both legs pulled up to the body. The left lower arm crossed over the body and the right arm was extended alongside the body. SK 543 was a female adult positioned on her right side, facing south, with both legs pulled up to the body and her right hand resting besides its head. This skeleton was selected for radiocarbon dating and returned a calibrated date ranging between AD 1225 and 1276 (UBA-14995). SK 524 was also an adult female and, despite poor preservation, she also appeared to have been buried lying on her right side with both legs pulled up to the body. The left lower arm crossed over the body and the right arm was extended alongside the body. The skull was not present but the head would have been orientated to the west. In addition, SK 1209, a young adult male, displayed a variation of a crouched burial in which the lower legs were tightly drawn up so that the feet would have lain beneath the buttocks. Crouched or tightly flexed burials are rare in early medieval and medieval contexts in Ireland. A number of burials at Whithorn in Scotland were interred in a tightly flexed position (Cardy 1997, 551), possibly reflecting a localised tradition (Gilchrist & Sloane 2005, 154). Another example of a crouched, adult inhumation, albeit one laid on its back and from an early medieval context, occurred at Knockea, Co. Limerick (O'Kelly 1967, 77, pl. III.i).

Twenty-eight burials at Ballyhanna were interred in supine positions—on their backs—with slightly flexed legs.[5] Although 15 of these supine flexed burials were of juveniles indicating a slight preference for burying children in this position, the practice is not considered to be meaningful. Burials interred in this position were found across all but the easternmost part of the main excavation area and the three examples which were sampled for radiocarbon dating (SK 182, SK 331 and SK 1224; see Appendix 1) provided a range of dates that spans the entire period of the graveyard's

5   SK 28, SK 68, SK 99, SK 120, SK 131, SK 176, SK 178, SK 182, SK 277B, SK 290, SK 298, SK 331, SK 347, SK 395, SK 438, SK 445, SK 501, SK 544, SK 559, SK 595, SK 627, SK 676, SK 784, SK 820, SK 926, SK 1061, SK 1208 and SK 1224.

use. It is probable that, for the majority of the supine flexed burials, the legs of the deceased were unintentionally displaced into a slightly flexed position as the body was lowered into the grave. Arguably, of more significance were the six burials, all located in relative close proximity to each other within Grid Squares Eiv, Ev, Fiv and Fv, that were either laid on their right-hand side (SK 55, SK 156, SK 376 and SK 348) or on their left-hand side (SK 98 and SK 133), with their legs in a slightly flexed position (for details see table included in the accompanying CD-ROM). These burials consisted of three young children (one to six years of age; SK 98, SK 156 and SK 376), two female adults (SK 55 and SK 428) and an unsexed adult (SK 133). One of the female adults (SK 55) was stratified between two skeletons (SK 70 and SK 31) that were dated to AD 1277–1395 (UBA-14985) and AD 1451–1634 (UBA-14996) respectively. A medieval date for the rite is consistent with the observations that one of the burials (SK 133) was stratified below a skeleton (SK 150) dated to AD 1410–55 (UBA-15971), whilst a third example (SK 428) was stratified above a burial (SK 484) dated to AD 1182–1379 (UBA-15982). The significance of the non-supine flexed burial rite is not obvious, but it is unlikely to have been the unintentional result of an accident during the interment of the body in the grave.

Two of the adult burials contained evidence to suggest that the integrity of the head within the grave was a concern. Both of these burials were furnished with 'head support' stones (Illus. 3.20). A young adult male was buried with two stones placed either side of his skull in an 'ear muffs' position (SK 1239B), whilst an older adult of indeterminate sex, was furnished with a cist-like structure around its skull (SK 972). The skeleton of the adult male (SK 1239B) was radiocarbon dated to between AD 1158 and 1252 (UBA-14984); in medieval burial contexts respect for the head is not unusual and the mid 12th- to mid 13th-century date for the furnishing of a grave with 'head support' stones is consistent with other closely dated examples of the practice in Ireland and Britain. For example, a number of burials ranging in date from the mid 11th to the mid 13th century from the graveyard of St Peter's, Waterford, were furnished with 'head support' stones (Hurley & McCutcheon 1997, 194–5, 208), as were over 100 burials at Mount Offaly, Cabinteely, Co. Dublin, where burial continued until the late 12th century (Conway 1999). Other Irish

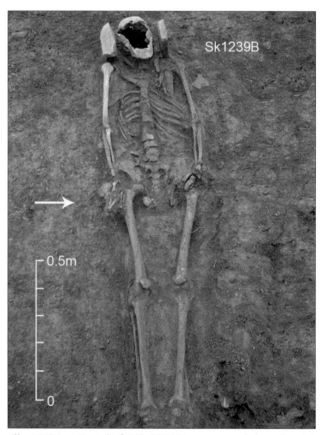

Illus. 3.20—Burial of SK 1239B, a young adult male, with two stones placed either side of his skull in an 'ear muffs' position (Photo by Irish Archaeological Consultancy Ltd, annotation by Libby Mulqueeny).

examples of the furnishing of graves with 'head support' stones occur at the medieval graveyard at Cove Street, Cork (Cleary 1996), and the cemetery at Knockea, Co. Limerick (O'Kelly 1967, 77, pl. IV.i). In England the practice is commonplace between the 11th and early 12th centuries AD, although there are a number of examples that indicate that the rite extended from the ninth century into at least the 16th century (Hurley & McCutcheon 1997, 195; Gilchrist & Sloane 2005, 138). Hurley and McCutcheon (1997, 195) considered that the practice was intended to ensure that the skull of the deceased did not roll to one side, presumably thereby ensuring that the deceased would be positioned facing the Risen Christ at the Last Judgement (Daniell 1997, 180–1). Daniell (ibid., 161, 175–81) has argued that between the late 11th and early 13th centuries theological belief about the afterworld changed, resulting in an increased emphasis on the bodily resurrection of the dead. The importance of maintaining the integrity of the head of a corpse, however, predates the 12th-century 'renaissance' in belief noted by Daniell. For example, the importance of maintaining the integrity of the head of a corpse was first noted in the eighth-century *Collectico Canonum Hibernensis* in which, with reference to the Resurrection, it is stated that where 'the head will have been, there all of the members [of the body] will be assembled' (Gilchrist & Sloane 2005, 139). The idea that one's place of burial was where one's head was buried is repeated by several 12th- and 13th-century liturgists (ibid.), suggesting that during the medieval period it was widely believed that at the Last Judgement it would not matter whether the body's other bones had been scattered or destroyed; provided that the material continuity of the skull had been maintained then the body could be physically resurrected in its entirety. Consequently, the furnishing of graves with 'head support' stones and cists that just extended around the skull, like the two examples from Ballyhanna, can plausibly be interpreted as reflecting a particular concern to maintain the integrity of the skull, and by extension the material continuity of the whole body, until the Last Judgement.

Whether exactly the same interpretation can be extended to burials in which the head of the deceased was rested directly upon a 'pillow' stone is doubtful. Although the furnishing of a grave with a 'pillow' stone may have tilted the head of a corpse so that it faced in the direction of the Risen Christ (Daniell 1997, 181), it is hard to see how the use of a 'pillow' stone would have protected the integrity of the corpse's head. At Ballyhanna only one burial, that of an older child (nine to 12 years in age) (SK 1117), was definitely laid out with its head upon a rectangular-shaped 'pillow' stone. The skeleton returned a date between AD 1447 and 1620 (UBA-11462). No other burials could be definitely identified as having been treated in this way, although it is possible that the head of an adolescent (SK 120) was also placed upon a 'pillow' stone. This second burial was stratified above a skeleton (SK 197) dated to between AD 779 and 965 (UBA-11442). Gilchrist and Sloane (2005, 146–7) note a number of English examples of furnishing burials with 'pillow' stones. These burials date from the 12th to at least the 15th century and where the sex of the deceased is identifiable are all of males. Gilchrist and Sloane (2005, 147) speculate that the rite may refer to Jacob and his dream of a stairway ascending to heaven or a spiritual display of humility in the act of laying one's head upon a hard rock.

Quartz

The excavators recorded, with varying degrees of certainty, that pieces of white quartz stone were associated with 52 of the adult and juvenile burials (Illus. 3.21; a table detailing all of these associations is included in the accompanying CD-ROM). Given the frequency of superimposition

Illus. 3.21—Site plan showing location of all skeletons associated with pieces of white quartz stone. Those burials for which the association is definite are represented in black, those for which the association is uncertain are represented in grey (Prepared by Sapphire Mussen and based on the original site plan by Irish Archaeological Consultancy Ltd).

of burial in the graveyard at Ballyhanna, the likelihood is that in many cases the quartz may have found its way into close association with burials through repeated disturbance of the graveyard soil during grave digging. In 18 cases, however, the association can be considered definite as the quartz stones were directly associated with either the hand bones of the skeleton or recovered from the pelvic region of skeletons where the hands had been placed over the pelvis. These 18 burials were all adult, with the exception of SK 1195, who was a 14–18-year-old adolescent, predominantly female, and restricted to the eastern half of the excavated area. The quartz stones were recovered from both the left and right hands of the skeletons. In the majority of cases the deceased were interred with one piece of quartz, however, in addition to a single piece recovered from the pelvic region, several quartz stones were also placed around the neck of one of the male burials (SK 780). Generally, in terms of burial rite, the skeletons definitely associated with quartz stones were otherwise indistinguishable from the other excavated burials, although one of the female examples (SK 1175) also—and uniquely for Ballyhanna—had a scallop shell placed over her right breast. The historical sources indicate that people from north-west Ireland undertook pilgrimages to Continental Europe during the medieval period (see Donnelly, this volume). The scallop shell is a symbol of pilgrimage to Compostela in north-west Spain and this raises the possibility that the woman had been on a pilgrimage there. Three of the skeletons definitely associated with the quartz stone rite (SK 495, SK 1201A and SK 1225) were sampled for radiocarbon dating (Table 3.1). These dates suggest that the rite extended from at least the end of the 14th century until the beginning of the 16th century, although it probably had a longer vogue. This date range is consistent with, but not refined by, the evidence provided by those other burials that were definitely associated with quartz stones and which were stratigraphically related to skeletons that had also been sampled for radiocarbon dating.

Table 3.1—Radiocarbon dates of skeletons definitely associated with quartz stones

Context	Laboratory no. / Radiocarbon age BP	Calibrated date range (two sigma)
495	UBA–14990 / 283 ± 27	AD 1499 to 1791
1201A	UBA–11451 / 347 ± 36	AD 1460 to 1638
1225	UBA–15985 / 649 ± 20	AD 1284 to 1390

In Ireland and western Britain there is a long association between Christian burial, in both ecclesiastical and non-ecclesiastical burial grounds, and the deposition of quartz stones and other white pebbles (e.g. O'Kelly 1958, 93–4; O'Kelly 1967, 77; Crowe 1980; Ivens 1989, 26, 59; O'Sullivan 1994, 334; Hill & Nicholson 1997, 472–3; Marshall & Rourke 2000, 111; Hurl 2002, 56; Macdonald 2005, 43–4; Marshall & Walsh 2005, 87–9; O'Sullivan & Ó Carragáin 2008, 270). This association usually takes one of two forms—either a mass of stones was deposited over the backfilled grave to form a visible cover, or a small number of stones were placed in the grave either with, or around, the body apparently as talismans. The former practice was largely restricted to the early medieval period, whilst the latter rite had a long floruit that extended from the early medieval period through to the relatively recent past. The small number of quartz stones recovered during the excavation at Ballyhanna, however, would suggest that the stones were 'burial talismans' and not the remains of disturbed grave covers.

The symbolic significance of placing white quartz stones with a body is debatable, although Hill and Nicholson (1997, 473) are almost certainly correct to suggest that the stones would have been considered to have a talismanic property. Marshall and Walsh (2005, 88–9) noted that, in the absence of any official Church statements about the liturgical use of white stones, their deposition was not part of an established protocol for a religious rite, but a spontaneous gesture based upon a popular belief. Casual references in ecclesiastical literature indicate that the colour white represented purity, innocence and a holy life (Marshall & Walsh 2009, 124). Alternatively, Gilchrist and Sloane (2005, 145) suggest that quartz stones associated with burials may have evoked apocalyptic imagery or represented protective amulets for the dead by citing Hildegard of Bingen who claimed in the 12th century that the devil hates and avoids all gemstones because they remind him of the City of God. It is tempting, although not provable, to equate a direct relationship between the rite of burying certain individuals with quartz stones and the reliquary at Ballyhanna which, as noted above, contained a large number of quartz stones. Although the burial rite at Ballyhanna involving interment of quartz stones with the deceased dates to the medieval period and the reliquary shrine is probably of early medieval date (see above) this should not necessarily negate a link between the two as the shrine was apparently respected, if not actively venerated, throughout the life of the graveyard. The medieval community that used the graveyard at Ballyhanna presumably would have believed that the quartz stones, by being placed as votives in the reliquary shrine, would become charged with the spiritual power of the venerated saint through being in contact with the corporal and associative relics once, or still, housed within the shrine. It may be that spiritually charged quartz stones were, on the occasion of certain burials, removed from the shrine and placed with the body of the deceased. Alternatively, it is also possible that the practice of including quartz stones with burials was unrelated to the votives deposited in the quadrangular shrine. The reason why the rite was largely restricted to female adults is not obvious, but may have been related to properties ascribed to the specific saint venerated at Ballyhanna. Unfortunately, osteoarchaeological analysis of the skeletons definitely associated with quartz stones did not identify any common link between them, apart from the fact that they were mostly adults and predominantly female (C J McKenzie, pers. comm.).

Summary

Archaeological analysis indicates that burial in the graveyard at Ballyhanna had begun, at the earliest, in the late seventh to early eighth century AD. There is no direct evidence to indicate whether the site included a church during this early medieval phase of its use, but the presence of a reliquary shrine suggests that it may have been a monastic foundation with a venerated founder and could have potentially become a place of pilgrimage. The site's position close to an important ford reflects the early Church's concern with being located on route-ways and it is possible that a chapel was originally established at the site in order for travellers to pray for, or give thanks for, a safe crossing. Regardless of the ecclesiastical status of the site, it apparently continued to be used to bury the local lay community into the medieval period, albeit with an apparent hiatus during the period between the early 11th century and the second half of the 12th century AD, which may have coincided with flooding of the site. Possibly after a period of abandonment associated with the flooding, a stone church was built at some point after the middle of the 13th century AD. This church was probably always a chapel-of-ease within the medieval parish of Enishmissaugh (Inishmacsaint) although, as the earliest historical references to the site date to the early 17th century, it is not possible to be certain. Burial activity continued at the site right through to its final abandonment in the 17th century, although from the mid 15th century it appears that burial was restricted to the eastern half of the excavated area.

4

LIFE IN MEDIEVAL BALLYHANNA—INSIGHTS FROM THE OSTEOLOGICAL AND PALAEOPATHOLOGICAL ANALYSIS OF THE ADULT SKELETONS

Catriona J McKenzie

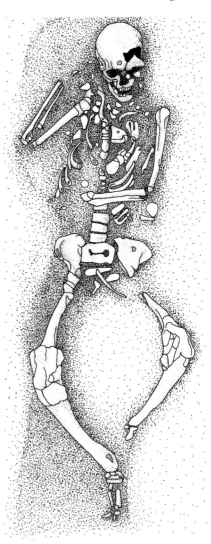

Stylised depiction of a young adult male, whose skeleton displayed numerous palaeopathological lesions owing to the congenital condition multiple osteochondromas (SK 331) (Sapphire Mussen).

Bioarchaeology, the scientific study of human skeletal remains, provides important information about how people lived in the past. A detailed examination of human skeletal remains has the potential to reveal insights into burial practices, health, diet, economy, interpersonal violence and warfare in past populations. This chapter presents the results of the comprehensive osteological and palaeopathological analysis of 869 adult skeletons excavated from the medieval graveyard at Ballyhanna, Co. Donegal. The adult skeletons were analysed as part of doctoral research undertaken by the author (McKenzie 2010) at Queen's University Belfast under the auspices of the Ballyhanna Research Project. The primary aim of the doctoral research was to elucidate new information about the health, diet and lifestyle of the medieval Gaelic community buried at Ballyhanna through an examination of the skeletal remains. To this end, a biocultural approach was adopted in the analysis of the skeletons. The biocultural approach integrated scientific data, gathered through the analysis of the physical skeletal remains, with contextual data about the culture of the population under study.

In total, there were 1,296 individuals excavated from the Ballyhanna burial ground. Of these, 869 were adult individuals and 427 were juveniles. This chapter examines the results of the analysis of the adult individuals only—the juveniles are discussed in Chapter 5. The analysis of the 869 adult skeletons was undertaken by the author with the assistance of Róisín McCarthy between July 2006 and July 2008. The adult skeletons were analysed using standardised osteological methodologies. For each skeleton a detailed inventory was prepared recording the bones which were present for analysis, the state of preservation, and the degree of fragmentation of the bones. Information was collected concerning the sex, age-at-time-of-death and the estimated living stature of each skeleton. In addition, for a sample of 400 skeletons, cranial and post-cranial metric and non-metric traits were recorded. A detailed palaeopathological examination recorded all of the pathological lesions and traumatic injuries apparent in the bones and teeth of every skeleton. This information was then collated and analysed with reference to historical and archaeological information relating to medieval Donegal. For the purposes of this chapter the results from Ballyhanna are compared with data obtained from the contemporary skeletal collections of Ardreigh, Co. Kildare (Troy 2010) and Wharram Percy, Yorkshire (Mays 2007).

The people

In the osteological analysis of any skeletal collection the amount of information retrieved is largely dependent upon the completeness, fragmentation and preservation of the skeletal collection. At Ballyhanna, the graveyard was relatively small—the main area of excavation was approximately 30 m (east–west) by 18.5 m (north–south)—and there was extensive disturbance of earlier graves by later interments. Of the 869 adult skeletons present for analysis, 42.9% (373/869) had less than 25% of their expected skeletal elements present for analysis and only 23.3% (202/869) of the adults were represented by complete—or almost complete—skeletons. In addition, the skeletons were frequently badly fragmented; approximately 44.3% (385/869) of the adult skeletons had greater than 75% of their skeletal elements fragmented. Missing data, due to poor completeness and fragmentation, is a significant limitation in this study and interpretations about the Ballyhanna population need to be formed around this caveat. Overall the surface preservation of the bone at Ballyhanna was excellent and the majority of the adult skeletons (67.9%; 590/869) were identified as having only minimal damage to the outermost (cortical) surface of their bones.

Of the 869 adults excavated from Ballyhanna it was only possible to estimate the sex and age of 62% (539/869) of the population. An almost even distribution of sex was apparent for the 655 adults for whom it was possible to assign a sex—49.2% (322/655) were male and 50.8% (333/655) were female. These figures indicate that the sex ratio at Ballyhanna was 0.97:1; that is about 97 males would have been born for every 100 females. This is close to the modern-day sex ratio of approximately 105 males born for every 100 females (Chamberlain 2006, 18).

Estimating the age-at-time-of-death in adult skeletons is notoriously difficult and there are many complications with the current standard methodologies (Cox 2000). As such, current guidelines suggest that adult individuals should be allocated to broad age brackets to compensate for inaccuracies in the various methodologies (Buikstra & Ubelaker 1994, 36; O'Connell 2004, 18). For the purposes of this study the age brackets used were: Young Adult (18–35 years), Middle Adult (35–50 years) and Old Adult (50+ years). The age and sex distribution of the adult individuals from Ballyhanna is shown in Table 4.1. These data show that the highest proportion of adults in the Ballyhanna population were dying in the young age bracket and that very few were surviving to 50 years of age or older. Of the 539 skeletons of determinable age and sex, 52.1% (281/539) died in young adulthood before they reached 35 years of age, approximately 39.7% (214/539) lived into middle age, while only 8.2% (44/539) survived until 50 years of age or older. The high proportion of adults who died before the age of 35 years is indicative of a population in which there was considerable poor health. The general health of the community at Ballyhanna has been previously discussed (see McKenzie & Murphy 2011 for further details) and, as such, will not be outlined again in detail in this chapter.

Table 4.1—Age and sex distribution of the adult skeletons

	Male		Female		Unsexed		Total	
	n/total number	%	n/total number	%	n/total number	%	n/total number	%
Young	148/869	17.0	133/869	15.3	31/869	3.6	312/869	35.9
Middle	94/869	10.8	120/869	13.8	15/869	1.7	229/869	26.4
Old	16/869	1.8	28/869	3.2	3/869	0.3	47/869	5.4
Adult★	64/869	7.4	52/869	5.8	165/869	19.0	281/869	32.3
Total	**322/869**	**37.1**	**333/869**	**38.3**	**214/869**	**24.6**	**869/869**	**100.0**

★ *The adult age category was used for individuals who were skeletally mature, but who could not be allocated to a broad age category.*

Overall, the high proportion of deaths in young adulthood would have had a significant wider socio-economic impact. It is likely that the nuclear family at Ballyhanna would have consisted only of two generations and that many children in the community would have lost one or both parents at a relatively young age. In medieval Gaelic Ireland concepts of lineage and kinship were of primary importance. It is possible that this emphasis on the extended family was due partly to the demographic structure of society, as many of the children living in Ballyhanna at this time would have been dependent upon their extended families or the wider community for their welfare. Community life at Ballyhanna would also have been adversely affected by the high percentage of deaths among the young adults—as the young adults are those who should have been among the healthiest and the most economically productive in the community. It is likely that every member of the medieval community at Ballyhanna would have played a role in the production of food and subsistence activities, and this would have been particularly important in a community which was affected by high rates of death among the young adult individuals.

Diet

In addition to the historical evidence for diet (see Donnelly, this volume) and the chemical evidence for diet (see McGowan & Bashir, this volume), it is also possible to examine the dentitions and skeletons to gain insights into the diet and nutrition of the medieval population at Ballyhanna. In the dentitions, two of the main dental diseases which may provide an indication of diet are dental calculus and dental caries.

Dental calculus is mineralised dental plaque which is attached to the surface of a tooth (Hillson 1996, 255). It is formed through the failure to remove living plaque deposits from the teeth and, as such, is often thought to be an indicator of poor oral hygiene (ibid., 259). Dental calculus has been linked to diets that are high in carbohydrates (ibid.) and also diets which are high in protein (Lieverse 1999, 224).

The prevalence rate of dental calculus among the adult individuals from Ballyhanna was very high as 96.1% (342/356) of adults with dentitions present for analysis displayed dental calculus. There was no significant difference between the prevalence of dental calculus on the adult males' dentition (96.2%; 153/159) and the female adult dentitions (96%; 167/174). Dental calculus was recorded on a similar percentage (96.3%; 497/516) of the adult dentitions present for analysis in the Ardreigh skeletal collection (Troy 2010, 22). In the Wharram Percy skeletal collection 89.2% (240/269) of adult skeletons were affected by dental calculus; however, this figure was probably an underestimation of the true prevalence as calculus deposits may have been accidently removed during post-excavation cleaning and handling of the skeletal remains (Mays 2007, 138). Overall, a high prevalence of dental calculus was recorded in all three of the medieval skeletal collections.

The second dental disease which is strongly influenced by diet is dental caries. Carious lesions are cavities in the teeth which are caused by demineralisation of tooth enamel by acid which is present in living plaque deposits (Hillson 1996, 269). This process occurs more frequently in diets which are high in carbohydrates (starches and sugars). In the Ballyhanna skeletal collection some 37.6% (134/356) of adults displayed one or more carious lesions in their dentitions. This prevalence rate was significantly lower than the rate recorded for Ardreigh (66.9%; 345/516) (Troy 2010, 22) and Wharram Percy (67.8%; 190/280) (Mays 2007, 134).

Previous research undertaken on archaeological populations has indicated that populations that eat diets which are high in carbohydrates display both high rates of dental calculus and high rates of dental caries (Keenleyside 2008, 265), while those that have a high protein and low carbohydrate diet have high levels of dental calculus and low levels of carious lesions (Lillie 1996, 140). It is likely that the diet among the Ballyhanna population was based upon a mixed subsistence economy, with both carbohydrates—such as oats, wheat and barley—and protein from milk, cheeses, fish and meats playing a significant role in the diet. The higher prevalence rates of dental caries in the Ardreigh and Wharram Percy populations would tend to suggest that the diet of these communities contained higher levels of cereals.

Tuberculosis

Among the adults at Ballyhanna there was only one specific infectious disease identified—tuberculosis. Tuberculosis is a chronic infectious disease which in the past was either spread between humans or transmitted from animals to humans. Tuberculosis may be caused by a variety of mycobacteria but in archaeological populations the most common mycobacteria were probably *Mycobacterium tuberculosis* or *Mycobacterium bovis* (Aufderheide & Rodríguez-Martín 1998, 118). *Mycobacterium tuberculosis* is transmitted between humans and is a droplet infection which is spread by coughing, sneezing, spitting and speaking (Roberts & Buikstra 2003, 5). This form of tuberculosis is most common among people living in close proximity with one another. As an airborne infection, *Mycobacterium tuberculosis* initially affects the lungs causing a pulmonary disease. In most individuals the infection will spread no further than the lungs; however, in a small percentage of individuals the infection will spread to the lymph nodes and from there throughout the body via the lymphatic system. Clinical symptoms of pulmonary tuberculosis include weight loss, coughing, coughing up blood, fatigue, night sweats and breathlessness. *Mycobacterium bovis* is transmitted between animals (commonly cattle) and humans. In this case the disease is spread not by droplet infection but through the consumption by humans of affected meat and dairy products. As children often consume more milk products than adults the infection is more common in childhood. *Mycobacterium bovis* may be common in populations in which there are infected cattle who live in close proximity to humans (Murphy et al. 2009, 2,029). Clinically, *Mycobacterium bovis* affects initially the gastrointestinal tract and infected patients present with slightly different symptoms than those infected by *Mycobacterium tuberculosis*. From the gastrointestinal tract the infection spreads to the lymph nodes and through the lymphatic system throughout the body affecting other tissues, including occasionally bone (Roberts & Buikstra 2003, 5). In addition to sweats, weight loss and fatigue people suffering from gastrointestinal tuberculosis may also experience vomiting, diarrhoea and anorexia.

In the pre-antibiotic era it has been estimated that skeletal manifestation of tuberculosis only affected approximately 3–5% of individuals with the disease (Aufderheide & Rodríguez-Martín 1998, 118). Among the adults at Ballyhanna there were six cases of probable tuberculosis (0.7%; 6/869) and this indicates that tuberculosis would have been a significant health concern in this community (see also Murphy, this volume). Relatively high rates of tuberculosis were also found in the rural Wharram Percy skeletal collection where 2.5% (9/360) of adult skeletons displayed lesions indicative of this specific infection (Mays 2007, 166). Six individuals from the Ardreigh skeletal collection were identified with lesions indicative of probable tuberculosis but only one of these was an adult individual (0.1%; 1/820) (Troy 2010, 65–7).

In skeletal remains the lesions indicative of tuberculosis are found most commonly in the spinal column, followed by the hip, knee and ankle (Aufderheide & Rodríguez-Martín 1998, 134). A

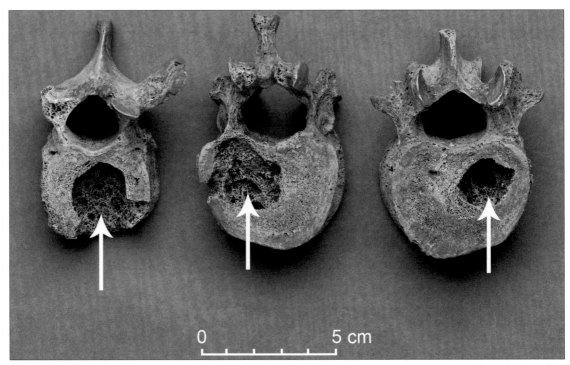

Illus. 4.1—Lesions caused by tuberculosis in the vertebrae of SK 566, a young adult male (Photo by Jonathan Hession, annotation by Libby Mulqueeny).

possible early example of tuberculosis was apparent in the vertebrae of SK 566, a young male adult (Illus. 4.1). The lytic lesions may have been caused by the formation of abscesses during life. In addition, SK 566 also exhibited periosteal new bone formation on the inner or visceral surface of six of his right ribs and on one of his left ribs. The new bone formation in this location is likely to have been caused by the transmission of the infection from the lungs, through the pleura (the membrane which attaches the lung to the ribs) to the internal surface of the ribs.

Pulmonary infections

In addition to the skeletons that displayed clear diagnostic lesions of tuberculosis there were also a number of individuals with periosteal new bone formation apparent on the inner or visceral surface of their ribs. Lesions in this location may be indicative of a pulmonary infection such as pulmonary tuberculosis or lobar pneumonia (Roberts et al. 1998). The infection in this instance is thought to be spread from the lungs through the pleura to the ribs. Some 8.2% (40/487) of the adults at Ballyhanna with ribs present displayed lesions which were indicative of a pulmonary infection.

Accidental injuries

In skeletal remains, many of the scrapes, scratches and bruises which occur as part of everyday life are unidentifiable unless the underlying bone has been affected (Roberts & Manchester 2005,

85). As such the injuries which are most commonly identified in skeletal remains are fractures and dislocations. Accidental injuries which occurred during everyday life may provide an insight into the day-to-day activities of those in the rural community at Ballyhanna. Among the adult individuals at Ballyhanna 8.5% (74/869) of adults displayed a fracture in one of their long bones. When the sexes are compared it is clear that the males (12.4%; 40/322) at Ballyhanna were more susceptible to accidental fractures than their female (7.5%; 25/333) counterparts. In the Ardreigh skeletal collection there was no marked difference between the prevalence of fractures in the male adults (7.6%; 24/316) compared with the female adults (7.3%; 24/341) (Troy 2010, 77). The overall prevalence rate for long-bone fractures among the Wharram Percy skeletal collection was noticeably different to Ballyhanna; in the Wharram Percy skeletal collection only 4.2% (14/334) of adult individuals exhibited a long-bone fracture (Mays 2007, 150). Given that these three rural populations are likely to have been partaking in similar farming activities it may be considered surprising that the Wharram Percy adults sustained far fewer injuries.

In the Ballyhanna skeletal collection the bones which were most commonly fractured were the bones of the forearm; the ulnae (3.6%; 15/422) and the radii (2.2%; 10/458). The majority of the injuries which occurred in the upper limb are likely to have been caused by either a fall onto the shoulder or onto an out-stretched arm. However, there are also fractures evident in the forearms which may possibly have been caused by a direct blow; these are called parry fractures.

Injuries in the lower limb occurred less frequently than those in the upper limb and the majority of lower limb injuries were relatively minor, probably caused by twisting the knee or ankle on uneven ground. One female, SK 151B, however, exhibited a serious injury consisting of a compression fracture in her left knee joint affecting both the left femur and tibia (Illus. 4.2). This injury was probably caused by her having landed on her feet following a jump or fall from a height. The fracture was healed but the joint surface had been altered by the fracture and secondary osteoarthritis had developed in this location. Two further individuals, a male and an unsexed adult were also identified with fractures in the mid-shaft of their femora. The femur is one of the most robust bones in the human skeleton and, as such, excessive forces are required to fracture this bone. Accidents which occur commonly in farming activities such as falling or having been thrown from an animal, falling from a height, being kicked by a cow or horse, being stepped on or trampled on by a large animal may all provide sufficient force to break a femur. Once fractured, the femur is a particularly difficult bone to re-align as the surrounding muscles contract; this causes displacement of the lower portion of the bone. A middle-aged male, SK 234, displayed a misaligned healed fracture to his left femur, which would have resulted in an obvious physical deformity as the left leg would have been significantly shorter than the right leg. Unfortunately the right femur was missing—removed during the later cutting of a grave—and so the difference in lengths between the left leg and the right leg could not be measured. A second individual, SK 939 an unsexed adult, exhibited a fracture which had failed to join—this is known as non-union—at the fracture site. The fracture was most likely an open or compound fracture as there was a deep bone infection evident at the site of the fracture affecting both ends of the bone. It is likely that the individual would have been unable to place any weight on his or her leg following the accident.

One particularly serious dislocation was identified in the skeletal collection; an intra-pelvic dislocation in a middle-aged male (SK 606). This injury involved an anterior dislocation at the hip

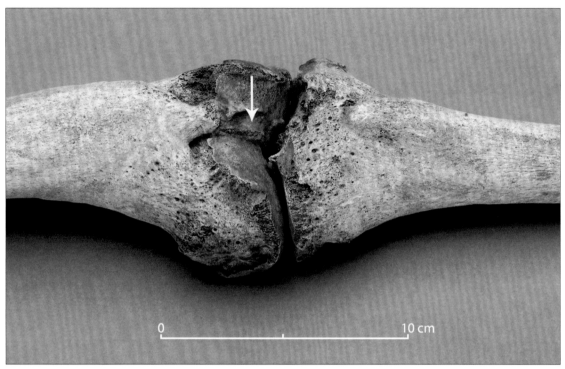

Illus. 4.2—Fractured distal left femur and proximal left tibia in SK 151B, a young adult female (Photo by Jonathan Hession, annotation by Libby Mulqueeny).

joint which displaced the femur at approximately a 90° angle. The man would not have been able to use his leg following the injury.

Among the Ballyhanna adults the hand phalanges (the bones of the thumbs and fingers) were commonly fractured. Males (71.4%; 10/14) were affected by fractured hand phalanges more frequently than females (28.6% 4/14). In modern populations the most common causes of hand fractures are: sports in adults between the ages of 10 and 29 years, accidents when using machinery in adults between the ages of 40 and 69 years, and falls in adults over 70 years of age (Jonge et al. 1994, 168).

During the medieval period in Ireland games which were common included field games, particularly stick and ball games (Gleason 1995, 193). The early Irish text *Meallbhreatha*—judging relating to games—suggests that there were over 20 different ball and stick games (O'Sullivan 1998, 32). In the north of the country the game *camánacht* was played using a narrow stick and a small hard ball (ibid.). Hurling (*horlinge*) is mentioned in the medieval period in the Statutes of Kilkenny in 1366 and again in the Statutes of Galway in 1527 in which the game is deemed a wasteful pursuit, in an attempt to suppress the Anglo-Irish adopting the native game. In addition to the written documents there is a clear pictorial representation of a curving *camán* with a long handle and a narrow boss and ball on the grave slab of Magnus MacOrristin a Scottish galloglass; this grave memorial (Illus. 4.3) is thought to date to the 15th or 16th century and is located in Clonca, Inishowen, Co. Donegal (ibid., 33). The image suggests that Magnus MacOrristin was both an able soldier and sportsman (Gleason 1995, 193).

In modern-day hurlers the metacarpals are the most commonly fractured hand bones, followed by the first proximal phalanges. Some 7.4% (15/204) of all adult males from Ballyhanna who had one or more hand bones present for analysis displayed an injury. It is likely that the game *camánacht* was played during the medieval period in Donegal and it is possible that some of the injuries identified at Ballyhanna were sustained during participation in this game.

In addition to the fractures of the appendicular skeleton there were also fractures identified in the axial skeleton—in the cranium, vertebrae and ribs. It is not always possible to differentiate between injuries which were accidentally caused and those that were caused on purpose during a violent encounter. Blunt force trauma on the skull, for example, can be caused by either an accident through a fall or by being hit with a blunt implement during a fight. A total of 5.1% (17/334) of adults with a cranial bone present for analysis displayed blunt force cranial trauma and males (6.5%; 10/154) were affected more commonly than females (3.9%; 6/154).

Fractures in the vertebral column are commonly caused by compressive forces acting on the spine or are secondary to other pathological conditions such as osteoporosis. Some

Illus. 4.3—Grave slab of Magnus MacOrristin from Clonca, Inishowen, Co. Donegal (Courtesy of Neil Jackman).

5.8% (32/552) of all adults with one or more vertebrae present for analysis displayed a fracture in their spinal column. It was clear that females (9.0%; 23/255) were affected by vertebral fractures more frequently than males (2.1%; 5/240); and that older adults (17.9%; 7/39) were affected more commonly by a vertebral fracture than younger adults (1.6%; 4/251). The pattern in the data indicates that the majority of vertebral fractures were caused by a weakening of bone strength due to ageing or an underlying disease process, such as osteopenia or osteoporosis.

Osteoporosis is a disease which is characterised by a reduction in the quantity and quality of bone which results in increased bone fragility and the susceptibility of developing non-traumatic fractures (Consensus Development Conference 1991, 107). In modern populations osteoporosis is particularly common among post-menopausal women, and both males and females who are older than 70 years of age (Agarwal et al. 2004, 33). Identifying individuals affected by osteoporosis in archaeological skeletal collections from examining the bones alone for fractures is complicated (Brickley 2000, 191). In the Ballyhanna skeletal collection a probable diagnosis of osteoporosis was suggested when individuals had light bones (indicative of osteopenia or bone loss), and the presence of two or more fractures evident in the vertebrae, the distal radius, or the proximal femur. In total, seven of the middle-aged or older females were identified with probable osteoporosis as they exhibited light bone and multiple fractures in their skeletal elements.

Interpersonal violence

The purpose of warfare for much of the medieval period in Gaelic Ireland was not to conquer new lands but to gain dominion over new people in order to increase wealth through the imposition of tributes and exactions (Simms 1975–6, 100). As such the primary aim of warfare in Ireland for much of the medieval period was not necessarily to kill people but rather to negotiate the submission of the people of a territory to the overlord. To this end, there were two main practices both of which aimed to conquer people—harrying and cattle raiding (ibid.). The practice of harrying involved the demand for submission through wanton destruction, by burning houses, trampling down corn and killing farm animals. This was a direct attack on the civilian population which aimed to terrorise them into submission (ibid.). Cattle raiding, as the term suggests, involved the stealing of cattle as these were the most valuable mobile commodity in medieval Ireland. By driving herds of cattle away it was possible to force the submission of a people and to negotiate tributes, in exchange for their safe return.

While there are clear examples of weapon trauma and interpersonal violence among the adult skeletons from Ballyhanna the frequencies of injuries caused by weaponry are very low. This may reflect the methodology of warfare outlined above—that the main aim of warfare was not to kill— or it may be indicative of a largely peaceful settled community at Ballyhanna. In total, only 1.7% (15/869) of adults displayed evidence of weapon trauma in their skeletons. The weapon injuries were mainly caused by swords (80%; 12/15), two adults sustained injuries caused by a skayne or dagger (13.3%; 2/15) and one may have been shot with an arrow (6.7%; 1/15). Similar low rates of sharp force trauma (0.9%; 7/820) were evident in the crania of the adults from Ardreigh (Troy 2010, 77) and in the adults from Wharram Percy (0.8%; 3/360) (Mays 2007, 164–5).

Sword and skayne injuries

In total 12 adults (1.4%; 12/869) displayed one or more injuries caused by a sword. Of these, nine (75%; 9/12) were males, two (16.7%; 3/12) were females and one (8.3%; 1/12) was an unsexed adult. The injuries were most commonly located on the skull bones, with 10 (83.3%) adults having been affected in this location. Nine of the adults (75%) had received their injuries at or around the time of death (peri-mortem) (Illus. 4.4), while three adults (25%) displayed injuries which had healed. One young female adult, SK 670, displayed two injuries on her skull, both of which had healed, showing that she had survived for some time after the attack (Illus. 4.5). Of the 10 individuals affected by cranial injuries, six (60%) displayed a single injury, while four adults (40%) displayed more than one injury. Only two adults displayed sword injuries to bones in their post-cranial skeleton. A young male, SK 289, exhibited two blade wounds in his right leg affecting the femur and patella, both of these injuries occurred peri-mortem. A young unsexed individual, SK 641, had his or her lower forearm completely severed during an attack involving a sword. The cut-marks apparent on the humerus of the individual indicate that the lower arm had been removed by a single swing of the sword. Perhaps unsurprisingly, this adult failed to recover from the significant injuries that he or she had sustained during the attack.

Two adults displayed injuries which may have been caused by a dagger or skayne. A young male, SK 81, displayed three horizontal slicing blade wounds on one of his cervical vertebrae. The cervical

Illus. 4.4—Peri-mortem sharp force trauma on the left parietal and occipital in SK 325, a male adult (Photo by Jonathan Hession, annotation by Libby Mulqueeny).

Illus. 4.5—Healed sharp force trauma on the frontal and left parietal bones in SK 670, a young adult female (Photo by Jonathan Hession, annotation by Libby Mulqueeny).

vertebrae are found in the neck region and it is likely that the individual had his throat cut and that this was the cause of his death. No other blade wounds were identified on the remaining bones of his skeleton. The second young male, SK 852, displayed two stab blade injuries on his left metacarpal bones (the bones in the palm of the hand). The hands and forearms are common places to find weapon injuries as these are locations which get injured when attempting to defend oneself against an attack. No additional injuries were identified on this individual but, as there is no evidence of healing, it may be assumed that the man died during, or shortly after, the attack.

A possible projectile injury

Only one possible projectile injury was identified among the adults at Ballyhanna. A young male, SK 208, was found to have an iron arrow-head associated with his skeleton during post-excavation washing. This male had iron staining on the inner (visceral) surface of the sixth, seventh and eighth right ribs. Unusually there was no penetrating fracture to indicate that the arrow-head had lodged in the ribs. It is therefore possible to propose two explanations to account for the presence of the arrow-head. Firstly, the arrow-head may have been fired during an attack but lodged only in the soft tissues, missing the skeletal elements or, secondly, the arrow-head may have been included in the grave on purpose or by accident by those responsible for the burial of the young man.

Activity patterns

It is not possible to identify exactly which occupations people undertook from looking at their skeletal remains. However, it is possible to ascertain whether a skeletal population led an active physical lifestyle, as opposed to a sedentary lifestyle, through an examination of the physical remains.

Osteoarthritis

Osteoarthritis is one of the most common debilitating joint diseases in the modern world. There are numerous factors which may contribute to the development of osteoarthritis including: age, weight, mechanical loading, genetics, hormones, biomechanics and behaviour (Resnick & Niwayama 1995a, 1268). In the past attempts have been made by osteoarchaeologists to identify certain activities which individuals may have performed through an examination of the pattern of joints which exhibit osteoarthritis (see Jurmain 1991; Jurmain 1999). The underlying theory was that if a joint was being repetitively used in a certain activity then there would be greater wear and tear at that joint surface and, as such, there would be a stronger likelihood of the joint developing osteoarthritis. These attempts to identify specific activity patterns through the presence of osteoarthritis have been largely abandoned as the cause of osteoarthritis is recognised to be multi-factorial (Weiss & Jurmain 2007). The main factor which affects the development of osteoarthritis is age. It is widely acknowledged that, while osteoarthritis is not a good indicator for identifying specific activity patterns, it may be considered to be more likely to develop in a population which is undertaking heavy physical labour and especially if heavy work is undertaken early in life.

In the Ballyhanna adult skeletal population 11.5% (100/869) of the individuals displayed osteoarthritis in one or more of their appendicular joints. This figure may seem low but it is important to remember that the main factor in the development of osteoarthritis is age and that the Ballyhanna skeletal population was largely a young adult population. Females (13.2%; 44/333) were more susceptible to developing osteoarthritis than males (12.7%; 41/322), however, the difference between the sexes was not statistically significant. A higher percentage of young males (8.8%; 13/148) displayed lesions indicative of osteoarthritis when compared with the young females (3.0%; 4/133). In this age bracket it may be suggested that the higher percentage of osteoarthritis among the male individuals may be due to heavy physical work at a younger age than the females. Overall there was a marked increase in prevalence of osteoarthritis with age, with 5.4% (17/312) of young adults affected by lesions indicative of osteoarthritis, while 40.4% (19/47) of the older adults displayed osteoarthritis in their joints.

The joints most commonly affected by osteoarthritis were the hands (5.1%; 38/746) and the hips (4.8%; 43/902), followed by the acromioclavicular joint of the shoulder (4.4%; 18/406) and the wrist joints (3.4%; 25/734). In modern populations osteoarthritis in the hand joints is most commonly caused by age. In the hip joints in modern populations there is a correlation between the early development of osteoarthritis in the hip and farming activities (Weiss & Jurmain 2007, 443). It is possible that at Ballyhanna some of the cases of osteoarthritis of the hip joint may be linked to the rural lifestyle of the medieval community.

A total of 37.7% (208/552) of all adults with one or more vertebrae present for analysis displayed osteoarthritis or degeneration at the apophyseal (small lateral and posterior) joints in their vertebrae. Both males and females displayed lesions in their spines which suggested that both sexes were involved in heavy physical labour from a relatively young age. Among the young adult age bracket 26.7% (67/251) were affected by degeneration in the spine, while in the older age bracket 53.8% (21/39) of individuals showed evidence of degeneration or osteoarthritis. When examining osteoarthritis, direct comparison between different skeletal collections is problematic as different researchers record and present the data for the condition in a variety of manners. In general, however, a larger proportion of individuals recorded with osteoarthritis was identified in the Wharram Percy skeletal collection but this may merely reflect differences in the age structure of the population under study. In the Ballyhanna skeletal collection approximately 91.8% of the skeletal collection was less than 50 years of age at-time-of-death, while in the Wharram Percy skeletal collection 60% of adults were over 40 years of age at-time-of-death (Mays 2007, 157).

Schmorl's nodes

Schmorl's nodes are indentations which are found in vertebral bodies. They are caused by herniation of the intervertebral disc into the adjacent vertebrae creating the indentation. Schmorl's nodes are commonly found in skeletal collections and are indicative of heavy loading of the vertebrae in early life (Jurmain 1999, 165). The vertebrae which are most commonly affected are the weight bearing vertebrae in the lower thoracic and lumbar regions.

Some 38.8% (207/533) of adults with vertebral bodies present for analysis displayed evidence of a disc herniation at one or more locations within the spinal column. A higher proportion of males (45.6%; 108/237) displayed the defect, when compared to females (38.1%; 93/244), which may suggest there was a division of labour with males having undertaken more of the work which involved heavy loading. The frequency of Schmorl's nodes was nonetheless high and is indicative that heavy physical labour was also undertaken by females in the adult population.

Treatment and disability

It is clear from the historical records that there were practising physicians working in Ireland during the early medieval and the later medieval periods. The role of physician was a hereditary position and the skills and knowledge were passed through the oral tradition of apprentice training. In Donegal the Dunlevy lineage provided the service of physician to the O'Donnell lineage (Simms 2004, 37). Practising physicians at this time had a knowledge of plants and herbs which may have been used to remedy certain conditions. However, there is also evidence in the Ballyhanna skeletal population of an advanced surgical procedure—a trepanation. In addition, two males exhibited a very rare inherited condition known as multiple osteochondromas in their skeletons. In one of these adults the condition would have resulted in obvious physical deformities.

Trepanation

The term trepanation refers to a surgical procedure in which a perforation is made in the skull. One young female, SK 1242, from Ballyhanna exhibited a possible trepanation on her cranial vault (Illus. 4.6). The perforation is large and ovoid in shape, and the original edges of the lesion measured approximately 87 mm antero-posteriorly by 73 mm medio-laterally. The original margins of the lesion have healed indicating that the woman survived for a time after the initial operation. By examining the skeletal remains it is not possible to identify the reason why the operation was performed—it may have been undertaken to relieve intra-cranial pressure on her brain following a traumatic injury; or perhaps it was undertaken to relieve migraines or epilepsy (see Murphy 2010). In addition to the probable healed trepanation, SK 1242 also exhibited a severe chronic infection in her left femur and in two of her lumbar vertebrae. It is not possible to determine whether the woman had been suffering from the infection before the surgery was undertaken or whether the infection was post-operative. Interestingly, this individual was the earliest dated skeleton excavated in the burial ground and radiocarbon dates indicated that she is likely to have lived during the late

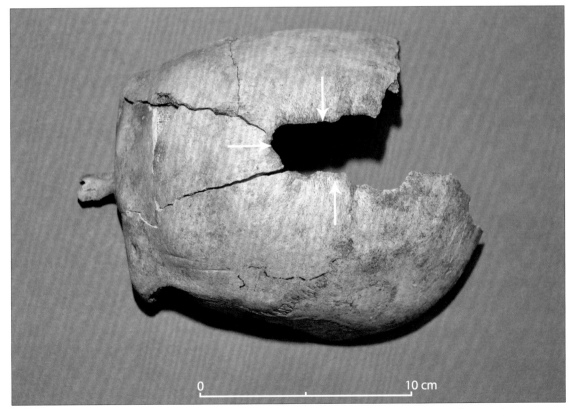

0   10 cm

Illus. 4.6—A probable healed trepanation in SK 1242, a young adult female (Photo by Jonathan Hession, annotation by Libby Mulqueeny).

seventh or eighth century (AD 670–772, UBA-11453; see Appendix 1). A healed trepanation was also discovered in the cranium of a juvenile in the Ardreigh skeletal collection (Troy 2010, 124). Ó Donnabháin (2003) conducted a review of the reported Irish cases of trepanation; at that time a total of 18 cases had been reported from Irish contexts and the majority of these dated to the historic periods.

Multiple osteochondromas

This chapter has highlighted that everyday life in Ballyhanna must have been difficult and physically demanding for all members of the community, but even more so for those with an obvious physical impairment. Two males in the Ballyhanna skeletal collection were identified with a very rare inherited condition known as multiple osteochondromas (Murphy & McKenzie 2010). This condition is characterised by the development of multiple bony growths located predominantly at the ends of the long bones (Aufderheide & Rodríguez-Martín 1998, 361). The growths are normally benign but can occasionally turn cancerous (malignant) and they may also be accompanied by a number of orthopaedic deformities.

The first male, SK 197, was radiocarbon dated to AD 779–965 (UBA-11442). SK 197 was between 35 and 49 years of age at-time-of-death and was of average height measuring 166.8 ± 2.99 cm (c. 5'6"). In this male the condition was relatively discreet and it is possible that there would have been no obvious physical deformity. A number of mostly small and medium-sized osteochondromas were identified throughout his post-cranial skeleton. In addition to the bony growths SK 197 also displayed: disparity in the lengths of his radii; slight curvature of his ulnae; fusion at the sacral-iliac joints; asymmetry of the pelvic girdle, coxa valga (in which the angle between the head and neck regions of the femora is abnormally large) and slight valgus deformity at the knee joints (knock-knees).

The second male, SK 331, lived in Ballyhanna at some time around AD 1057–1254 (UBA-11443). The individual was a young adult (probably 25–35 years) male and had an estimated living stature of 158.3 ± 2.99 cm (c. 5'2")—a little shorter than average. In this individual the condition was of greater severity—there were extensive large bony growths in his post-cranial skeleton which were particularly pronounced on his upper and lower limb bones. In addition to the multiple osteochondromas he also displayed: severe orthopaedic deformities of his left forearm (Illus. 4.7), disparity in long-bone lengths (affecting the clavicles, humerii, ulnae, radii, and fibulae), fusion at the sacral-iliac joints; coxa valga, marked valgus deformity at the knee joints and at the left ankle joint, and fusion between the two lower leg bones (the tibia and fibula) affecting both the left and right leg (Illus. 4.8).

Modern clinical data indicate that individuals with multiple osteochondromas commonly experience pain, muscular injuries, restricted range of motion at affected joints, and impinged nerves (including compression of the spinal cord). It is likely that the two individuals from Ballyhanna suffered from similar symptoms. In the case of SK 331 the large size of the osteochondromas and the associated orthopaedic deformities would have meant that the man would have been recognised as having a physically debilitating condition, very probably from a relatively young age. It is not possible to imagine how SK 331 was treated during life, but in death he seems to have been treated with respect and accorded much the same burial rights as the rest of the community at Ballyhanna.

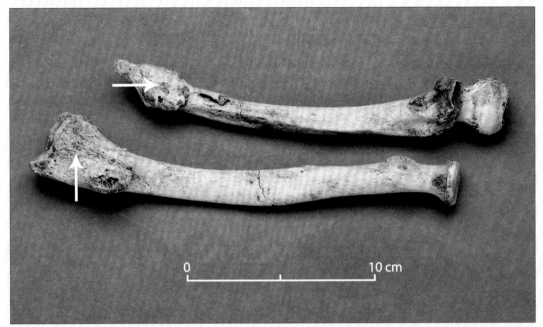

Illus. 4.7—Orthopaedic deformities of the left ulna and radius—caused by the rare condition multiple osteochondromas—evident in SK 331, a young adult male (Photo by Jonathan Hession, annotation by Libby Mulqueeny).

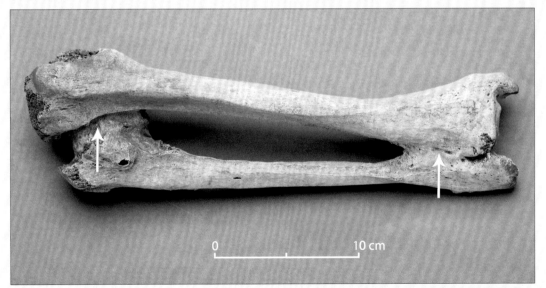

Illus. 4.8—Large benign bony tumours in the right tibia and fibula of SK 331—one of the two individuals affected by multiple osteochondromas (Photo by Jonathan Hession, annotation by Libby Mulqueeny).

Conclusions

This chapter aimed to present some of the insights that may be revealed through a detailed analysis of an archaeological population of adult human skeletons. Life at Ballyhanna during the medieval period would undoubtedly have been difficult and the data suggest that poor health and nutritional stress was the norm at this time at Ballyhanna and also in other Irish and English rural medieval communities. The high mortality rate of the young adults at Ballyhanna would have had a profound effect on the community at large and may have played a role in the emerging importance of the extended family during the medieval period. The diet would have varied according to what was available seasonally and the richer classes would have had greater access to foods which were better in quality. Carbohydrates and protein were the main components in the diet and the most likely sources of these were through the consumption of oats, meat, fish and milk products. Tuberculosis is likely to have been a significant health concern in the community at Ballyhanna. For those suffering from chronic illnesses their roles in the community must have altered as the diseases progressed and their capabilities decreased.

Injuries which may have occurred during both work, and possibly play, were apparent in the adult skeletons. However, the vast majority of the injuries identified were relatively minor. Males were more likely to sustain injuries to their limb bones than their female counterparts and the injuries apparent in the males were often of greater severity than those identified in the female adults. It is likely that some of the accidents were caused during the day-to-day interaction with large animals such as cows and horses. Males were also more likely to sustain blunt force trauma to their cranial bones than their female counterparts. In contrast, females were affected by vertebral injuries more commonly than their male counterparts and it is likely that a number of the older females had suffered from osteoporosis. While there is clear evidence of interpersonal violence in the adult skeletal collection from Ballyhanna it is important to emphasise that the frequencies of injuries were very low. This may be considered evidence of a fairly peaceful settled community or it may be indicative of the aims of medieval warfare in Ireland. Certainly there is no large-scale evidence of battle trauma among those buried at Ballyhanna and the injuries outlined above were more likely to have been sustained during small-scale interpersonal skirmishes. Identifying specific activities through the presence of osteoarthritis in skeletal remains is not recommended, however, it is possible to assess whether members of a community were involved in strenuous physical activity. The collective data from Ballyhanna suggest that all individuals of the society would have been involved in physical activities from a relatively young age—as would be expected in a medieval rural community.

Evidence of surgical intervention was apparent in the case of a trepanation in a young female adult and, although we do not know why the procedure was undertaken, we do know that the woman survived for a period of time following the operation. Two individuals were identified with a very rare inherited disorder—multiple osteochondromas—and it is likely that these individuals were in some way related, although the radiocarbon dates indicate that they were separated by several generations. Through this study it is apparent that the examination of the adult skeletal remains has the potential to reveal many stories about the individuals who lived, worked and died by the banks of the River Erne.

5

LIVES CUT SHORT—INSIGHTS FROM THE OSTEOLOGICAL AND PALAEOPATHOLOGICAL ANALYSIS OF THE BALLYHANNA JUVENILES

Eileen M Murphy

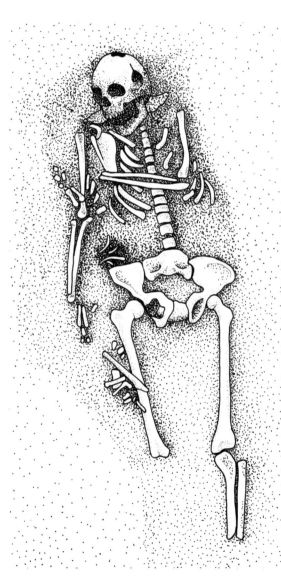

Stylised depiction of a young adult female, with the remains of a full-term foetus within her abdomen, both of whom likely died during the birthing process (SK 227 and SK 339) (Sapphire Mussen).

Discussions of children are rare within the archaeological record for Ireland. This situation is undoubtedly, at least partly, due to the approaches and interpretations employed by archaeologists, and when evidence is re-evaluated it is possible to catch at least glimpses of these children (e.g. McKerr 2008). It is obvious that every adult was once a child and that medieval Ireland would have been full of youngsters, but sometimes this reality is not reflected in archaeological discussions of the period. The discovery of a large population of juveniles, such as that at Ballyhanna, is a veritable goldmine when it comes to learning more about the lives and deaths of Ireland's medieval children. Although the juveniles buried at Ballyhanna are the non-survivors—those individuals who failed to adapt to the pressures of their environment and to successfully reach adulthood—there is still much to be learned about life in this rural Irish community from the study of their remains. The survival of the young in any population, whether past or present, is influenced by a myriad of biological, environmental, economic and social factors that operate in a complex manner. This is even the case for the unborn infant who experiences the impact of these interactions indirectly through its mother (Saunders & Hoppa 1993, 146). The following chapter will explore a variety of key aspects of the Ballyhanna juvenile population. Where possible, the findings will be compared to those derived from contemporary juvenile populations, particularly those from the rural populations of Wharram Percy, Yorkshire, and Ardreigh, Co. Kildare, which lies within an area of Anglo-Norman influence.

Age-at-death

The age-at-death of the juveniles was estimated using a combination of epiphyseal fusion data, the diaphyseal (shaft) lengths of long bones, dental eruption and dental calcification (Moorrees et al. 1963; Smith 1991; Scheuer & Black 2000), with most emphasis placed on the more reliable age estimates derived on the basis of dental development (Ferembach et al. 1980, 530; Smith 1991, 143). The Ballyhanna population also contained a substantial number of perinatal and neonatal infants who were aged using the linear regression equations of Scheuer et al. (1980) or, when this was not possible, those of Fazekas and Kósa (1978). Each juvenile was assigned to one of the following broad biological age categories (after Scheuer & Black 2000, 468–9):

- Preterm   < 37 weeks from conception
- Full term   37–42 weeks
- Neonatal   c. 40–44 weeks
- Infant   1 month to 1 year
- Younger child   1–6 years
- Older child   6–12 years
- Adolescent   12–18 years

Preterm babies were those who had an age-at-death of less than 37 weeks and who would probably not have been sufficiently well developed to have survived in the past, while full term individuals were those aged around 37–42 weeks. The perinatal period lasts from around 24 weeks' gestation to seven post-natal days, while the neonatal periods extend from birth to 28 days (Scheuer & Black 2000, 468).

Proportion of adults to juveniles

The Ballyhanna population comprised 869 adults (67%) and 427 juveniles (33%). Chamberlain (2006, 90–1) provided ageing data for four archaeological populations—in all cases the frequency of children aged less than 14 years was greater than 40%. He also provided age-at-death information for two groups of foragers and two groups of agriculturalists, based on historical demographic data. The frequencies of children aged less than 14 years in these groups ranged from almost 50% to approximately 67%. Since only 33% of the Ballyhanna population had an age-at-death less than 18 years it would appear to be the case that juveniles are somewhat under-represented in the population. This is not an unusual finding, however, and the medieval population at Ardreigh, Co. Kildare, was found to comprise 34.9% (439/1259) juveniles less than 18 years of age (Troy 2010, 15), while some 45% of the medieval population of Wharram Percy, Yorkshire, had age-at-death values less than 16 years (Mays 2007, 89).

The under-representation of juveniles, particularly infants and young children, is a major feature of archaeological populations even for burial grounds that have produced large numbers of individuals and are expected to have included the remains of individuals of all ages. This finding has been explained as a consequence of the poorer preservation potential of the skeletons of juveniles as well as the greater tendency for their remains to be misidentified during excavation (Saunders 2000, 136; Chamberlain 2006, 89). The Ballyhanna juveniles displayed a wide range of states of preservation, and many individuals were highly incomplete. As such, it is highly probable that their under-representation in the population is related to the densely crowded nature of the burial ground, which was in use for a substantial period of time, in conjunction with the less robust nature of certain juvenile bones.

Juvenile age-at-death profile

Analysis of child mortality trends can provide insights concerning the activities in which children engaged and their exposure to risk and disease at different ages. Details of the age-at-death determinations for the Ballyhanna juveniles are presented in Illustration 5.1.

A small number of preterm babies (1.6%; 7/427) were represented in the assemblage, while a relatively large proportion of the infants comprised full term or neonatal babies (9.4%; 40/427) and a smaller frequency consisted of infants between one month and one year of age (5.2%; 22/427). It is evident that almost half of the juvenile population had died between the ages of one and six years (46.4%; 198/427), and this appears to have been a particularly vulnerable age for the Ballyhanna juveniles. If they survived past this age they appear to have had a better chance of survival to adulthood since smaller proportions appear to have died during older childhood (21.3%; 91/427) and adolescence (16.1%; 69/427). The age-at-death profile for Ballyhanna is compared to those of the contemporary sites of Ardreigh and Wharram Percy in Table 5.1.

Table 5.1—Details of the juvenile age-at-death profiles for Ballyhanna, Ardreigh (Troy 2010, 15) and Wharram Percy (Mays 2007, 88)

Site	Preterm % (n/total no.)	Full term/ Neonate % (n/total no.)	c. 1 mth–1 yr % (n/total no.)	1–6 yrs % (n/total no.)	6–12 yrs % (n/total no.)	12–18 yrs % (n/total no.)
Ballyhanna	1.6 (7/427)	9.4 (40/427)	5.2 (22/427)	46.4 (198/427)	21.3 (91/427)	16.1 (69/427)
Ardreigh	0.7 (3/434)	9.2 (40/434)	13.4 (58/434)	36.8 (160/434)	25.6 (111/434)	14.3 (62/434)
Wharram Percy	9.8 (32/327)	13.5 (44/327)	7.6 (25/327)	32.4 (106/327)	26.0 (85/327)	10.7 (35/327)

The age-at-death profiles for all three populations followed a generally similar pattern which involved a gradual increase in numbers from young babies to a peak in frequency for younger children followed by a gradual decline in frequency for older children and adolescents. The Ballyhanna and Ardreigh populations contained very small numbers of preterm infants, while the proportion for Wharram Percy was notably higher (9.8%; 32/327). The frequency of full term/ neonates and infants was lower at Ballyhanna (14.5%; 62/427) when compared to Ardreigh (22.6%; 98/434) and Wharram Percy (21.1%; 69/327). Although the greatest proportion of individuals in

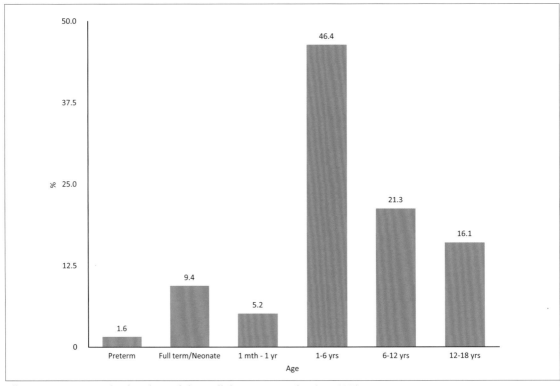

Illus. 5.1—Age-at-death values of the Ballyhanna juveniles (n=427).

all three populations had died at 1–6 years of age, the frequency for Ballyhanna was notably high (46.4%; 198/427) and it would appear to be the case that young children in this population were more susceptible to death when compared to their counterparts in Ardreigh and Wharram Percy. Similar levels of older children (21.3–26%) and adolescents (10.7–16.1%) were represented in each population.

When we look at Barbara Hanawalt's (1986, 272) summary of data relating to accidents contained within English medieval coroners' rolls it is not really surprising that younger children were at greatest risk of death. In a study of 750 children the findings indicate that risk notably increased from the age of 0–1 years (7.7%; 58/750), to 1–2 years (16.9%; 127/750) and peaked at 2–3 years (32.4%; 243/750), after which time it fell for 3–4-year-olds (17.5%; 131/750) and continued to fall for 4–6-year-olds (10%; 75/750), only to rise again for 7–12-year-olds (15.5%; 116/750). The majority of children aged less than one year were probably initially swaddled (although not continuously) and then tied within their cradles. Many of the infants seem to have been left unattended since a high proportion of them died as a result of house fires (33%; ibid., 175). Writing in the 12th century Geraldus Cambrensis commented that the Irish did not swaddle their babies although it has been suggested that the author was not entirely objective and this statement was made in the context of a general criticism of Irish child-rearing practices. The depiction of a swaddled infant in a 13th-century cathedral carving in Wexford (the Bambino of Ross) may suggest otherwise, although it is possible that this situation had occurred because of Anglo-Norman influences (McKerr 2008, 44). As with modern children, when medieval children became toddlers—and more mobile and curious—they undoubtedly would have been more accident prone. The English coroners' rolls indicate that greater frequencies of children aged over one year died outside the home, and the majority of 1–3-year-olds died as a result of accidents involving water, pots, fire and when playing with other children or when out walking (Hanawalt 1986, 178–80). Accidents could happen very easily as in the case of a two-year-old girl, for example, who was simply eating a piece of bread outside her house. A small pig came up, tried to take the bread from her and ended up pushing her into a ditch and causing her death (ibid.).

The coroners' roles are also informative in that they provide information relating to the chores that children were expected to undertake. By 2–3 years of age children appeared to be engaging in gendered activities—some of the accidents for girls occurred during play related to gathering food, drawing water or working with pots—while boys of the same age suffered accidents while playing and observing men working. By the age of 4–5 years details of the accidents suggest these youngsters were charged with tasks, such as babysitting younger children, and by the age of 6–12 years they had proper roles, and both helped their parents and supplemented the household income through fishing and gathering activities (ibid., 157–8). The medieval English peasant home and environs were full of hazards for small children and it is no doubt the same was also true for their counterparts in medieval Ireland. It seems highly probable that many of the 1–6-year-old children in the Ballyhanna cemetery population would have died as a result of misadventure, although there is also ample evidence that some of them would have died as a consequence of malnutrition and disease (see below).

Children in medieval England appear to have been charged with greater responsibility from the age of around six years and it is possible that some of them left the home at this time to take up apprenticeships (ibid., 157). In medieval Gaelic Ireland, there was a tradition of fosterage in which children of all echelons of society were fostered from the age of around seven years. The rationale behind this practice was to educate the child for their role in later life. Girls were taught in matters relating to cooking and the tending of sheep and young livestock, while boys were schooled in farming activities (Ní Chonaill 1997, 29). While a smaller proportion of the Ballyhanna juveniles died at 6–12 years, the early documents suggest that children of this age were warned against the dangers of livestock, cliffs, precipices and lakes, as well as the risk of injury caused by spikes, spears, sticks and stones (ibid., 30), thereby suggesting that these older children were not immune to injury and death by misadventure.

Perinatal infants

In the modern world most neonatal deaths are considered to be due to 'endogenous' (internal) factors caused by genetic and maternal influences, such as developmental defects, prematurity, low birth weight and birth trauma. Post-neonatal infant deaths are thought to be a reflection of 'exogenous' (external) factors, such as disease, poor nutrition and trauma. It is possible to obtain a crude estimate of deaths due to endogenous as opposed to exogenous factors by comparing the numbers of individuals who died at 38–40 lunar weeks as opposed to 41–48 lunar weeks (Lewis 2007, 84–6; Illus. 5.2).

The majority of perinatal infants from Ballyhanna had died prior to the age of 41 lunar weeks (65.4%; 34/52). This finding would tend to suggest that endogenous factors were largely responsible.

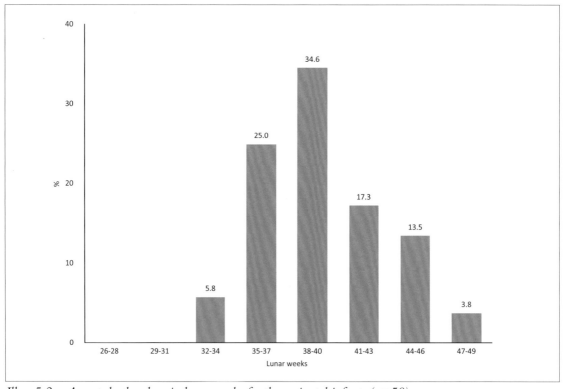

Illus. 5.2—Age-at-death values in lunar weeks for the perinatal infants (n=50).

At Ardreigh, the majority of infants who had died at less than two months of age also appear to have died as a result of endogenous factors since 83.7% were classed as foetal (3/43) or perinatal (33/43) as opposed to neonatal (7/43; birth to two months) (Troy 2010, 15). Gélis (1991, 251) has stated that: 'It was quite an achievement to come safely through the first month, so many and so fearsome were the threats'. Many babies would have had to recover after a difficult birthing process and would have been in constant risk of infection due to poor standards of hygiene. Their best chance of survival was their ability to successfully breastfeed (ibid.). Breastfeeding affords the newborn infant with protection against exogenous factors and research on a series of early modern populations from Germany demonstrated that death as a result of external factors, such as infection and diarrhoea, was much lower in societies which practised breastfeeding compared to those in which it was less common or discontinued shortly after birth (Knodel & Kinter 1977).

Deaths during or shortly after childbirth

If we turn to the burial record it is possible to ascertain further information about the cause of death for a number of the perinatal infants from Ballyhanna. It is also possible to glean insights concerning society's attitude towards these very young infants. Two of the perinatal infants were recovered from within the abdomens of adult females and had clearly died, along with their mothers, while they were still in utero. SK 60A, was a preterm infant with an age-at-death of 30–34 lunar weeks. Unfortunately, the state of preservation meant that it was not possible to establish the position of the baby in utero. It is possible that the mother—SK 60B, a middle-aged adult female—and her unborn baby had died as a result of premature labour. Interestingly, the pelvic bones of the individual were notably androgynous (did not have a notably female morphology) and this may have prevented the woman from successfully delivering the baby. It is also feasible, however, that the mother had succumbed to a disease unrelated to her pregnancy or that she had died as a result of an accident. SK 339 was a full term infant with an age-at-death of 39 lunar weeks. Excavation photographs clearly show that the baby's head was pushed tightly against the mother's (SK 227, a young adult) pelvic bones and it would seem highly probable that both the mother and baby had died during the birthing process (Illus. 5.3). In the excavation notes for SK 784, a full term infant with an age-at-death of 37 lunar weeks, it is recorded that 'most of the upper half [of SK 784] was also lying on a piece of pelvic bone' and that one side of an adult pelvis was located to the right of the skeleton. It is possible that these remains are those of a further pregnant female and that SK 784 had also been an unborn infant.

SK 978 (a young adult female) appears to have survived the birth of baby twins (SK 986 and SK 979), only for all three of them to have died shortly after (Illus. 5.4). SK 986 had an age-at-death of 36 weeks, while SK 979 was aged at 37 weeks thereby clearly illustrating the dangers of assigning precise age-at-death values to perinatal infants on the basis of diaphyseal measurements. Modern ultrasound tests frequently indicate size discrepancies in unborn twins which can arise as a result of the unequal distribution of amniotic fluid or differences in blood flow (Piontelli 2002, 43). As such, it is quite probable that SK 979 had been afforded an advantageous situation in the womb relative to the smaller SK 986. Neither baby displayed any palaeopathological lesions. In the modern world twins are considered to have reached full term at around 36–37 weeks *in utero*, by which time the intrauterine environment is no longer considered sufficient to continue sustaining their growth

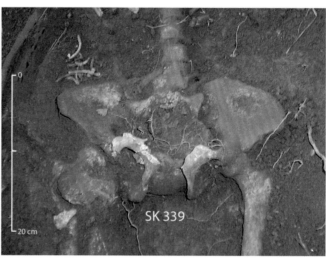

Illus. 5.3—A young adult female (SK 227) with the cranium of a full term infant (SK 339) clearly pressing tightly against her pelvic bones. It is probable that both individuals died during the birthing process (Photos by Irish Archaeological Consultancy Ltd, annotation by Libby Mulqueeny).

(ibid., 25). SK 978 appears to have been a very petite young adult, with an estimated living stature of only 144.4 cm (4' 9"). It is possible that, in the absence of modern medical intervention, the delivery of twin babies was simply too difficult for her and that she and the babies had died as a result of the birthing process. Even in the modern world twins form a high proportion of prenatal and perinatal deaths. Both twins are presented in the favourable vertex position in only 40% of cases and even then there can be complications—after delivery of the first twin the second twin has more room to move around and frequently changes position, making a spontaneous delivery impossible (ibid., 22, 52). This burial was especially poignant since the three bodies appear to have been laid out in a particularly careful manner. The babies were positioned to the left of the mother; the head of SK 986 rested on her chest, while the head of SK 979 was laid on her abdomen. The mother's arms appear to have been deliberately arranged so that she cradled both babies. While it is possible that the woman may not have been the mother of either baby (see below), or may have been the mother of only one of the infants, the careful positioning of the three bodies would tend to suggest this is unlikely.

Childbirth is thought to have been hazardous for mother and infant alike during the Middle Ages. The birth would have taken place at home and been attended by a midwife, whose skill would have meant the difference between life and death for the mother and her baby (Gélis 1991, 229–32). Death during childbirth, or shortly after, would have been frequently caused by haemorrhaging or infection or have been related to the malpositioning of the baby in *utero* (ibid., 238–50). The situation would potentially have been exacerbated for poor women who may have been malnourished and probably had to undertake heavy physical work until a short time before the birth of the baby (see Nic Suibhne 1992, 4).

The inclusion of both heavily pregnant and newly delivered women, as well as the remains

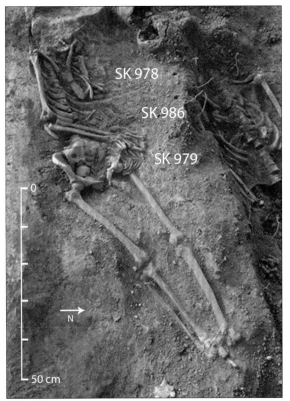

Illus. 5.4—A young adult female (SK 978) with possible baby twins (SK 986 and SK 979). The three bodies appear to have been laid out in a particularly careful manner. The babies were positioned to the left of the mother; the head of SK 986 rested on her chest, while the head of SK 979 was laid on her abdomen. The mother's arms appear to have been deliberately arranged so that she cradled both babies (Photo by Irish Archaeological Consultancy Ltd, annotation by Libby Mulqueeny).

of tiny preterm babies, in the burial ground at Ballyhanna is a clear indication that these women and their babies were not excluded by the Church and society at their time of death. Indeed, it would appear to be the case that all members of society—including miscarried and stillborn infants—were interred within consecrated ground at Ballyhanna. During the Counter-Reformation in the 16th and 17th centuries the situation appears to have changed quite dramatically and later Church teachings required that such individuals were prevented from burial within consecrated ground. This resulted in the proliferation of unconsecrated children's burial grounds (*cillíní*) throughout Ireland where the remains of unbaptised babies and pregnant women were laid to rest (Donnelly & Murphy 2008; Murphy 2011).

Health and nutritional status

Growth profiles

Studies of modern children have repeatedly revealed that growth is a sensitive index of the health and nutritional status of a population (Tanner et al. 1966, 454; Eveleth & Tanner 1990, 191; Bogin 1999, 304). The final height attained by an individual is the result of a combination of both genetic and environmental factors. Recent trends have revealed a gradual increase in stature between succeeding generations and these findings have been interpreted as an indication that modern improvements in nutrition and standards of health care have contributed to populations reaching increasingly higher proportions of their genetic potential (Garcia & Quintana-Domeque 2007; Perry et al. 2009). During periods of nutritional shortage the growth rate of an undernourished child slows down (Eveleth & Tanner 1990, 191), while prolonged periods of infection can also result in weight loss and have a negative impact on growth (see Saunders & Hoppa 1993, 134–5). Other environmental factors, such as, psychological and physiological stress, the levels of sanitation, water quality, education and health care can also have an impact on growth (Eveleth & Tanner 1990, 198–207; Miles & Bulman 1994, 132). As such, the linear growth of long bones has been used in many studies as a non-specific indicator of the overall health of a population (e.g. Saunders & Hoppa 1993; Mays 1999).

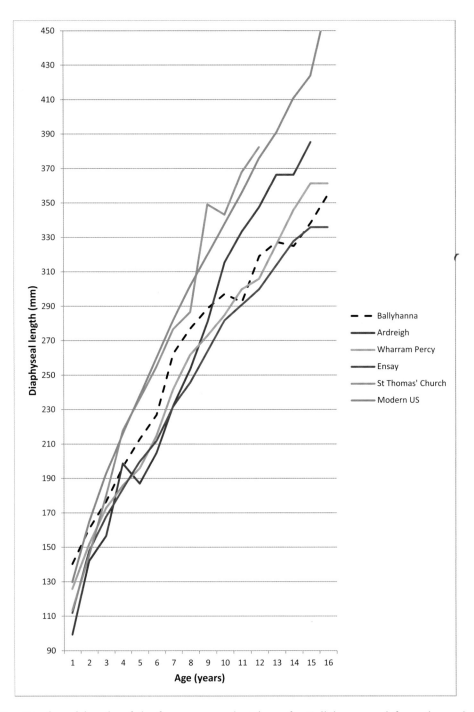

Illus. 5.5—Diaphyseal lengths of the femora versus dental age for Ballyhanna and four other archaeological populations (Medieval—Ardreigh, Co. Kildare (C Troy, pers. comm.), n=170; Wharram Percy, Yorkshire, England (Mays 1999; 2007), n=117; late/post-medieval—Ensay, Outer Hebrides, Scotland (S Mays, pers. comm. based on data included in Miles & Bulman 1994), n=118; post-medieval—St. Thomas' Church, Belleville, Ontario (Saunders et al. 1993), n=241) and data for recent US children (Maresh 1955).

For the purposes of producing skeletal growth profiles, mean diaphyseal (bone shaft) lengths were plotted against dental age determinations. Dental development is considered to be an extremely reliable technique for determining the age of juveniles (Smith 1991), while it is clear that the diaphyseal lengths of the long bones can be influenced by the various factors discussed above. The Ballyhanna individuals were each assigned to a one-year age category in which the age is the midpoint of the age category in years and were then compared to other archaeological and modern groups (Illus. 5.5). The work of Eveleth and Tanner (1990, 196) has demonstrated that the femur and tibia are among the fastest growing bones in the body resulting in the legs being very sensitive to environmental stress so the femoral diaphyseal lengths were utilised in the Ballyhanna analysis. So that a relatively modern comparative population could be included in the study, the methodology of Mays (1999, 294) was applied to Maresh's (1955) data for living, white American children. This technique involved minor adjustment to take into account magnification of the bones that was introduced by the radiographic process (Feldesman 1992, 450).

The number of juveniles from Ballyhanna (n=88) suitable for inclusion in the comparative analysis was substantially lower than the comparator populations. As such, the data may not be entirely representative of the growth of the population—this is particularly the case for individuals aged between 12 and 17 years. Nevertheless, a number of trends warrant discussion. The Ballyhanna juveniles were more similar in size to the medieval populations from Ardreigh, Ensay, Outer Hebrides and Wharram Percy than those from 19th-century St Thomas' Church, Belleville, Ontario, or the modern American children. Interestingly, they generally appeared to be positioned at the taller end of the medieval populations. The paucity of juveniles from Ballyhanna with an age-at-death of 0.5–0.99 years (n=1) appears to be having an impact on the size of the infants recorded for the 0.5–1.49 age category since the majority of individuals (n=7) included in this category were 1–1.49 years of age and at the older end of the scale. This situation has very likely skewed the results so that older, and presumably larger, children are being over-represented compared to their younger, and presumably smaller, counterparts. This has produced a probable anomalous trend in which the Ballyhanna one-year-olds are larger than their post-medieval or modern counterparts. For Ardreigh, the converse was the case and all nine of the individuals in the one-year age category had died at 0.5–1 year which has resulted in the infants from Ardreigh appearing overly small.

Juvenile statures

Following the methodology advanced by Mays (1999, 297) the statures of the Ballyhanna juveniles aged between eight and 17 years were compared to statures of the medieval population buried at Wharram Percy in Yorkshire. The mean total lengths of the femora were calculated for each age group based on the underlying premise that the diaphyseal length—the length of the long-bone shaft—represented approximately 91% of the total length of an immature femur. Averaged girl/boy femur:stature ratios derived from Feldesman (1992, table 5) were then used to convert the total lengths into statures. Comparative data from a study of factory children in the Manchester and Stockport areas of England undertaken by Samuel Stanway and JW Cowell in 1833 are also included in Illustration 5.6. These children were from the poorest levels of societies and would have worked long hours—when writing about factory labour a contemporary social critic stated that: 'The slave trade is mercy compared to it' (Tanner 1981, 145). Modern comparative data derived

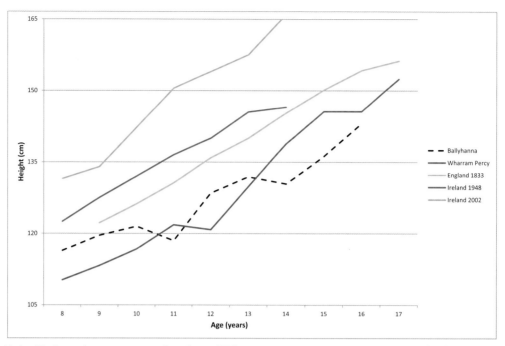

Illus. 5.6—Estimated stature versus dental age (Wharram Percy—Mays 2007, 99; England 1833—Tanner 1981, 148; Ireland—Perry et al. 2009).

from research on the heights of Irish children in 1948 and 2002 was also included. It should be noted that Irish children were not subject to rationing during World War II or in the immediate post-war period so the results will not be skewed as a result of the war (Perry et al. 2009, 262).

As expected the height values of modern Irish children are the greatest, followed by those of Irish children from the middle of the 20th century. It is thought that Irish children living in the late 1940s were probably somewhat undernourished due to the lack of variety of the habitual diet, and this might explain why heights have increased in the period between 1948 and 2002 (Perry et al. 2009, 262). Factory children from early 19th-century England were all smaller than the later Irish children but taller than the two medieval populations. As discussed above, life would by no means have been easy for these 19th-century children, many of whom would have been expected to work long hours and would have lived in a potentially overcrowded urban environment. It can perhaps be extrapolated from this finding that life must have been even more perilous, with even poorer standards of health and nutrition, for the rural children of both medieval England and Ireland.

Nutritional deficiency and physiological stress

One of the traditional ways that palaeopathologists can identify evidence of nutritional deficiency and physiological stress in past populations is through the evidence for cribra orbitalia (pitting in the roofs of the eye sockets), porotic hyperostosis (pitting on the outer layer of bone of the skull vault) and linear enamel hypoplasia (lines, grooves or rows of pits in the tooth enamel) (e.g. McKenzie & Murphy 2011 for the Ballyhanna adults). A recent study by Walker and colleagues (2009) has suggested that porotic hyperostosis is due to a variety of anaemias which most commonly arise from deficiencies of

114

vitamin B$_{12}$ and vitamin B$_9$ (folic acid). They indicate that the situation concerning cribra orbitalia is less clear cut and that the lesions may have been caused by a multitude of conditions, which include chronic infections and deficiencies of vitamins B$_{12}$, C and D (Walker et al. 2009, 115, 119). A total of 71 of 163 juveniles from Ballyhanna, with one or more preserved orbits (eye sockets), displayed cribra orbitalia, providing a prevalence of 43.6%. This is notably higher than the prevalence at Ardreigh of 21.7% (52/240) (C Troy, pers. comm.). Lewis' (2002, 82) study of four English juvenile populations from the historic period found frequencies of cribra orbitalia ranging from 55–57%, while she recorded a prevalence of 38.5% for Roman Poundbury (Lewis 2010, 410). It would appear to be the case that, while the Ballyhanna juveniles were more prone to nutritional deficiencies than those at Ardreigh, they were affected to a similar or lesser degree than their peers at historic sites in England. Porotic hyperostosis occurred with a relatively low frequency of 4.8% (10/210) for the Ballyhanna juveniles—a typical finding for an archaeological population (Aufderheide & Rodríguez-Martín 1998, 350). At Ardreigh, the lesion occurred with a frequency of 2.5% (8/316) among the juveniles (C Troy, pers. comm.). Of the seven affected individuals with observable orbits from Ballyhanna, six displayed both cribra orbitalia and porotic hyperostosis. If it is accepted that these lesions have different causes (see Walker et al. 2009), this finding would tend to suggest that at least these six juveniles had been suffering from multiple vitamin deficiencies.

The frequencies of linear enamel hypoplasia (lines, grooves or rows of pits in the tooth enamel) can also provide insights concerning the health of a population. The hypoplastic defect acts as a memory to an incident of systemic physiological stress—such as congenital and infectious disease, changes in diet, malnutrition and premature birth—during childhood (Goodman & Martin 2002, 23; Griffin & Donlon 2009). Studies of living children have consistently demonstrated an inverse relationship between poor nutrition and low socio-economic status and the frequency of linear hypoplasias (e.g. Goodman et al. 1991). The frequencies of linear enamel hypoplasias in archaeological populations have been interpreted in contradictory ways, however, with some authors arguing that a high prevalence is indicative of high levels of childhood stress. Conversely, others have suggested that the presence of the lesions is an indication that the affected individuals were able to survive and recover from physiological stress, thereby suggesting that they were potentially healthier than individuals with no lesions who had died during childhood. When attempting to interpret linear enamel hypoplasia it is important to examine the results from a biocultural perspective and to also consider the frequencies of other non-specific stress indicators. It was possible to analyse the permanent dentitions of 76 Ballyhanna juveniles for hypoplastic defects, and some 67.1% (51/76) of these individuals displayed the lesions. In a medieval population from Nova Rača, Croatia, the frequencies of linear hypoplasias in the permanent dentitions of the juveniles (69%; 29/42) was notably higher than the corresponding rate for adults (27.8%; 50/180). It was concluded that the frequency of linear hypoplasias was strongly correlated with age-at-death—individuals with the lesions were much more likely to die young (Šlaus 2000, 201). A very similar situation appears to be the case for medieval Ballyhanna where the frequency for adults (11%; 26/237) was also notably lower.

Rickets

Rickets is a disease which occurs in infancy and young childhood as a result of a deficiency of vitamin D. Such deficiency largely arises as a consequence of a prolonged lack of exposure to sunlight and/or a lack of foodstuffs in the diet containing vitamin D (e.g. eggs, milk, liver and oily fish) (Mays et al. 2006, 362; Brickley & Ives 2008, 75–6). Insufficient exposure of the skin to the sunlight is believed to be the most common reason for the development of rickets (Ortner & Mays 1998, 46). Previously, palaeopathological cases of rickets were only identified in the skeleton on the basis of bending deformities (e.g. Power & O'Sullivan 1992) but recent research has indicated that a suite of lesions can arise, largely as a result of the body's response to the deficient mineralisation of osteoid (Ortner & Mays 1998, 46). A suite of some 10 features—which largely relate to bony porosity, metaphyseal flaring and biomechanical deformation of bones—is now considered to be characteristic of the condition (Mays et al. 2006, 363). One infant (SK 823) and three younger children (SK 253, SK 820 and SK 1213) from Ballyhanna are considered to display lesions compatible with a diagnosis of rickets, providing a prevalence of 0.9% (4/427).

None of the four individuals from Ballyhanna were particularly well preserved and in all cases the lesions were most obvious in the cranium, where diffuse porosis and thickening was evident in most bones of the vault and the orbital surfaces (Illus. 5.7). SK 253, SK 820 and SK 823 all displayed porosity at their metaphyses and SK 253 and SK 820 displayed roughening of the surfaces of their long-bone growth plates. In all four cases where spongy bone was exposed it had a coarsened appearance with sparse trabeculae. SK 820 was the most complete of the four individuals and also displayed metaphyseal flaring and changes to the neck region of the femora (thigh bones). None of the individuals displayed obvious bending deformities but it is possible that these were obscured due the poor preservation of the remains.

Mays et al. (2006, 369–73) reported a prevalence of 2% (8/327) for rickets amongst the Wharram

Illus. 5.7—Extensive porosis in the parietals of a 1–2-year-old younger child (SK 1213) which are probably indicative of rickets (Photo by Jonathan Hession, annotation by Libby Mulqueeny).

Percy juveniles and a frequency of 13% (21/164) for the 19th-century juvenile population of St Martin's from Birmingham. A number of differing trends were apparent for the two populations. At Wharram Percy all of the individuals with active rickets were infants or young children whereas at St Martin's children as old as 4.5 years displayed characteristic lesions. They considered the occurrence of lesions in children who were presumably old enough to spend a lot of their time outdoors as an indication of poor environmental conditions (dark, polluted environment) which resulted in inadequate synthesis of vitamin D. They suggested that the occurrence of healed and recurring rickets was a sign that the disease was probably a common ailment amongst the children of St Martin's that was not necessarily life threatening. It is considered probable that the medieval inhabitants of the village at Wharram Percy would have led a largely outdoor existence. The occurrence of rickets amongst very young children has been interpreted as evidence that these children were sickly and, as a consequence, had been kept indoors in dark, smoky houses which meant they did not experience direct exposure to the sunlight. The lesions at Wharram Percy seemed to be generally more severe that those at St Martin's and this was considered to be further evidence that the affected individuals at Wharram Percy had been completely excluded from sunlight, whereas those at St Martin's simply lived in an environment which was marginal for vitamin D synthesis.

Not surprisingly, the findings from Ballyhanna are very similar to those from Wharram Percy—the cranial lesions, in particular, are notably severe and only the very young are affected. As such, it seems probable that the children with rickets at Ballyhanna were also sickly and, as a response to their poor health, they had been kept indoors as part of the care afforded to them by their families. Unfortunately, this course of action appears to have exacerbated their ill health, leading to the development of rickets which undoubtedly contributed to their untimely deaths.

Tuberculosis

Tuberculosis was the only definite specific infective disease apparent in the juvenile population at Ballyhanna. The natural history of tuberculosis has already been introduced in Chapter 4 since at least nine of the Ballyhanna adults appear to have suffered from the disease. The Ballyhanna children were not immune to the disease and at least two of them—SK 755, a 7.5–9-year-old child and SK 1155, an 8.5–10.5-year-old child—displayed pronounced lesions characteristic of long-standing tuberculosis. Both of these children would have been extremely ill before their untimely deaths—SK 1155 had suffered a collapsed spine and would have quite probably been paraplegic, while SK 755's right arm and left leg would no doubt have been extremely swollen and very probably painful and he or she most likely had to endure the presence of large weeping sores on these limbs (Illus. 5.8).

The prevalence rates of tuberculosis may appear very low—0.7% (6/869) for adults, 0.5% (2/427) for juveniles and 0.6% (8/1296) overall—but it needs to be remembered that bone changes as a result of tuberculosis infection only occur in 3–5% of a tuberculosis-affected population (Resnick & Niwayama 1995b, 2462) and it is possible that many more of the Ballyhanna individuals had been suffering from the disease but without having developed skeletal lesions associated with the disease.

Unfortunately, it has not been possible to ascertain through aDNA analysis the type of tuberculosis that had affected the Ballyhanna individuals (see Tierney and Bird, this volume). A total of 1.3% (9/687) of individuals, all of whom were adults, displayed evidence of tuberculosis at Wharram Percy.

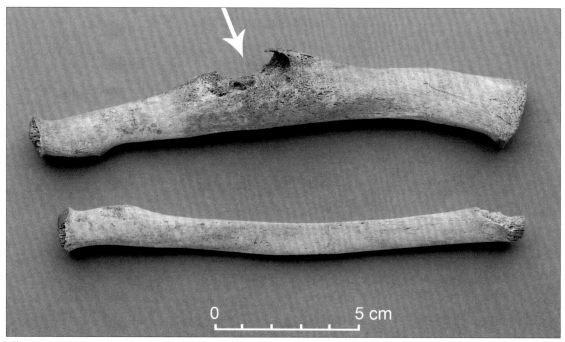

Illus. 5.8—Tuberculous lesion (spina ventosa) in the right radius of a 7.5–9-year-old child (SK 755) with the unaffected left radius included for comparison (Photo by Jonathan Hession, annotation by Libby Mulqueeny).

Despite an expectation that this rural farming community, who shared their houses with their cattle, would have been suffering from the bovine form of the disease, aDNA analysis revealed evidence only of infection by *Mycobacterium tuberculosis*—the human to human form of the disease. This finding was interpreted as an indication that the cattle herds may have been free from tuberculosis and that it was possible for the human form of the disease to be maintained even in relatively scattered populations. It was suggested that York, one of the largest cities in England at that time and located only 20 miles away from Wharram Percy, may have acted as a reservoir of tuberculosis infection which then spread to the small rural communities in its hinterland (Mays 2007, 163–6). The people buried at Ballyhanna would have lived in the hinterland of the town of Ballyshannon (see Donnelly, this volume) and it is possible that it would have served as a reservoir for the human form of the infection. In modern developing countries a child's risk of infection by *Mycobacterium tuberculosis* is related to their likelihood of being exposed to an infectious individual—usually an adult or an older child with pulmonary disease. Social factors, the prevalence of tuberculosis within the child's community and their age determine when exposure to the disease is most likely to occur. The majority of cases in young children arise in the home, whereas older children are more likely to acquire the disease outside their household (Newton et al. 2008, 498). The occurrence of childhood infection by *Mycobacterium tuberculosis* within a population is a warning event since it is indicative that the active transmission of the disease is occurring within a community (Walls & Shingadia 2004, 13). Indeed, in mid 19th-century Ireland Sir William Wilde reported that pulmonary tuberculosis was 'by far the most fatal affection to which the inhabitants of this country were subject' (Wilde 1843, xxviii).

Within the context of rural Ireland one might anticipate that the bovine form of tuberculosis is more likely to be responsible for the lesions evident at Ballyhanna since livestock was clearly of paramount importance to the people of Gaelic medieval Ireland (see Donnelly, this volume). The occurrence of spinal lesions is not incompatible with the bovine form of the disease and, in a study of Iron Age pastoral nomads from southern Siberia, individuals with pulmonary infection, including a 9–11-year-old juvenile, were confirmed through aDNA analysis as having suffered from the bovine form of the disease (Murphy et al. 2009). In the urban centres of 19th-century Ireland tuberculosis appears to have been rife amongst cattle although it is generally considered that bovine tuberculosis affected a relatively small number of humans compared to the human to human form of the disease (Jones 2001, 102–3).

Violence

Two possibly male adolescents displayed unhealed weapon injuries. In SK 14 (14–18 years) unhealed sword injuries were visible on the left humerus and scapula (Illus. 5.9), while in SK 35 (15–18 years) two unhealed knife cuts were visible on the ribs and were suggestive that the individual had been stabbed at least twice in the chest. The occurrence of definite weapon injuries in these two teenagers at Ballyhanna is interesting since it would tend to suggest that young males of this age may have been as susceptible to death during skirmishes as adult members of the population (see McKenzie, this volume). Indeed, studies of groups of medieval skeletons considered to be professional soldiers often include small numbers of adolescents, such as the remains of the mariners on board King Henry VIII's warship the *Mary Rose* (Stirland 2000, 122) or the soldiers buried in a

Illus. 5.9—Unhealed sword cut in the scapula of a 14–18-year-old adolescent (SK 14) (Photo by Jonathan Hession, annotation by Libby Mulqueeny).

mass grave associated with the Battle of Towton (Boylston et al. 2000, 53). In England a 14th-century law existed which required practically all males aged between seven and 60 years to learn how to use the longbow (Stirland 2000, 122).

Conclusions

Analysis of the younger members of the Ballyhanna population has provided some tantalising glimpses relating to life in rural medieval Gaelic Ireland. The age-at-death profile generally mirrored those for contemporary Irish and English sites, with the 1–6-year-olds having the greatest risk of death. While disease may have played a part in this increased risk it is probably also the case that increased mobility and curiosity caused many of these youngsters to die as a result of misadventure. The young babies of the society seem to have been largely susceptible to death as a consequence of genetic factors, difficult births and poor maternal health.

The growth study revealed that the Ballyhanna children were of comparable size to those of Ardreigh and Wharram Percy and they would have been much smaller than their peers in the modern world. While higher than the frequencies obtained for Ardreigh, the levels of cribra orbitalia were similar to those from a range of English historic sites and it would appear to be the case that the young throughout medieval Britain and Ireland suffered from generally low standards of health. The occurrence of rickets in four very young individuals appears to be indicative that these children had been kept completely indoors by their families in a tragic attempt to help them overcome their poor health. The occurrence of tuberculosis amongst the juveniles is suggestive that this disease may well have been a major problem for the people of medieval Ballyhanna.

The presence of a number of women at Ballyhanna who had died while pregnant, or during or immediately after giving birth, serves to remind us of the dangers of childbirth faced by medieval women. The manner in which such women and their infants were treated, however, can also provide us with glimpses of the depth of the loss experienced by the living. This is exemplified in the burial of a petite young woman with, presumably, her newborn twins. The three bodies had been carefully laid out in their grave so that the woman was cradling the infants. This arrangement was made by the living—perhaps the husband, sister or even mother of the woman; the father, aunt or grandmother of the babies—and is perhaps a reflection of the way they may have imagined her holding her babies had they all survived. One can only imagine the sorrow felt as these three individuals were laid to rest. Indeed, much of the research on English and Irish medieval societies has tended to suggest that children were at the very least regarded as a highly valued asset in the peasant economy (Hanawalt 1986, 148) and anthropological accounts certainly indicate this was the case in early modern Ireland (Nic Suibhne 1992, 2). Although probably largely relating to the upper and middling echelons of society, Ní Chonaill's (forthcoming) review of child-centred law in medieval Gaelic Ireland would tend to suggest that much scholarship and concern was invested in the consideration of child-rearing practices. Indeed, 'child-rearing was regarded as one of the four corner-stones of stability and social order' (Ní Chonaill forthcoming). The death of many, if not all, of the 427 juveniles buried at Ballyhanna would undoubtedly have involved some degree of disappointment, and, very probably, sorrow—the hopes of the living were not to be realised because of the deaths of these children. Even the very youngest members of society were present in the Ballyhanna burial ground—no-one was excluded from this Christian community.

6

DISARTICULATED HUMAN REMAINS AT BALLYHANNA

Róisín McCarthy

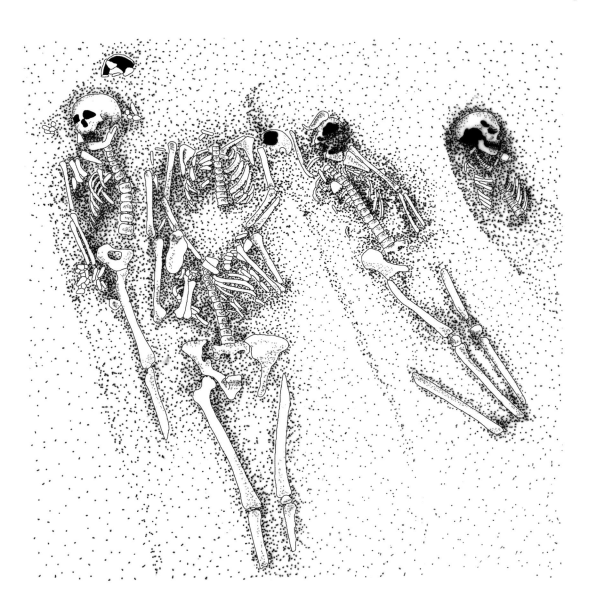

Stylised depiction of a typical group of skeletons at Ballyhanna, demonstrating the crowded nature of the burial ground and the extensive intercutting of the burials (Sapphire Mussen).

Archaeological excavations at the Ballyhanna medieval burial ground uncovered not only the several hundred juvenile and adult skeletons described in previous chapters, but also a large volume of loose bones for which a primary grave could not be assigned. These bones were meticulously collected during the excavation process and bagged according to individual excavation areas within the cemetery boundaries. The resulting collection of skeletal material is referred to as the Ballyhanna disarticulated bone assemblage. This chapter focuses on the osteological methods used to collect data from the

Illus. 6.1—Intercutting of graves in the burial ground (Irish Archaeological Consultancy Ltd).

Ballyhanna disarticulated bone assemblage and on some of the most interesting interpretations about the medieval population of Ballyhanna drawn exclusively from these data.

The term 'disarticulated bone' refers to those bones that over time become disassociated from the skeleton and their primary burial context (e.g. the grave), usually as a result of a variety of factors ranging from animal activity and erosion to human intervention. In the case of Ballyhanna, a burial ground in use over the course of many generations but with restricted space, burial density was high and intercutting of graves was commonplace (Illus. 6.1). Grave digging to make way for new interments was, therefore, a major contributing factor to the large volume of disarticulated bone recovered during the archaeological excavations. The Ballyhanna disarticulated bone assemblage included many thousands of both adult and juvenile bone fragments and teeth, as well as some animal bone. Owing to the large size of the assemblage a detailed osteological analysis of the material was undertaken by the author in order to determine if the assemblage was reflective of the articulated skeletal assemblage overall and if new and interesting contrasts in relation to health or lifestyle could be drawn. Although limited in its scope, the osteoarchaeological analysis of the Ballyhanna disarticulated assemblage provided some useful data pertaining to the grave-digging practices employed during the graveyard's use as well as several examples of pathological bone representing diseases not encountered in the articulated assemblage.

Osteological analysis and results

Minimum number of individuals

The process of collecting data in the most effective way from a disarticulated assemblage as large as that of Ballyhanna proved to be a challenging prospect. It was imperative that a clearly defined strategy of data collection was employed in order to glean the most useful information for comparison with the articulated assemblage. The first step of the analysis process was to separate all material according to age group—in this case the adult bone was separated from the juvenile bone, then the skeletal elements were separated by relative completeness, and finally the bones were sorted into categories which represented the components of the human skeleton (long bone, hand/foot, cranial etc.). A total of 4,312 complete adult bones and 935 juvenile complete bones were present. Information relating to skeletal element, side (left or right) and age were entered into a skeletal inventory to further aid interpretation of the data. The resulting figures illustrated a definitive predisposition towards the presence of complete foot bones (44.3% of total complete elements), followed by hand bones (22.4% of total complete elements). Exhumation practice has been cited previously as a factor affecting the variability of skeletal element recovery in disarticulated bone assemblages (Ubelaker 2002, 331). It would appear that those individuals digging new graves at Ballyhanna had taken care not to disturb existing burials by avoiding, as much as possible, the removal of the larger, more noticeable bones, such as the arm and leg bones (6.1% and 2.3% representation respectively), with the result being that the smaller, less noticeable, bones of the extremities were moved in the process.

The next stage of analysis involved the construction of a basic demographic profile of the assemblage. The first step in this process was to determine the minimum number of individuals (MNI) represented by the assemblage. The MNI count is one of the most popularly applied systems of quantification and is often the main objective in the analysis of any type of disarticulated assemblage. To calculate the MNI all complete bones (i.e. bones that were ≥75% intact), which shared a unique landmark (i.e. a distinctive feature on the bone), were 'sided' according to left and right. The total number of the most recurrent bone in the assemblage was then taken to equal the MNI represented by the disarticulated assemblage. The right fifth metatarsal bone (i.e. the bone preceding the 'little toe' in the foot) was the most recurrent adult bone of the assemblage (n=121), whilst the left pelvis was the most recurrent juvenile bone (n=51), giving an overall minimum number of 172 individuals. If, for example, all 121 adult right fifth metatarsals are assumed to belong to skeletons already accounted for in the articulated adult assemblage of 869 individuals, then at the very least one in seven adult burials on average was disturbed at some point during the lifetime of the Ballyhanna burial ground. Although crude, this rate is testimony to the high density of burials at Ballyhanna and to the significant length of use of the graveyard.

Age and sex trends

To determine the number of individuals present beyond duplication of skeletal element and side it was considered useful, where possible, to consider the age and sex of at least some of the adults represented. This meant putting aside complete bones that could help to provide this information during the sorting process. Complete lower jawbones and pelves were separated to determine age and biological sex. The most recurrent bone deemed observable for the purpose of assessing age and sex in the material was the left pelvis. Using standard osteological ageing and sexing methodologies (Lovejoy et al. 1985, 15–28; Buikstra & Ubelaker 1994, 15–21) a total of 28 adult pelves could be aged with 13 adult pelves suitable for the determination of biological sex. Each of the adult specimens was assigned to one of three adult age categories and five sex categories as outlined in Table 6.1. The pattern of recovery of pelves appeared to be evenly dispersed according to age and sex, with perhaps a slight bias towards pelves assigned to the young adult age category (46.4%;

13/28). The sex trend appeared to indicate that both sexes were likely to die in early to middle adult years, however, no females were identified in the older age category.

For juvenile remains, long-bone lengths and epiphyseal fusion rates were assessed to determine age-at-death (Scheuer & Black 2004) and the juvenile MNI according to age category. The application of these methods allows for individuals to be assigned to much narrower age ranges than in the case of adults. The juvenile age categories utilised in the current study were as follows: <40 lunar weeks, 0–0.5 years, 0.6–2.5 years, 2.6–6.5 years, 6.6–10.5 years, 10.6–14.5 years and 14.6–17 years. In total, discounting bone duplication, 45 juveniles could be assigned to one of the above age categories, with a further one individual falling between the age categories of 10.6–14.5 years and 14.6–17 years. Due to the absence of reliable sexing methodologies for juvenile skeletal material, the juvenile age-at-death trend could not be correlated with biological sex. The results obtained are outlined in Table 6.2.

Of the total number of aged juvenile individuals, by far the largest proportion (37.0%; 17/46) fell into the 2.6–6.5 years age category followed by the 0.6–2.5 years category at 21.7% (10/46). Individuals falling into the <40 weeks, 0–0.5 years and 10.6–14.5 years groups were all represented equally accounting for 10.9% each of the overall total of ageable skeletal elements. A general trend of improved survival rates beyond the age of 6.5 years was apparent.

Table 6.1—Summary of adult age-at-death and sex assessment

No. of individuals	Age range (yrs)*	Sex**	Adult age category
13	18–35	1F, 1F?, 3M	Young Adult
9	35–50	4F, 1M, 1I	Middle Adult
6	50+	1M, 1I	Old Adult
Total = 28		Total = 13	

Key: * *Broad age ranges were used as recommended by Buikstra & Ubelaker (1994, 9).* **F = female, F? = probable female, M = male, M? = probable male, I = indeterminate sex.*

Table 6.2—Summary of juvenile age-at-death assessment

No. of individuals	Age range
5	<40 weeks
5	0–0.5 years
10	0.6–2.5 years
17	2.6–6.5 years
3	6.6–10.5 years
5	10.6–14.5 years
1	14.6–17.0 years
Total = 46	

Health and disease in the disarticulated assemblage

During the sorting process bones of particular interest, usually those exhibiting pathological changes, were set aside and recorded separately. Each bone was assigned a unique bone code at this stage for ease of identification. The health and disease trend of the adult disarticulated material reflected that of the articulated skeletons in so far as pathological changes on the bones were relatively common. Juvenile pathology was somewhat less common, perhaps as a reflection of high rates of mortality before bony changes can take place and the smaller sample size.

The limitations associated with palaeopathological analyses of disarticulated bone often mean that the prevalence rate of various diseases according to age/sex is impossible to determine. Crucially, the absence of articulating skeletal elements means that the distribution of lesions across the affected individual's skeleton cannot be assessed, thereby inhibiting the osteoarchaeologist's ability to offer a differential diagnosis of what the underlying disease(s) may have been. Despite these limitations it was considered important to record pathology in the disarticulated assemblage where present as a source of supporting research data and also to highlight diseases potentially not represented in the articulated bone assemblage. It is not within the scope of this chapter to discuss each case individually, however, two of the most interesting examples, unique to the Ballyhanna disarticulated assemblage, are discussed below.

Of the 149 adult bones exhibiting pathological changes the percentages represented according to primary cause were as follows: 31% (46/149) infection, 28% (42/149) joint disease, 21% (31/149) trauma, 10% (15/149) metabolic, 5% (7/149) miscellaneous disease, 4% (6/149) congenital disease and 1% (2/149) neoplastic disease. Of a total of 15 juvenile bones exhibiting pathological changes the percentage rate according to primary cause was 73% (11/15) infection, 13% (2/15) metabolic disease (the diseases which affect bone formation, bone remodelling or bone mineralisation), 7% (1/15) congenital disease and 7% (1/15) neoplastic disease (cancers).

From the percentage rates outlined above it was clear that non-specific infection was the most frequently encountered lesion type in the disarticulated assemblage. Of all the levels of bone inflammation, osteomyelitis (deep bone infection) is perhaps the most distinctive lesion in appearance but was found to occur most infrequently with only two cases identified overall, specifically osteomyelitis of an adult left pelvis and a possible involucrum (i.e. sheath of infected long bone) which had become disassociated from its primary site of infection. The former case of osteomyelitis presented as extensive new bone formation and expansion of the hip bone resulting in severe deformity (Illus. 6.2). Multiple cloacae (i.e. holes which are caused by pus draining from the infection) were observable across the outer surface of the bone. Bony inflammation had also spread to involve the sacroiliac joint surface. Although the hip joint socket was not present for analysis due to post-mortem damage, the extent of the overall lesion indicated that this joint surface was probably also inflamed. The pathological changes in this particular case were so extensive that reliable ageing and sexing of the individual was not possible.

Clinically, osteomyelitis is a rare condition with an incidence rate of 2–11% of all bone infections (Rand et al. 1993, 733). The largest of the three pelvic bones, the ilium, is the most commonly affected. Symptoms such as severe intermittent pain, tenderness and limited range of motion at the hip joint, fever, nausea and vomiting all commonly present in cases of osteomyelitis of the pelvis. The exact cause of the condition is not wholly understood, however, it is thought to arise in some cases as a result of gastrointestinal infections and trauma. Crohn's disease has been cited previously as a possible cause of osteomyelitis of the pelvis (ibid.). This disease is one of a group of conditions termed enteropathic arthropathies which cause chronic ulceration (Aufderheide & Rodríguez-Martín 1998, 105). Joint surface changes in connection to osteomyelitis of the hip have previously been cited as secondary to septic arthritis or a ruptured pubic symphysis as a result of blood poisoning, or

Illus. 6.2—Left pelvis displaying osteomyelitis (Photo by Jonathan Hession, annotation by Libby Mulqueeny).

puerperal septicaemia (Ortner 2003, 192). In this particular case it was impossible to determine the cause of the initial infection. Extensive remodelling and partial healing of the bone indicated that the infection was a long-standing condition. The degree of malformation arising from the lesion would almost certainly have had a considerable debilitating effect on the individual who suffered with it.

The second, and perhaps the most notable example of a pathological lesion from the Ballyhanna disarticulated bone assemblage was observed in the form of a large ovoid bony lesion at the right maxilla (upper jaw) of a young child (Illus. 6.3). The shape and characteristics of the lesion indicated neoplastic disease as a possible cause. Neoplastic diseases involving the skeleton can be broadly categorised as primary bone tumours (i.e. those that develop initially in the bone), secondary bone tumours (i.e. those that spread to the bone) and finally soft tissue tumours that result in a bony response (Anderson 2000, 199). The precise cause of the majority of neoplastic diseases is unknown, however, it is generally accepted that cancerous tumours arise due to a combination of physical, chemical and/or viral agents (Aufderheide & Rodríguez-Martín 1998, 372). Primary bone tumours, particularly those of a malignant form, are reported relatively infrequently in the archaeological literature in comparison to diseases of other aetiologies.

In this specific case, the upper jaw was so disfigured by the lesion that it lacked distinguishing features most notably the palatine process (part of the palate) and tooth sockets—it appeared to be the case that much of the maxilla had failed to develop. The bony growth itself was made up of shiny compact bone, ivory-like in appearance. Four large holes were present on the various surfaces of the lesion with irregularly shaped bony outgrowths concentrated on its external surface and also within three

126

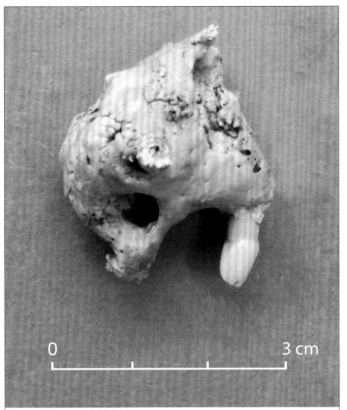

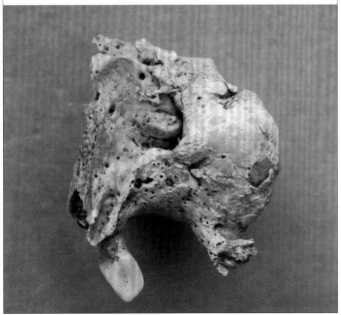

Illus. 6.3—Possible cemento-ossifying fibroma lesion on a right juvenile maxilla (top is the anterior view, bottom is the posterior view) (Photo by Mícheál Cearbhalláin, annotation by Libby Mulqueeny).

of the four holes. A single malformed deciduous tooth (possibly a canine) protruded from the inferior aspect of the jaw, most likely from the bone as with normal upper jaw morphology and development. A second tooth appeared to be embedded within the ovoid bony growth. Part of a possible tooth root—most likely belonging to the same—was partially exposed on the distal/posterior aspect of the ovoid bony growth. A third possible tooth extended from the jaw but was largely encased in bone.

The morphology of the lesion was highly unusual and lacked comparable specimens in the osteoarchaeological literature. This indicated not least, that the lesion was a very rare specimen. Several possible diagnoses emerged as to the underlying cause, but perhaps most applicable was a diagnosis of a benign fibro-osseous neoplastic lesion. Fibro-osseous lesion is the generic term for a group of jaw disorders which include cemento-ossifying fibromas, epidermoid cysts, desmoid fibromas and fibrous dysplasia (Colard et al. 2008, 195). Of all of these possible differential diagnoses, this particular case was morphologically characteristic of a cemento-ossifying fibroma lesion (COF). COFs are clinically very rare benign bony tumours primarily of the lower (70% of cases) and upper jaws that can develop at any stage of life, but are more commonly seen in young children. The juvenile form of the condition is the most aggressive clinically and these lesions can grow at a rapid rate (MacDonald-Janowski 2004, 11–25). Secondary complications depend on the size of the lesion. In severe cases the tumour can extend into the floor of the eye socket resulting in ptosis (i.e. outward protrusion of the eye) resulting in a limited range of eye movements (Colard et al. 2008, 196). Unfortunately due to disarticulation it was impossible to assess this lesion relative to the remaining portion of the maxilla. At the time of analysis only one previous case of a COF had been reported from a palaeopathological context. This lesion was identified at the right maxilla of an adult female dating to the Merovingian Period (i.e. sixth–seventh centuries AD) from Magnicourt-en-Comte, France (ibid., 195–201). The causative factors resulting in COFs are largely unknown but a previous history of trauma has been reported in a number of clinical cases (ibid.).

Conclusion

Detailed osteological analyses of disarticulated bone assemblages are not typically undertaken in cases where a substantial sample of articulated bone from the same cemetery is available. Despite this universally prevailing attitude, it was considered pertinent to the integrity of the Ballyhanna Research Project research framework to maintain a level of analysis of the highest quality throughout. Detailed osteoarchaeological analysis of the Ballyhanna disarticulated assemblage ultimately proved to be a very rewarding, although challenging, endeavour, without which many unique cases of disease and patterns in exhumation practices may never have been revealed in relation to the Ballyhanna population. The extensive volume of osteological data retrieved for comparison with the articulated assemblage was testimony to the usefulness of the disarticulated assemblage in creating a better understanding of the Ballyhanna medieval population overall.

7

ANCIENT DNA ANALYSIS OF THE BALLYHANNA HUMAN REMAINS

Sheila Tierney & Jeremy Bird

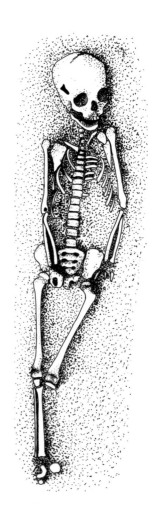

*Stylised depiction of a 6.5–7.5-year-old child, buried in a typical extended,
supine position with the head to the west (SK 144) (Sapphire Mussen).*

Ancient DNA (aDNA) is the term used to describe fragments of DNA recovered from preserved biological material, ranging from human and animal remains, to plant material and preserved microbes (Brown 2000, 457). This is a relatively new area of science which has presented archaeologists with an alternative means of investigating past societies (Hofreiter et al. 2001; Kaestle & Horsburgh 2002; Cipollaro et al. 2005). The study of aDNA has the potential to reveal new insights into human evolution, population movements, ancient diseases and the domestication of plants and animals (Brown 2000, 455). Ancient DNA analysis is a growing area of research which is of considerable interest to both the scientific community and to the general public.

The Ballyhanna Research Project (BRP) provided an exciting opportunity for aDNA analysis to be undertaken on individuals from the medieval community at Ballyhanna (Illus. 7.1). The aim of the project was to develop a reliable biomolecular method for the extraction and analysis of aDNA. The recovered aDNA extract would then be analysed to establish the sex of a number of adult and juvenile members of the community. At present, reliable sex estimates cannot be established for immature individuals using standard osteological methodologies (Brickley 2004, 23). The promising results from this initial analysis allowed the aDNA project on the Ballyhanna skeletons to develop, which resulted in two further collaborative strands of research. Firstly, work was undertaken on the Ballyhanna skeletons as part of a wider project concerning the origins of cystic fibrosis, led by Professor Philip Farrell from the University of Wisconsin, Madison. Secondly, research was conducted,

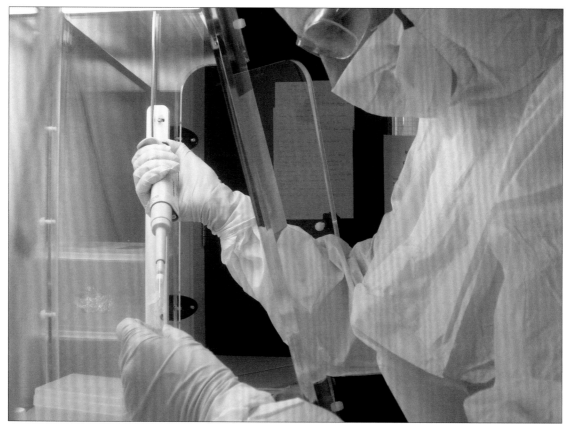

Illus. 7.1—Sheila Tierney extracting ancient DNA at the Institute of Technology, Sligo (Jeremy Bird).

with assistance from Dr Mike Taylor of the University of Surrey, to identify whether it was possible to extract ancient pathogen DNA, specifically *Mycobacterium tuberculosis* or *Mycobacterium bovis,* from the Ballyhanna skeletons.

Ancient DNA: problems and solutions

Contamination

Contamination in aDNA studies refers to the introduction of DNA from an outside source that has a similar sequence to that of the target aDNA. In terms of human skeletal remains archaeologists involved in the excavation, washing and curation of the bone often handle the skeletal remains before any aDNA analysis has been undertaken. Modern human DNA may therefore contaminate the bones from which aDNA is to be extracted at numerous stages prior to the analysis. Contamination may also be introduced during the extraction and amplification of the aDNA within the laboratory. This is a major problem as a similar, or identical, modern DNA template could then be indiscriminately extracted and mistaken to be authentic aDNA (Yang & Watt 2005, 332).

In order to minimise the likelihood of contamination there are strict protocols which are followed by those undertaking aDNA analysis. The prevention of contamination requires laboratory facilities which are devoted solely to the extraction and analysis of the ancient material (ibid., 333). Contamination is always a threat but, by following the standardised recommendations, it is possible to minimise the likelihood of contamination from outside sources thereby increasing the chances that the extracted DNA results reflect ancient sequences (O'Rourke et al. 2000, 225).

Degradation of aDNA

A second problem associated with aDNA is that it is often highly degraded with only minute quantities of DNA surviving in archaeological specimens. Polymerase Chain Reaction (PCR) is a molecular method used to selectively and consistently copy a specific fragment of DNA numerous times, resulting in millions of copies of the fragment of interest. By copying the DNA fragment numerous times the PCR creates sufficient DNA for further analysis. Real Time PCR (RT-PCR), a new adaptation of PCR, allows simultaneous quantitation and detection of the DNA. This is crucial to aDNA studies as it allows the analyst to determine the original quantity of DNA surviving in the archaeological specimen and identifies if enough DNA has been recovered for further analyses such as sequencing.

DNA sequencing

DNA sequencing involves using biochemical methods to determine the order of nucleotide bases which are the building blocks of a DNA sequence. The majority of the human genes are identical across all individuals, however, there are regions within the genes which vary from one person to another. A technique known as STR (Short Tandem Repeat) analysis takes advantage of these regions of variation and, when a number of these regions or STRs are screened, an individual's unique DNA profile can then be determined. The probability of two unrelated individuals having identical STR profiles when 13 STRs are analysed is approximately one in a trillion (Butler 2001, 62). By using these highly variable genetic markers in aDNA studies it is possible to detect whether there has been contamination of the original material. The extracted aDNA is analysed in two geographically isolated laboratories and, if both laboratories succeed in producing the same aDNA profile, then it is clear that laboratory contaminants have not affected the results. The chances of contamination are further eliminated as all personnel involved in the analysis ranging from the osteoarchaeologists to the laboratory staff are screened prior to the aDNA analysis and this information is input into a staff elimination database. Each individual's unique DNA profile is then compared to the aDNA extract. If each aDNA sample profile is unique (i.e. not matched with the DNA of a known person who has handled the bones), and is verified in a second independent laboratory, then this will aid in the authentication of the aDNA sample sequence.

Authentication

When working with aDNA it is particularly important to confirm the results come from the ancient material sampled as opposed to a contemporary contaminant source (O'Rourke et al. 2000, 225). A protocol to aid in the authentication of aDNA has been established and is routinely followed by all aDNA researchers. Some of the key requirements for aDNA studies are outlined below.

- Physically isolated work area—aDNA work normally takes place in at least two separate laboratories. In the first laboratory the aDNA is extracted and the pre-PCR work is conducted (Pääbo et al. 2004, 656). In the second laboratory, RT-PCR and genetic sequencing is completed (Illus. 7.2). This system means that the pre- and post-PCR work spaces are kept separate to avoid the risk of contamination from amplified products.

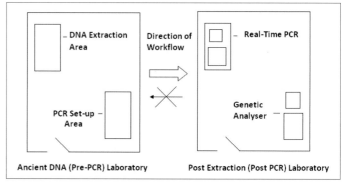

Illus. 7.2—Laboratory setup and direction of work flow (Sheila Tierney).

- Extraction and PCR controls—multiple negative controls are used in the extraction and the amplification process to differentiate between sporadic contamination which may occur during the extraction or pre-PCR preparation (ibid.). The negative control samples do not contain any DNA extract—water is added in its place—but otherwise they are treated the same as the DNA samples.
- Reproducibility—each extraction and amplification is repeated to verify that the results are reproducible and to further detect the presence of contamination (ibid.).
- Independent replication—the reproduction of the results in a second independent laboratory is extremely important as it can detect laboratory contaminants which may not have been

obvious in the original analysis. This is particularly significant in studies concerned with human aDNA analysis (ibid.).

- Quantitation—quantitating the number of aDNA molecules within an extract using RT-PCR identifies if there are sufficient molecules present for further investigations, such as STR analysis.
- Appropriate molecular behaviour—as DNA is degraded over time it is unusual to recover large fragments of aDNA. In cases when large fragments are identified they are usually suspicious and are treated with caution, as they more than likely came from modern contaminating sources (ibid.).

Ancient DNA analysis: applications in archaeology

DNA-based sex identification

Identifying sex is one of the basic requirements for the reconstruction of social or demographic structures in past populations. In human skeletal remains there are key differences between the sexes which may be identified in the skull and pelvis of adult individuals. In general, male skulls are more robust than their female counterparts and male skeletons typically display more prominent muscle markings. In the pelvic area, males often have high, narrow pelves which are adapted for effective bipedal locomotion, while females have wider and lower pelves to accommodate the carrying of a child during pregnancy (Mays 2010, 40; Mays & Cox 2000, 118). The biological differences apparent in human skeletal remains develop after puberty, and are therefore identifiable in adult skeletal remains. Before puberty, juveniles exhibit little sexual dimorphism in their skeletons which means it is not possible to identify which skeletons were male and which were female through looking at the bones alone. In addition to the juveniles, it may also not be possible to determine the sex of incomplete adult skeletal remains, particularly if they are missing the skull and pelvis.

Developments in molecular biology in the past 10 years have presented archaeologists with the opportunity to establish the sex of juvenile and incomplete or fragmentary remains using aDNA analysis (Hagelberg et al. 1991, 399). In humans, genetic sexing is confirmed by targeting a gene known as the amelogenin gene which is found on both the X and Y chromosomes. Males have one X and one Y chromosome, whilst females contain two X chromosomes. The X and Y versions of this gene are not identical (the gene is smaller on the X chromosome when compared to the Y chromosome) and methods were therefore designed to identify these differences.

Genetic diseases

In the last decade new work has also been undertaken on the examination of genetic diseases, as the recent advances in aDNA analysis have allowed studies into genetic disorders to be undertaken on archaeological skeletal remains. Archaeological evidence of genetic disorders is quite rare as many genetic diseases affect only the soft tissues in the body. Thus many inherited diseases would never be detected by conventional osteoarchaeological methods as the underlying skeletons are unaffected.

Ancient DNA analysis therefore provides an exciting opportunity to identify such genetic disorders in past populations.

The inherited genetic disorder cystic fibrosis is one of the most common life-threatening autosomal recessive diseases in European and Euro-American populations (Farrell et al. 2007, 2). Modern-day Ireland has the highest incidence of cystic fibrosis in the world at 1 in 1,353 births (Farrell 2008, 451). In total, over 1,500 mutations have been discovered for this disease, but most are rare (Farrell et al. 2007, 3). The most common genetic mutation is known as the F508del mutation (Kerem et al. 1989, 1073).

Cystic fibrosis is caused by an error or mutation in a gene known as the Cystic Fibrosis Transmembrane Conductance Regulator, or CFTR gene (Riordan et al. 1989, 1066). When an individual inherits only one copy of the F508del mutation they are known as a heterozygote carrier and are unaffected by the disorder. However, when two copies of the cystic fibrosis F508del mutated gene are inherited (known as homozygotes) this individual will manifest cystic fibrosis (Collins 1992, 774). Cystic fibrosis patients are principally affected by chronic respiratory infections.

It is still not clear why this mutation has such a high incidence rate in Caucasian populations compared to other ethnic groups (Southern et al. 2007, 58). We have to assume that there is some explanation for the mutation, as it would not be so common if there was not some advantage to it occurring. It has been suggested that the genetic mutation may have originated in past populations to give a selective advantage to individuals carrying the mutated gene. Many hypotheses have been proposed to explain the high incidence of cystic fibrosis, and the selective agent responsible for the probable evolutionary advantage of the F508del mutation has been widely discussed (Bertranpetit & Calafell 1996, 97; Farrell et al. 2007, 2; Poolman & Galvani 2007, 97).

It has been hypothesised that increased resistance to infectious disease in heterozygote carriers has retained the cystic fibrosis mutation at high levels in some populations (Bertranpetit & Calafell 1996; Poolman & Galvani 2007). A number of studies have proposed that persistence of this mutation may be caused due to resistance in the heterozygote carrier to infectious diseases such as typhoid fever and cholera (Pier et al. 1998; Bramanti et al. 2000). However, research conducted by Poolman and Galvani (2007) suggests that the tuberculosis pandemic, which broke out in Europe at the beginning of the 17th century, could be responsible for the modern incidence of cystic fibrosis in Ireland and Europe. Clinical evidence supports the association between cystic fibrosis and resistance to tuberculosis, as low incidences of tuberculosis have been observed in cystic fibrosis patients (Anderson et al. 1967; Smith et al. 1984; Kilby et al. 1992). The historico-geographical distribution of *M. tuberculosis* also supports this hypothesis, as the origin and the duration of the tuberculosis pandemic in Europe at the beginning of the 17th century meant that the maximum selective pressure was thus applied there. This may account for the modern gradient in cystic fibrosis incidence between Europe and the rest of the world (Poolman & Galvani 2007, 95). Further investigations into ancient human populations in Europe using genetics have the potential to further explore such hypotheses. A recent study conducted by Farrell and colleagues (2007) reported three cases of the F508del mutation from 32 Iron Age skeletons in Austria and confirmed that the F508del mutation was present more than 2,000 years ago in central Europe.

As Ireland currently has the highest incidence of cystic fibrosis in the world a collaborative partnership was formed between the Institute of Technology, Sligo (ITS), and the University of Wisconsin, Madison (UW), to investigate whether the cystic fibrosis mutation, F508del, was present among the medieval Ballyhanna population. This work was undertaken as part of a wider research project at UW where an international interdisciplinary team are investigating the ancient origins of cystic fibrosis.

Palaeopathology: identification of tuberculosis using aDNA analysis

Another strand of investigation in which aDNA analysis can play an important role is in the study of micro-organisms which cause diseases. This is an area of research which has been particularly popular over the last 10 years and a number of studies have successfully identified the causative bacterial agents of infections in human skeletal remains (see Drancourt et al. 1998; Taylor et al. 2007; Murphy et al. 2009).

Tuberculosis is a chronic infectious disease which has been present in human populations since the Neolithic period (Hershkovitz et al. 2008, 2). Skeletons exhibiting lesions consistent with a diagnosis of tuberculosis were recovered during the osteoarchaeological analysis of the Ballyhanna human remains (see Illus. 4.1 and 5.8). The disease may be caused by a variety of mycobacteria but those which most often affect humans are *M. tuberculosis* and *M. bovis*. The lytic bone lesions that arise as a result of tuberculosis have been found to be a source of residual mycobacterial DNA (Donoghue et al. 2004, 585). Screening archaeological skeletons for *Mycobacterium tuberculosis complex* (MTBC) DNA involves using two specific markers which amplify repetitive DNA elements (short repeated DNA sequences) exclusive to the tuberculosis complex called IS*6110* and IS*1081* (Dziadek et al. 2001, 569). Ancient extracts which are IS*6110* or IS*1081* positive should subsequently be analysed using further genetic markers—oxyR28 and pncA159. Analysing these can distinguish between *M. bovis* and *M. tuberculosis* infections (Scorpio et al. 1997, 106).

Ancient DNA analysis was conducted on six adult skeletons with lesions identified through osteological analysis, to confirm that the lesions were consistent with tuberculosis and to distinguish between infections caused by *M. tuberculosis* or *M. bovis*. This work was conducted in collaboration with Dr Mike Taylor from the University of Surrey.

Methodology

Before any aDNA extractions could commence, a specific aDNA facility had to be developed for the purpose of this project. A new laboratory was set up as a pre-PCR area for conducting aDNA extractions and pre-PCR work only. This entire room was thoroughly decontaminated with 10% sodium hypochlorite and all equipment moved into the laboratory was also decontaminated. The laboratory was then designated a 'clean room' with restricted access to authorised personnel who could only enter when wearing the correct protective clothing (Illus. 7.1). A protocol was written to ensure that the correct procedure would be maintained when entering and working inside the aDNA laboratory. Each day, before any work commenced in the laboratory, all surfaces and equipment were thoroughly decontaminated with bleach. Surfaces, equipment and reagents used in the extraction process were also exposed to ultraviolet light, which subsequently crosslinks (alters) any contaminant DNA present on the surfaces or in molecular reagents, thus preventing them from amplifying with the aDNA during PCR. All consumables used were sterile and validated DNA free and the materials were sourced from companies which have been used by other researchers engaged in aDNA research.

At the time of the Ballyhanna excavation it was not anticipated that the human skeletal remains would later undergo aDNA analysis. As such, the bones were handled by archaeologists throughout the excavation, washing, and osteoarchaeological study. This undoubtedly contaminated the archaeological remains with modern DNA. The first step in the aDNA analysis, therefore, involved the decontamination of the bones and teeth through chemical destruction of the surface contaminant DNA.

Initially adult disarticulated pelvic bones were selected for aDNA analysis, however, following a number of unsuccessful attempts to detect aDNA in these bones it was decided that teeth might be a preferable sampling material. The protective outer enamel layer of teeth seems to provide a degree of protection to the DNA and also protects against penetration of contaminant DNA. Teeth also have the advantage of providing multiple independent samples per individual. As such, all aDNA analysis was conducted using teeth, except in relation to tuberculosis.

The teeth chosen for aDNA analysis were selected and ranked (i.e. A, B and C) according to quality and preservation (Illus. 7.3). Teeth which were deemed to be very well preserved were used for aDNA analysis where possible. A mould was made of each tooth before destructive analysis. The tooth was then cleaned using sterile scalpels and bleach, and washed in a decontamination solution before being ground into a fine powder for DNA extraction.

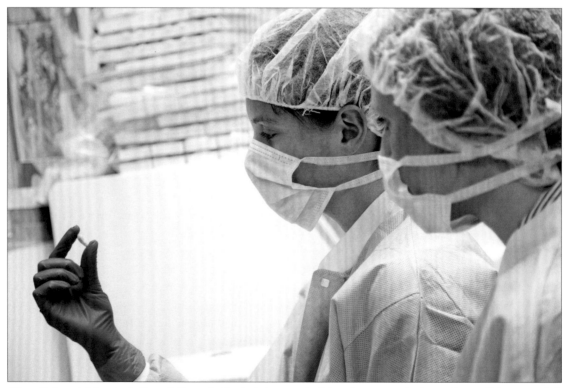

Illus. 7.3—Ashley Pokallus (left) and Sheila Tierney (right) selecting teeth from the Ballyhanna adult assemblage for analysis at the University of Wisconsin (Phil Farrell).

Comparative analyses were conducted to find the extraction method which would recover the most DNA from the archaeological teeth. A total demineralisation Silica method was determined to be the most sensitive method for the Ballyhanna samples (Rohland et al. 2010).

Results

Sex determination of adult skeletons

DNA was extracted from 50 teeth from articulated adults and the sex of each was identified using molecular methods—a sample of these is shown in Tables 7.1 and 7.2. All of the teeth were sourced from individuals whose sex had previously been determined using standard osteological methods. All molecular data was verified in the UW, which conducted second centre independent analysis using a second tooth from each skeleton included in the study.

Table 7.1—Results of the quantitative RT-PCR assay from the Ballyhanna adults sampled in ITS

Skeleton number (Adult)	Tooth grade	Sex: osteological analysis	Centre 1: RT–PCR detecting human and male DNA	Centre 2: RT–PCR detecting human and male DNA	Sex: DNA analysis
137	B-	Female	Human DNA detected No male DNA detected	Human DNA detected No male DNA detected	Female
142	A-	Male	Human DNA detected Male DNA detected	Human DNA detected Male DNA detected	Male
367	A	Female	Human DNA detected No male DNA detected	Human DNA detected No male DNA detected	Female
401	B	Male	Human DNA detected Male DNA detected	Human DNA detected Male DNA detected	Male
426	B-	Male	Human DNA detected Male DNA detected	Human DNA detected Male DNA detected	Male
452	A-	Male	Human DNA detected Male DNA detected	Human DNA detected Male DNA detected	Male
454	B-	Female	Human DNA detected No male DNA detected	Human DNA detected No male DNA detected	Female
606	B	Male	Human DNA detected Male DNA detected	Human DNA detected Male DNA detected	Male
826	A	Female	Human DNA detected No male DNA detected	Human DNA detected No male DNA detected	Female
882	A	Female	Human DNA detected No male DNA detected	Human DNA detected No male DNA detected	Female

Table 7.2—Consensus STR profiles from a sample of the Ballyhanna adults screened in ITS and in the second centre laboratory in the UW

Skeleton number (Adult)	Sex: STR – amelogenin analysis	STR profile (Top: Centre 1, IT Sligo (ITS); Bottom: Centre 2, University of Wisconsin (UW))			
	AMEL	D18S51	D8S1179	TH01	FGA
SK 137	ITS: X X–Female	14, 17	13, 14	7, 9.3	21, 22
	UW: X X–Female	14, 17	13, 14	7, 9.3	21, 22
SK 142	ITS: X Y–Male	13, 14	10, 12	8, 9.3	22, 23
	UW: X Y–Male	13, 14	10, –	–, 9.3	22, 23
SK 367	ITS: X X–Female	13, 16	12, 14	9, 9.3	19, 21
	UW: X X–Female	13, 16	12, 14	9, 9.3	19, 21
SK 401	ITS: X Y–Male	13, 14	11	8, 9	20, 22
	UW: X Y–Male	13, 14	11	8, 9	20, 22
SK 426	ITS: X Y–Male	12, 16	10, 13	8, 9.3	19, 23
	UW: X Y–Male	12, 16	Undetected	8, 9.3	19, 23
SK 452	ITS: X Y–Male	15, 19	14, 16	6, 9.3	22, 24
	UW: X Y–Male	15, –	14, 16	6, 9.3	22, 24
SK 454	ITS: X X–Female	12, –	Undetected	7, 9.3	22, 23
	UW: X X–Female	12, 15	10	7, 9.3	22, 23
SK 606	ITS: X Y–Male	12, 15	11, 13	8, 9.3	20, 22
	UW: X Y–Male	12, 15	11, 13	8, 9.3	20, 22
SK 826	ITS: X X–Female	10, 17	9, 10	6, 9	–, 23
	UW: X X–Female	10, 17	Undetected	6, 9	21, 23
SK 882	ITS: X X–Female	14, 15	13, 14	6, 9.3	21, 23
	UW: X X–Female	14,15	13, 14	6, 9.3	21, 23

Tables 7.1 and 7.2 show that the sex of the Ballyhanna adult skeletons as determined using osteological methodologies corresponds to the sex identified using two DNA-based sex determination methods—RT–PCR and STR–amelogenin analysis. The RT-PCR assay simultaneously detects and quantifies the total amount of human DNA and human male DNA in a sample. This is a very

sensitive assay that can detect levels of DNA as low as 23 picograms/µl. If well-preserved human and/or male DNA is present in an aDNA extract then it should be detected and quantified. A second confirmatory method—the STR–amelogenin method—was also used to verify the sex of the skeletons. As the amelogenin gene is found on both the X and Y chromosomes it is routinely used in molecular tests to determine sex. Since males have one X and one Y chromosome they can be distinguished from females who have two X chromosomes.

A unique STR profile was also identified for each skeleton using the STR–amelogenin method. The DNA profile from each tooth sampled in ITS matched the profile from the corresponding tooth sampled in UW (Table 7.2). This verified that the results were reproducible in separate laboratories and thus fully authenticates the results. All negative PCR and extraction blank controls were negative thereby indicating that no contamination was detected.

Sex determination of juvenile skeletons

Once it had been verified that the DNA-based methods were accurate for sexing the adult individuals, the techniques could then be used to determine the sex of a sample of Ballyhanna juvenile remains (Tierney & Bird 2015). Nineteen immature individuals ranging in age from 5–7 years up to 16–18 years were randomly selected for screening. Second centre analysis of the juvenile samples was conducted in a second laboratory in ITS, which was located in a spatially separate building to where the first centre analysis was performed and was carried out by an independent researcher. Table 7.3 provides details of the results of the sex determination using Real Time PCR, while Table 7.4 provides the corresponding results from the STR-amelogenin assay.

Table 7.3—Results of the quantitative RT-PCR assay from the Ballyhanna juveniles sampled in both centres of analysis in ITS

Skeleton number	Tooth grade	Centre 1: RT–PCR detecting human and male DNA	Centre 2: RT–PCR detecting human and male DNA
10	B	Human DNA detected No male DNA detected	Human DNA detected Male DNA detected
53	C/B-	Human DNA detected Male DNA detected	Human DNA detected Male DNA detected
56	C	Human DNA detected Male DNA detected	Human DNA detected Male DNA detected
164	C	Human DNA detected Male DNA detected	Human DNA detected Male DNA detected
232	A-/B+	Human DNA detected Male DNA detected	Human DNA detected Male DNA detected
305	B-	Human DNA detected Male DNA detected	Human DNA detected Male DNA detected

Table 7.3—Results of the quantitative RT-PCR assay from the Ballyhanna juveniles sampled in both centres of analysis in ITS (cont'd)

Skeleton number	Tooth grade	Centre 1: RT–PCR detecting human and male DNA	Centre 2: RT–PCR detecting human and male DNA
319	C	Human DNA detected No male DNA detected	Human DNA detected Male DNA detected
536	A-/B+	Human DNA detected Male DNA detected	Human DNA detected Male DNA detected
600	C	Human DNA detected Male DNA detected	Human DNA detected Male DNA detected
627	C	Human DNA detected Male DNA detected	Human DNA detected Male DNA detected
668	B	Human DNA detected Male DNA detected	Human DNA detected Male DNA detected
687	B	Human DNA detected Male DNA detected	Human DNA detected Male DNA detected
691	B-	Human DNA detected No Male DNA detected	Human DNA detected only No Male DNA detected
694	C	No DNA detected	No DNA detected
730	B	Human DNA detected Male DNA detected	Human DNA detected Male DNA detected
772	B-	Human DNA detected No male DNA detected	Human DNA detected No male DNA detected
859	C	Human DNA detected No male DNA detected	Human DNA detected Male DNA detected
865	C	Human DNA detected Male DNA detected	Human DNA detected Male DNA detected
870	C	Human DNA detected Male DNA detected	Human DNA detected Male DNA detected

Table 7.4—Consensus STR profiles from the Ballyhanna juveniles sampled in both centres of analysis in IT Sligo

Skeleton number	STR–amelogenin analysis	STR profile Top: IT Sligo Centre 1 (C.1); Bottom: IT Sligo Centre 2 (C.2)				
	AMEL	D18S51	D8S1179	TH01	FGA	Molecular sex*
10	C.1: XY–Male	12, 15	10, 14	7, 8	22, 22.2	Probable male
	C.2: XY–Male	12, 15	10, 14	7, 8	22, 22.2	
53	C.1: undetected	Undetected	Undetected	Undetected	Undetected	Probable male
	C.2: XY–Male	12, 17	8, 13	6, 9.3	21, 2	
56	C.1: XY–Male	15	10	7	22, 23	Probable male
	C.2: XY–Male	15	10	6, 7	22, 23	
164	C.1: XY–Male	14, 17	10, 14	7, 9	23, 25	Male
	C.2: XY–Male	14, 17	10, 14	7, 9	23, 25	
232	C.1: XY–Male	15, 16	13	7, 9.3	20, 25	Male
	C.2: XY–Male	15, 16	13, 15	7, 9.3	20, 25	
305	C.1: XY–Male	15,16	10, 13	7, 9.3	21, 22	Male
	C.2: XY–Male	15,16	10, 13	7, 9.3	21, 22	
319	C.1: XY–Male	14	14, 15	9.3	23, 25	Probable male
	C.2: undetected	14	Undetected	9.3	25	
536	C.1: XY–Male	12, 21	10, 11	8, 9.3	22, 23	Probable male
	C.2: undetected	Undetected	Undetected	8, 9.3	Undetected	
600	C.1: undetected	Undetected	Undetected	Undetected	Undetected	Inconclusive
	C.2: XY–Male	12	13	9, 9.3	21	
627	C.1: XY–Male	12, 18	8, 10	7	21, 23	Inconclusive
	C.2: X,Y only	12, 18	8, 10	7	21, 23	
668	C.1: XY–Male	18, 19	13	6, 9.3	20, 21	Probable male
	C.2: undetected	Undetected	Undetected	Undetected	Undetected	
687	C.1: XY–Male	16, 20	12, 15	9.3	20, 23	Probable male
	C.2: XY–Male	16	12	9.3	20, 23	

Table 7.4—Consensus STR profiles from the Ballyhanna juveniles sampled in both centres of analysis in IT Sligo (cont'd)

Skeleton number	STR–amelogenin analysis	STR profile Top: IT Sligo Centre 1 (C.1); Bottom: IT Sligo Centre 2 (C.2)				
	AMEL	D18S51	D8S1179	TH01	FGA	Molecular sex★
691	C.1: undetected	Undetected	Undetected	Undetected	Undetected	Inconclusive
	C.2: XY–Male	15, 18	Undetected	7, 9.3	22	
694	C.1: undetected	Undetected	Undetected	Undetected	Undetected	Inconclusive
	C.2: undetected	Undetected	Undetected	Undetected	Undetected	
730	C.1: XY–Male	12, 18	11, 14	6, 7	22, 23	Probable male
	C.2: XY–Male	12, 18	11	6, 7	22	
772	C.1: XX–Female	12, 15	8, 10	6, 7	21, 24	Probable female
	C.2: XX–Female	12, 15	8, 10	6, 7	21, 24	
859	C.1: XY–Male	13, 19	10, 13	9.3	18, 20	Probable male
	C.2: XY–Male	13, 19	Undetected	9.3	18	
865	C.1: XY–Male	14	12, 13	7, 9.3	21, 24	Probable male
	C.2: XY–Male	14	12, 13	7, 9.3	21, 24	
870	C.1: XY–Male	13, 16	12, 13	6	21	Male
	C.2: XY–Male	13, 16	12, 13	6	21	

Note: ★Some of the samples were sexed as 'probable' males or females as the results were not replicated in more than two samples in the two centres of analysis and therefore could not be verified in full. The sex of some of the individuals was identified as 'inconclusive' as the molecular sex could not be confirmed since little or no amplifiable DNA was detected.

From assessing the overall results of both sexing methods in the two centres of analysis and using strict interpretation criteria, we determined that four of the juveniles were male, 10 were probable males, one was a probable female and four were inconclusive. The sex of some of these individuals could not fully be confirmed due to the degraded state of the DNA profiles. The Powerplex STR assay verified that the results were genuine as the DNA profiles were reproduced in both centres of analysis, with the exceptions of SK 668, SK 691 and SK 865 whose DNA profiles were only detected in one centre. The fragile and unpredictable nature of aDNA can be seen in such samples where no profile, or only a partial profile, was obtained in one centre, while a full profile was obtained in another. This highlights how important it is to undertake multiple replications of each ancient extract.

Results of the screening for the cystic fibrosis F508del mutation

Some 60 individuals from the Ballyhanna skeletal collection were sampled and screened for the F508del mutation in UW, and these results were confirmed in ITS. Approximately one in 19 people in Ireland today are carriers of the F508del cystic fibrosis mutation (Cashman et al. 1995). Therefore, if the frequency of the mutation has not changed in the last 500 years, we would expect to find three individuals from the 60 sampled with the mutation. Of the 60 individuals from Ballyhanna screened for the mutation at UW and ITS, no cystic fibrosis heterozygote carriers were identified.

Results of the aDNA analysis of lesions characteristic of tuberculosis

From the six bones sampled which showed lesions indicative of tuberculosis, extracts from four of these bones were found to be IS*1081* negative, while extracts from two of the bones, SK 182 and SK 885, showed positive results for the IS*1081* marker. However, the results from SK 885 were not repeated when the PCR was replicated. The extracts were then screened using the second marker specific to the MTB complex, IS*6110*. All extracts were found to be negative except for SK 182 which again showed amplification products of the desired fragment size. However, the second centre analysis conducted by Dr Mike Taylor in the University of Surrey found all six samples to be IS*1081* and IS*6110* negative.

Discussion and conclusions

Ancient DNA research can add significant information to archaeological investigations, often providing answers to previously unresolved hypotheses and therefore benefiting archaeological interpretations immensely. This was the main reason for conducting the aDNA study as part of the BRP. The research represents the first biomolecular archaeological evaluation of a medieval assemblage in Ireland to date.

The preliminary analysis conducted in the early stages of the project demonstrated that aDNA could only be successfully recovered from four out of 11 disarticulated pelvic bones. Subsequent analysis identified that teeth from the Ballyhanna individuals were a superior source of preserved aDNA to the bone material. A comprehensive investigation of the aDNA extraction and PCR amplification methods applied to the Ballyhanna skeletal material was conducted. This comparative study identified which extraction method was most sensitive and enabled reproducible and reliable high quantitative DNA yields from the Ballyhanna remains. In addition, by changing from conventional PCR methods to newer, more advanced, quantitative RT-PCR techniques, a more sensitive, accurate and precise amplification method was established to detect and quantify aDNA from the Ballyhanna material. Through conducting this preliminary comparative analysis early in the project, the factors which can limit aDNA studies such as degradation, contamination and inhibition, were thus assessed and strategies to overcome them were developed and implemented.

The results from the molecular analysis carried out on the 47 Ballyhanna adult skeletons (sexed using morphological methods) successfully confirmed the sex of 25 of these individuals using two genetic sexing methods and two independent centres of analysis. The molecular sex of 10 adults could not be fully confirmed due to our strict interpretation criteria which required both sexing assays to reproduce the results in more than two replicate samples. These 10 individuals could therefore only be assigned a probable sex, mainly due to poor amplification of the aDNA which was a consequence of poor DNA preservation in these samples. The sex of the remaining individuals could not be confirmed as little or no amplifiable DNA was detected—a direct consequence of the degraded state of the DNA. The sex of these individuals was therefore inconclusive. The results from this study demonstrated how the precautionary measures taken against modern contamination appear to have been efficient, as all non-template controls and extraction blank controls were negative. The STR profiles of the Ballyhanna adults also exhibited no evidence of contamination from modern human DNA as no matches were observed against the staff elimination database and each profile appeared to be unique and was replicated in the second centre. Appropriate molecular behaviour was also observed as an inverse relationship between the DNA fragment size and its quantity was seen throughout the analysis. The core objective to develop a reliable, rapid and unambiguous sexing system for the Ballyhanna human remains was thus achieved and meant that these methods could be used with a high degree of certainty on the unsexed juvenile remains.

As juvenile human skeletons exhibit little sexual dimorphism, attempts to develop osteological techniques to determine the sex of such individuals have been difficult. It was for this reason that an alternative method was required to sex the juveniles from Ballyhanna, and this was the basis for conducting this aDNA study. By testing and validating the accuracy and reproducibility of our molecular sexing methods using osteologically sexed adult remains, it was established that these methods could thus be used reliably on unsexed juveniles from the assemblage.

Reliable sex identification of juvenile human skeletal remains is extremely significant as it allows us to build up a picture of the structure of past populations. Strands of research may be developed through the ability to sex immature remains, such as, exploring whether there are dietary differences apparent between the sexes. It also permits the social treatment of males and females during childhood to be examined. Reliably determining the sex of children within a society can inform us about their preferential treatment, their susceptibility to disease, their place in society through burial rite and grave inclusions, the degree and division of labour and at what age boys and girls became accepted as adult members of a community (Lewis 2007, 48). It is also important to archaeological inquiry to establish if there was any significant difference in the morbidity and mortality rates of young males and females within an assemblage. As no morphological method for sexing juvenile skeletons is currently widely accepted, aDNA analysis has the potential to be a significant and necessary tool for sex determination and thus may finally answer these questions and open up new avenues of research.

A number of aDNA studies have successfully used DNA sexing methods on archaeological juvenile remains to answer specific research questions. Some studies have sexed infant remains thought to be victims of infanticide (Faerman et al. 1998; Waldron et al. 1999; Mays & Faerman 2001), while others have tried to link morphological sexing traits with molecular analysis (Waldron et al. 1999; Cunha et al. 2000) or develop an accurate morphological sexing method using aDNA (Zadzinska et al. 2008). With the exception of a study by Lassen and colleagues (2000) which reconstructed the sex ratio of neonatal and stillbirth infants, it appears that no other study has assessed the natural mortality ratio across the entire juvenile assemblage from a population using aDNA analysis until now. From the 19 juveniles sampled in the study, the sex of just four of these could be confirmed as males. However, the results derived from the other, less successfully amplified, samples still indicated that 10 of these juveniles were probable males and one was a probable female. Four individuals could not be sexed and were determined as inconclusive. Unfortunately, the sex of these 15 individuals cannot be substantiated fully due to the degraded state of the aDNA.

As the number of juveniles sampled was quite small, the results are therefore not representative of the entire juvenile population at Ballyhanna. A larger sample size would have been more representative but was not possible within the remit of the current study. Increasing the sample number and conducting further genetic sexing analyses would provide us with more conclusive results and present a more detailed picture of the mortality ratio of the boys and girls of medieval Ballyhanna. Nevertheless, the results from the research are quite tantalising as they potentially indicate that more young males than females were dying at a young age in medieval Ballyhanna, which could be due to a mortality disadvantage of some kind towards males.

In relation to the cystic fibrosis F508del screening study, the F508del mutation was not detected amongst the individuals sampled from Ballyhanna. This suggests that the F508del mutation was not as prevalent in this medieval population as it is in Ireland today, which indicates that a more recent event was responsible for enriching the Irish population with the F508del mutant allele. If this is the case, the findings from this study support the hypothesis that the tuberculosis pandemic which spread throughout Europe in the 17th century could possibly have provided sufficient selective pressure to generate the modern incidence of cystic fibrosis (Meindl 1987; Poolman & Galvani 2007). We know that the mutation was present in Europe more than 2,000 years ago as it was identified directly using aDNA analysis in three out of 32 Iron Age skeletons in Austria (Farrell et al. 2007). The prevalence of the F508del in this Iron Age population, however, was substantially higher than the current carrier frequency of between 1 in 23 and 1 in 32 in European populations today (Morral et al. 1994, 169). Other aDNA studies conducted on historic populations in Europe (Sicily and Central Poland) showed similar results to the Ballyhanna study—no heterozygote carriers were identified in these populations (Bramanti et al. 2000; Witas et al. 2006). Such findings clearly open up debate as to what selective pressure was responsible for causing the current high incidence of cystic fibrosis. Conducting a more widespread investigation on ancient human populations throughout Ireland and Europe using aDNA analysis has the potential to explore such hypotheses further and help provide an explanation as to why this mutation is so common in Ireland and Europe today.

No mycobacterial DNA was detected from five of the six individuals exhibiting pathological lytic lesions consistent with tuberculosis. Mycobacterial DNA was detected in just one sample— SK 182—in the ITS centre but analysis in the second centre, conducted by Dr Mike Taylor in the University of Surrey, found that all samples were negative when screened with the IS1081 and IS6110 assays. It must always be remembered when conducting aDNA research that failure to obtain a positive signal for a particular pathogen does not necessarily provide definitive evidence of its absence from an archaeological specimen. The DNA of pathogenic micro-organisms will always be a minor component within a host so sampling directly from the lesion site where the pathogen would be localised is the best approach (Donoghue & Spigelman 2006). In this study, in order to preserve the lesions, bone samples could only be taken from behind or adjacent to the lesion site. This, as well as the uneven distribution of microbial pathogens within the samples (Donoghue et al. 2005) could explain the negative results in five out of the six lesions sampled. Another factor that may have attributed to the high occurrence of negative results from the Ballyhanna remains could be in relation to the bone type sampled. The bone which microbial DNA was detected from in SK

182—acromiale end of the clavicle—contained the greatest amount of cortical bone material from the area sampled near the lesion. The remaining five bones sampled contained only trabecular bone at the site of sampling. Trabecular bone has a spongy composition and is therefore much less rigid and dense. The denser nature of cortical bone assists in protecting and preserving the endogenous aDNA within, in turn providing more aDNA molecules for analysis than spongy bone (Yang & Watt 2005). Another possible explanation for the lack of amplifiable DNA detected in the second centre could be down to the extraction method used, which may not have the same level of sensitivity as the method used in ITS. Since the positive result for tuberculosis from SK 182 could not be replicated in the second centre of analysis, this result unfortunately could not be fully authenticated. All samples were also found to be negative for the pathogen responsible for brucellosis.

Through the aDNA study, we have answered key research questions relevant to the Ballyhanna assemblage by applying molecular techniques and interpreting the results within the archaeological context. The aDNA analysis has allowed us to look back in time and answer those important questions about our ancestors which previously could not be addressed using traditional archaeological methods.

8

INSIGHTS FROM THE CHEMICAL ANALYSIS OF HUMAN BONE FROM THE BALLYHANNA BURIAL GROUND

Ted McGowan & Tasneem Bashir

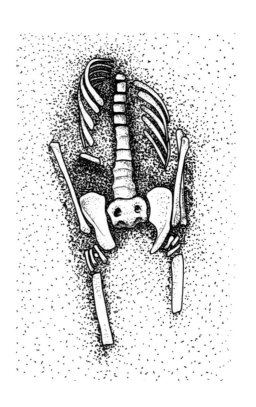

Stylised depiction of a middle-aged male, buried with quartz in his right hand (SK 993) (Sapphire Mussen).

Carbon, hydrogen, nitrogen and oxygen are essential to life on earth along with several of the 76 other stable elements; calcium and phosphorus are the main inorganic (i.e. not carbon based) elemental components of our bone structure. Also essential to health are many minor and trace elements, such as copper and zinc. Study of the elements of which our bodies are composed can give a chemical insight into the various natural processes affecting life (i.e. biogenic processes), including diet, health and indeed the location in which we have lived. In modern medicine the levels of biogenic concentration of various elements in our blood, bone and other body tissues can provide essential information for health diagnosis. As bone tissue in living adults is replaced over an estimated period of five to seven years, and maybe longer depending on the density of the particular bone, the examination of skeletons for the constituent elements provides indications of the diet over the final years of life (Tykot 2006, 136).

Following burial, while soft tissue (i.e. blood, skin and organs) generally decays rapidly, the robust structure of bone tissue preserves to some extent a chemical record of the individual. The degree of preservation of bone within the burial environment, and therefore the biogenic elemental information contained therein, will depend on the harshness of the burial conditions such as soil acidity. In archaeological studies, the alteration of the biogenic elemental profile in bone due to the burial environment is termed diagenesis (Pollard & Heron 2008, 10).

Techniques developed in the field of analytical chemistry and used in this research will explore whether the archaeological bone from the medieval Ballyhanna human skeletal remains tells the same story about their diet as the historical sources infer. The research has also addressed specific questions arising from discoveries made during the osteoarchaeological analysis of the Ballyhanna assemblage. Skeletons with evidence of cribra orbitalia (porosity or pitting in the roof of the eye sockets) and porotic hyperostosis (porosity or pitting on the outer surface of the cranial vault), which are believed to be indicative of vitamin and nutrient deficiencies (Walker et al. 2009, 114), were included in the study to investigate whether significant differences existed in the trace element profiles between these groupings.

The chemical analysis of bone is a vibrant area of modern research and both existing and new analytical techniques can yield a variety of health-related, dietary and environmental information. Table 8.1 provides an overview of the specific elements included in the Ballyhanna analysis and includes comments regarding the application of specific groups of these elements (Shafer et al. 2008, 146). Details of the individual skeletons included in the study are provided in Table 8.2. Supplementary material for this chapter is provided on the accompanying CD-ROM.

Table 8.1—Overview of the elements monitored in the Ballyhanna bone and their significance/applications

Element	Application
Calcium (Ca), Carbon (C), Barium (Ba), Hydrogen (H), Magnesium (Mg), Nitrogen (N), Oxygen (O), Strontium (Sr), Phosphorus (P)	Major bone structural elements (Ca, P); minor bone structural elements (Ba, Sr, Mg) which substitute for calcium in bone mineral; Calcium, Phosphorus and Strontium are often used to normalise other trace element data
Stable isotope of Carbon (^{13}C), and stable isotope of Nitrogen (^{15}N)	Elements used for paleodietary studies (Ba, Sr, ^{13}C, ^{15}N)

Table 8.1—Overview of the elements monitored in the Ballyhanna bone and their significance/applications (cont'd)

Element	Application
Boron (B), Bismuth (Bi), Molybdenum (Mo), Rubidium (Rb), Sodium (Na), Uranium (U)	Elements used to monitor for diagenetic alteration of bone and groundwater contact (B, Ba, Bi, Mo, Na, Rb, Sr, U)
Aluminium (Al), Iron (Fe), Manganese (Mn), and rare earth elements (i.e. Cerium (Ce), Dysprosium (Dy), Erbium (Er), Europium (Eu), Gadolinium (Gd), Holmium (Ho), Lanthanum (La), Lutetium (Lu), Neodymium (Nd), Praseodymium (Pr), Rhenium (Re), Ruthenium (Ru), Samarium (Sm), Terbium (Tb) and Thulium (Tm)	Elements used to monitor contamination, primarily sourced from soil and contaminates via groundwater Biogenic Iron (Fe) would provide useful physiological data if soil sourced interference was removed
Cobalt (Co), Chromium (Cr), Nickel (Ni)	Can be used both as tracers to monitor potential contamination in bone from the coring drill and also as nutritional indicators
Copper (Cu), Nickel (Ni), Zinc (Zn)	Used to monitor for essential trace elements; Zinc is a bone seeking element under strong physiological control
Arsenic (As), Cadmium (Cd), Lead (Pb)	Principal anthropogenic contaminant metals indicating toxicity

Table 8.2—Ballyhanna articulated bone samples selected for chemical analysis

Skeleton	Metabolic disease	Sex	Age	Femur grade	Cal AD date ranges or probable historical period
86	No	M	18–35	1	1403–1476
172	No	F	50+	0	Probable late medieval
263	No	F	18–35	0	Probable late medieval
322	No	F	Adult	0	Probable late medieval
471A	No	F?	Adult	2	Probable late medieval
484	No	M	18–35	1	1182–1379
910	No	F	18–35	0	Probable late medieval
971	No	F?	18–35	0	Probable late medieval
973	No	F	18–35	0	Probable late medieval
982	No	M	18–35	0	Probable late medieval
1014	No	F	18–35	1	Probable late medieval
1026	No	F	35–50	1	Probable late medieval

Table 8.2—Ballyhanna articulated bone samples selected for chemical analysis (cont'd)

Skeleton	Metabolic disease	Sex	Age	Femur grade	Cal AD date ranges or probable historical period
1027	No	F	18–35	1	Probable late medieval
1046	No	F?	Adult	0	Probable late medieval
1113	No	M	18–35	2	1280–1388
1125	No	F	50+	2	Probable early medieval
1159	No	F	35–50	1	Probable late medieval
1225	No	M	35–50	1	1284–1390
90	Yes	F	50+	0	Probable late medieval
150	Yes	M	35–50	1	1410–1455
198	Yes	M	35–50	0	1280–1389
295	Yes	M	18–35	2	1220–1277
418	Yes	F	35–50	0	Probable late medieval
425	Yes	?	Adult	2	Probable late medieval
478	Yes	F	35–50	0	Probable late medieval
532	Yes	F	18–35	0	Probable late medieval
566	Yes	M	18–35	1	779–966
571	Yes	M	18–35	0	1028–1161
608	Yes	F?	18–35	2	Probable late medieval
624	Yes	F	35–50	1	Probable late medieval
633	Yes	F?	50+	2	Probable late medieval
845	Yes	F	18–35	1	Probable late medieval
850	Yes	M	18–35	0	1455–1631
927	Yes	M	18–35	0	1429–1606
936A	Yes	M	35–50	0	1440–1633
1125	Yes	F	18–35	0	Probable late medieval
1151	Yes	M	18–35	0	1446–1632
1185	Yes	M	35–50	1	694–889

Note: calibrated date ranges are expressed at two sigma (95% probability) levels of confidence (see Appendix 1).

Other similar studies of archaeological human bone assemblages from around the world have successfully been used to gain insights into palaeodiet (e.g. Van Klinken et al. 2002; Jay & Richards

2006; Knudson et al. 2012, 317), geographical mobility (Knudson et al. 2012), the treatment of disease (Rasmussen et al. 2008) and metal toxicity (Grandjean 1988, 11; González-Reimers et al. 2003).

This chapter will present quantitative multi-elemental data from the chemical analysis of bones excavated from the cemetery at Ballyhanna. The chemical analysis was carried out with the aim of achieving the following research objectives:

1. To assess the state of preservation of human bone from Ballyhanna. The results from tests will provide information on the general structural integrity of the sampled bones including the inorganic crystal structure and organic content. The harshness of the burial environment in respect of bone preservation is evaluated through analysis of the surrounding burial soil, the results of which are also used to evaluate the potential for contamination of the skeletal remains due to elements from the soil.

2. To determine the concentrations of a range of major, minor and trace elements in the bone. These will include elements which provide information on the degree of bone diagenesis. The modern multi-element analysis methods used significantly increase the amount of data collected on contaminants. These data provide for both the clearer identification of interferences and the basis for removal of these interferences.

3. To develop correction methods for the removal of the contamination signal due to trace elements from burial soil and groundwater.

4. To estimate biogenic (i.e. natural pre-burial) concentrations of selected trace elements in bone. In order to interpret factors affecting the life of the individual the elemental data are corrected when required for identified interferences. Any limitations of these interference corrections are clearly outlined and potential errors highlighted.

5. To interpret biogenic elemental profiles for indications of diet, environmental conditions, health or disease that may have affected the Ballyhanna population. Discussions in this chapter will focus in particular on dietary inferences from the accumulated data. Results for the Ballyhanna human bone assemblage will be compared with modern human bone and with archaeological bone analysed as a part of other studies.

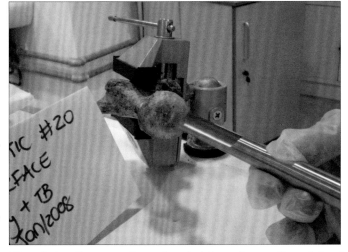

In order to avoid contamination from burial soil, an inner core of compact cortical bone from the femur head was sampled after removing a surface layer of bone. Both the inner bone coring strategy and the use of cortical bone provide for maximum avoidance of soil contamination (Illus. 8.1). The elemental analysis involved

Illus. 8.1—Core sampling of cortical bone from a femoral head using a manual coring drill (Ted McGowan).

the dissolution of the bone samples with concentrated acid. These solution samples were subsequently nebulised into a high temperature plasma flame and elemental concentrations measured from the specific emissions for each element.

Background to the study

Diagenesis and the degree of bone preservation

In the past doubt was cast on the results of trace element analysis of archaeological bone due to uncertainties arising from diagenesis. The term diagenesis refers to the chemical alterations which occur in the skeletons following death. All current studies, however, involve monitoring for diagenesis, and attempt to mitigate against any potential diagenetic interferences. Some approaches have used tooth enamel samples which are more inert to diagenesis than other forms of bone. However, unlike the cortical bone used in the current study, a disadvantage of enamel is that it is formed only once, in the early years of life and its elemental content is therefore representative only of this period (Knudson et al. 2012, 317). For the Ballyhanna research the impact of diagenesis is assessed using a combination of techniques similar to those applied in other recent comparative studies (Mays 2003, 732–4; Shafer et al. 2008, 153–6; Knudson et al. 2012, 316). These techniques 'build up a picture of the diagenetic change in the material under study' (Mays 2003, 733).

The following general processes have been identified in bone diagenesis (Turner-Walker 2008):

1. Chemical destruction of bone collagen—a protein which comprises approximately 90% of the organic component of bone (ibid., 5).
2. Chemical alteration of the calcium phosphate-based inorganic crystal structure, termed bone apatite.
3. Destruction of the bone matrix (mainly collagen) following microbial attack.

The greatest alteration in bone apatite can be attributed to chemical weathering. This involves the leaching of elements from the surrounding soil into the bone or, conversely, loss of elements from the bone to the soil—termed bone dissolution. Once bone is interred there are several factors which are capable of increasing the dissolution process. These factors include soil acidity, the degree of saturation of water with calcium and phosphate ions and the rate of groundwater movement (ibid., 11–16). Soil pH levels (i.e. used for soil acidity determination) and the concentration of labile trace elements (i.e. elements readily water soluble and available for transfer from soil into groundwater) are determined as part of this research.

The crystallinity and organic content of bone is regularly used by archaeological researchers to assess the degree of modification of ancient bone by diagenetic processes. The Crystallinity Index (CI), or Splitting Factor (SF), is a measure of the order of the crystal structure (Stiner et al. 2001; Thompson et al. 2009).

The levels of calcium (Ca) and phosphorus (P) (i.e. the main inorganic elements in bone tissue) also provide useful information on the degree of preservation of archaeological bone. The ratio of the amounts of these elements by weight (Ca/P) is a standard measure of bone integrity and is evaluated in most current studies in the field (Farnum et al. 1995; Zapata et al. 2006; Knudson et al. 2012, 315–16). The Ca/P ratio in modern bone, calculated from average results obtained from 45 autopsied individuals, is approximately 2.07 (Yoshinaga et al. 1995, 243).

Several elements, or groups of elements, in bone provide a quantitative measure of ingress from the surrounding burial soil (e.g. aluminium, iron, manganese and the rare earth elements (REE)) (Trueman et al. 2006, 4343–55; Shafer et al. 2008; Knudson et al. 2012, 315–16). The REE are those elements which are present at very low levels in soil and groundwater and range in atomic number (Z) from lanthanum (La) (Z=57) to lutetium (Lu) (Z=71) (Trueman 1999, 557). REEs are ubiquitous in bone pore waters—groundwater which may enter bone through pores in its structure—and are present in very low concentrations, in the order of parts per billion (ppb) or microgrammes per litre (ibid., 558). The REEs are also normally present at ppb levels in living bone (Shaw & Wasserburg 1985, 503; Trueman 1999, 557). As interred bone undergoes recrystallisation the adsorbed REE concentrations can increase by several orders of magnitude (Kohn & Cerling 2002, 457; Trueman & Tuross 2002). The amount of adsorbed REEs can therefore be used as tracer elements for the monitoring of soil contamination of buried bone. In this research, the concentrations of 14 REEs were determined in each analysed bone and both their individual and cumulative concentration ($\sum$ REE) reported.

The data generated from the large range of techniques used in this research on the Ballyhanna population have enabled a detailed evaluation of the diagenesis of the bones to be undertaken. The REE data set collected as part of the project is more comprehensive than that included in other similar studies and has provided additional opportunities for the use of interference correction techniques when required.

Trace elements and diet

Trace elements are mainly incorporated into bone apatite and originate from all sources of food (Tykot 2006, 138). Currently there are two approaches to the use of trace elements to determine diet. The first approach relies mainly on assessing levels of strontium and barium which are known to concentrate in the skeleton and to become part of the crystalline structure of the bone (Burton & Price 1990; Arnay-de-la-Rosa et al. 2009; Knudson et al. 2012, 315–17). Diagenesis affecting barium and strontium can be monitored and its severity usually does not significantly limit any dietary interpretations (Burton & Price 1990; Arnay-de-la-Rosa et al. 2009; Knudson et al. 2012, 315–17). The second approach involves the use of a diverse range of elements which would almost always include magnesium, copper and zinc (Ezzo 1994; Djingova et al. 2004). The particular elements monitored are chosen because of their apparent ability to distinguish between plant- and animal-based resources in the food chain (Gilbert 1985, 339–58; Baraybar & de la Rua 1997, 361–3). Some of these elements are, however, severely impacted by diagenesis from burial soil and therefore this latter approach has seen only limited application in recent archaeological research (Larsen 2002, 122). In addition, many of these elements previously considered useful for palaeodietary analysis are now considered unsuitable due to biological constraints (Burton & Price 2000, 162).

The ability of the gastrointestinal system to discriminate against strontium (i.e. not absorb it in equal ratio to calcium) develops with age (Mays 2003, 732–40). Mays has demonstrated this in a study of a juvenile population from the medieval village of Wharram Percy, Yorkshire. He also used strontium:calcium ratios (Sr/Ca) from infant bone to track the cessation of breastfeeding.

Element ratios such as those of Sr/Ca can provide significant information and have also been used in studies of diagenesis, past diet and migration. Other commonly used ratios in dietary studies are those of barium:calcium (Ba/Ca) (Burton et al. 1999, 609–16) and barium:strontium (Ba/Sr) (Knudson et al. 2012, 316). Plots of the Ba/Ca ratio versus Sr/Ca ratio also help to identify clusters of individuals with similar strontium and barium profiles. Indeed such plots have previously been used to identify populations within specific geological regions or those with similar diets (Burton et al. 1999, 610–15; Sponheimer et al. 2005, 150–5).

The Ba/Sr ratio (commonly expressed as log (Ba/Sr)) in bone is a particularly important indicator for the identification of marine-sourced food in diets since such food has relatively low levels of barium compared to food sourced from the land. Indeed the Ba/Sr ratio in bone that is reflective of a land-based diet is greater than that resulting from a marine diet by more than an order of magnitude (Burton & Price 1990, 548–9). Therefore, with the exception of establishing land-based diets from desert regions, the following generalisations are made regarding average barium:strontium ratios—mean log (Ba/Sr) values > −0.5[6] are indicative of mainly food sourced from the land in the diet, whereas mean log (Ba/Sr) values < −1.25[7] are indicative of a diet based predominantly on fish and other marine products (ibid., 550). Although Ba/Sr values are widely used and accepted for differentiating between marine and land-based diets, it is always necessary to consider the potential for diagenetic contamination via trace elements from soil in burial environments (Burton & Price 1990, 549–51; Fabig & Herrmann 2002, 115; Arnay-de-la-Rosa et al. 2009, 1979; Knudson et al. 2012, 312).

Carbon and nitrogen isotopes and diet

The stable isotope ratios of carbon ($\delta^{13}C$) and nitrogen ($\delta^{15}N$) are routinely monitored in studies of archaeological bone, providing information on both the types of plants being consumed and also whether the diet contains marine or land-sourced food (Smith & Epstein 1971; Knudson et al. 2012, 312). The stable isotope ratios of carbon and nitrogen for bone collagen, including tooth dentine, are mainly representative of the protein component of diet (Tykot 2006, 138).

The collagen $\delta^{13}C$ and $\delta^{15}N$ for bone samples obtained from selected males are listed in Table 8.3 and a preliminary account of the dietary interpretation for this selected group is provided on the accompanying CD-ROM.

---

6   i.e. Ba/Sr: > 0.32
7   i.e. Ba/Sr: < 0.056

Results and discussion

Barium, strontium and other trace elements in Ballyhanna bone

The average total concentrations of barium in articulated bone from the Ballyhanna graveyard (15 ± 7 ppm; n=36[8]) are above the range of 1.7–12.3 ppm reported for modern human bone (Beneš et al. 2000, 202). The total average strontium concentrations from the Ballyhanna bone (165 ± 37 ppm; n=36) are also greater than those from the autopsied modern specimens (23.4–117 ppm) (ibid.). They are, however, within a more general range for modern adults of 100–300 ppm (Mays 2003, 734). Higher than average strontium levels (249.6 ± 54.7 ppm; n=50) were reported for the medieval adult bones from the Wharram Percy cemetery (ibid., 733). Significantly, the relative variability (given numerically as the % rsd, which is the standard deviation for the strontium concentrations expressed as a percentage of the average strontium concentration) in strontium concentrations (16% rsd) for Ballyhanna is not large—it is similar to both the 21.9% rsd (24.7 x 100)/249.6) obtained for the Wharram Percy medieval adult population and the 24.3% rsd (19.6 x 100/80.5) derived from 45 modern human autopsied individuals (Yoshinaga et al. 1995, 243). Since the variability in strontium in the Ballyhanna samples is less than that for the modern autopsied bones, it would appear to reflect biogenic levels, acquired while living, and suggests that limited diagenesis had affected the strontium levels. The variability for barium (49% rsd) in the Ballyhanna bone is significantly greater than that of strontium (16% rsd). Like calcium, both strontium and barium are alkaline earth elements which are incorporated with calcium into the mineral structure of bone, reflecting dietary levels, and both are preferentially eliminated, relative to calcium, from the alimentary tract (Burton & Price 1990, 547). Therefore it is expected that the variability of barium and strontium levels within a population should be similar. In the Ballyhanna samples this is not the case and, as such, the larger variability found for barium indicates that the high concentrations of barium may be due to diagenesis. An important factor influencing barium diagenesis may be the much lower average concentration of barium in the bone (15 mg/kg) relative to the barium concentrations found in the surrounding burial soil at Ballyhanna (65 mg/kg) which would infer a greater probability for a transfer of barium from soil to bone. Conversely, the strontium concentrations in the Ballyhanna burial soil (64 mg/kg) are lower than those found in bone (165 mg/kg) indicating less potential for contamination of the bone from the soil.

Results for several trace elements—particularly aluminium, iron, manganese and potassium—appear elevated in the Ballyhanna samples, and well above what would be expected for biogenic bone, and it is clear that corrections for significant residual soil contamination will be required as part of any future research in order to extract useful and interpretable biogenic concentrations for these elements. The results for barium, copper, lead, strontium and zinc are, however, either comparable with, or less than, the reference values for biogenic bone (Beneš et al. 2000, 202) and this may indicate, with respect to these elements, only minor impacts due to ingress from the burial soil.

---

8   The limits (±) represent the uncertainty equivalent to one standard deviation for the 36 bone samples derived from articulated individuals at Ballyhanna.

Assessment of diagenesis and the degree of preservation of Ballyhanna bone

The main findings in relation to the degree of bone preservation and diagenesis at Ballyhanna may be summarised as follows:

1. Ca/P for articulated bone at 2.2[9] compares favourably with the 2.16 approximation for modern bone (LeGeros & LeGeros 1984) and also with the average of 2.07 (246 x 100/119) for 45 modern autopsy patients (Yoshinaga et al. 1995, 243). In addition the Ballyhanna results indicate marginally better preservation than that indicated by the 2.27 average Ca/P obtained for medieval Wharram Percy adults[10] (Mays 2003, 713).

2. The average Crystallinity Index (Splitting Factor) of the Ballyhanna samples of 3.38[11] is marginally above the upper limit of 3.25 for modern unaltered bone (Thompson et al. 2009, 910) and reflects a good state of general preservation within the cemetery.

3. The Ballyhanna results indicate that the strontium concentrations in the bones appear to be mainly of biogenic origin. This is supported by both the observed greater concentration of strontium in the bone relative to the surrounding burial soil and also the fact that strontium concentrations in the bone do not correlate with REE contamination tracer concentrations in the radiocarbon-dated bones (Table 8.3).

4. A larger relative concentration of barium in the Ballyhanna burial soil when compared to the bone favours a movement of barium ions from soil via groundwater into bone.

5. The dissimilar Ba/Sr ratio for the burial soil opposed to the bone—1.02[12] versus 0.1[13] respectively—is another significant indication that bone concentrations of these elements may be mainly biogenic.

6. Both the cumulative REE concentrations (13 ± 10 ppm; n=14) and the barium concentrations (14 ± 9 ppm; n=14) in the Ballyhanna bone generally increase with archaeological age, indicating that the burial soil has contributed to the concentration of these elements (Table 8.3). This is also indicated by the positive correlation ($R2 = 0.87$) for the plot of REE bone concentration versus barium bone concentration (Illus. 8.2).

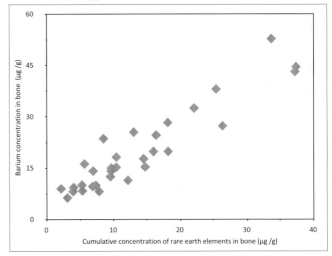

Illus. 8.2—Cumulative concentration of selected rare earth elements versus barium concentration in the bones of 31 articulated skeletons.

---

9   Ca/P: 2.20 ± 0.08; n=37
10 Ca/P: 2.27 ± 0.10; n=50
11 CI: 3.38 ± 0.19; n=38
12 Ba/Sr: 1.02 ± 0.08; n=5
13 Ba/Sr: 0.1 ± 0.08; n=53

Table 8.3—Isotopic and elemental data derived from bone samples from 14 male adults from Ballyhanna

Radiocarbon dates		Osteoarchaeological overview				Stable carbon and nitrogen isotope ratios			Major, minor and trace elements in bone					
Skeleton code	Cal AD date range	Grade[1]	Sex	Age	N	Material	Mean $\delta^{13}C$ collagen (V-PDB) (‰)[2]	Mean $\delta^{15}N$ collagen (AIR) (‰)	N	Ba (µg/g)[3]	Sr (µg/g)	Log (Ba/Sr)	∑ REE (µg/g)	Ca/P
SK 1185	694–889	1	Male	35–50	2	Tooth	−20.30	11.84	3	13.0	210.4	−0.9195	14.6	2.18
SK 571	1028–1161	0	Male	18–35	2	Tooth	−20.36	11.11	3	21.4	138.1	−0.7776	26.4	2.22
SK 484★	1182–1379	1	Male	18–35	2	Tooth	−20.89	10.75	3	33.6	180.5	−0.5152	37.2	2.28
SK 295	1220–1277	2	Male	18–35	2	Tooth	−20.46	10.91	3	28.9	140.5	−0.7035	29.6	2.17
SK 198	1280–1389	0	Male	35–50	2	Tooth	−21.14	10.49	3	11.0	134.9	−1.0950	9.7	2.27
SK 1113★	1280–1388	2	Male	18–35	2	Bone	−21.70	10.31	3	15.4	171.0	−1.0020	37.2	2.28
SK 1225★	1284–1390	1	Male	35–50	2	Bone	−21.04	10.98	3	12.0	165.4	−1.1770	10.4	2.17
SK 86★	1403–1476	1	Male	18–35	2	Tooth	−20.45	10.53	3	18.5	150.5	−1.0330	8.5	2.24
SK 150	1410–1455	1	Male	35–50	2	Tooth	−21.13	10.85	3	6.5	227.3	−1.3380	7.9	2.16
SK 927	1429–1606	0	Male	18–35	2	Tooth	−20.88	10.44	3	7.6	151.7	−1.1970	6.9	2.18
SK 936A	1440–1633	0	Male	35–50	2	Tooth	−20.53	10.38	3	6.5	161.9	−1.2890	4.0	2.23
SK 1151	1446–1632	0	Male	Adult	2	Tooth	−20.46	10.94	3	6.6	147.5	−1.2910	5.4	2.17
SK 850	1455–1631	0	Male	18–35	2	Tooth	−21.26	10.33	3	5.0	232.5	−1.3710	3.1	2.09
SK 982★	1494–1653	0	Male	18–35	2	Bone	−21.44	10.24	3	7.0	150.0	−1.4790	2.1	2.01

Key: ★ *Indicates skeletons which do not show indications of a metabolic disease. 1. Grade indicates degree of visual preservation when graded on the McKinley (2004, 14–17) scale. 2.* $\delta^{13}C$ *and* $\delta^{15}N$ *collagen values are derived from raw AMS (Accelerator Mass Spectrometry) stable isotope values:* $\delta^{13}C$ *reported relative to V-PDB (Vienna PeeDee belemnite) carbonate standard and* $\delta^{15}N$ *reported relative to air. Both are expressed in per mil (‰) (S Hoper, pers. comm.). 3. Minor and trace element (Ba, Sr and REE) concentrations are reported as microgrammes (µg)/gram (g) of dry bone.*

Ballyhanna dietary indications from barium and strontium element ratios

In addition to the comments above regarding specific elements in the Ballyhanna samples, observations can be made relating to dietary indications from an assessment of the elemental ratios—Sr/Ca, Ba/Ca and Ba/Sr. The log-transform of these ratios creates a more normal distribution and obviates some of the bias of anomalous outliers for statistical description (Burton et al. 1999, 210).

The log (Sr/Ca) for articulated bones from Ballyhanna is very consistent, ranging from –3.0 to –3.3.[14] This narrow range indicates that both calcium and strontium originate from a similar source associated with the diet of the individuals. Both the average log (Sr/Ca) and its low variability (as indicated by the standard deviation) are typical of the diets of omnivores (ibid., 612–13).

The very low values for the log (Ba/Ca) ranging from –3.72 to –4.67[15] are typical of land-based carnivores for the higher barium concentrations, to levels indicative of a barium depleted seafood diet (ibid., 611–15). The variability of the log (Ba/Ca) is greater than that for log (Sr/Ca) and indicates possible contamination by barium from soil.

As mentioned in the introduction, marine-sourced food contains less barium by up to a factor of 10 than food which comes from the land. This barium deficiency is reflected in the bones of a marine food consumer (Burton & Price 1990, 549) with log (Ba/Sr) values of < –1.25 being indicative of mainly marine resources in the diet (ibid.). The log (Ba/Sr) for Ballyhanna[16], which ranged from –0.51 to –1.48, therefore indicates the presence of significant marine resources in the diet of the Ballyhanna population. Based on these results, some individuals appear to have consumed relatively large amounts of marine products, particularly those high in calcium, during the last years of life (Knudson et al. 2012, 317). They are typical in profile to several coastal marine communities (Burton & Price 1990, 550)—a similar (but not quite as low) log (Ba/Sr) was also found for coastal dwelling individuals of La Gomera, Canary Islands[17] (Arnay-de-la-Rosa et al. 2009, 1978–9). Although the ratios between Ballyhanna and La Gomera are similar, the absolute strontium and barium concentrations found in the La Gomera bone were much higher (ibid.). Some 29% (11/38) of the Ballyhanna individuals have a log (Ba/Sr) of < –1.25, indicative of having consumed significant food based on marine fish and other marine products. The log (Sr/Ba) found for medieval ninth- to 12th-century AD bones from Dublin ranged from –1.12 to –0.055[18] (Knudson et al. 2012, 314–15). In this latter study, the authors also concluded that some individuals consumed relatively large amounts of marine products while others consumed calcium, strontium and barium from land sources (ibid., 317). It appears therefore that some individuals from Dublin and Ballyhanna have similarities in their diets with respect to the consumption of significant marine-sourced foods, though the significantly lower mean log (Ba/Sr) for Ballyhanna is much more indicative of marine-sourced food in the diet of the population.

The above data for barium levels from Ballyhanna are not corrected for any diagenetic interference and indeed some soil contamination is indicated by the positive correlation with REE tracer (Illus. 8.2) and other indications mentioned above. However, removal of the barium interference due to soil contamination would inevitably lead to even lower log (Ba/Sr) and therefore would further confirm,

---

14 log (Sr/Ca) = –3.19 ± 0.073; n=37
15 log (Ba/Ca) = –4.24 ± 0.244; n=37
16 log (Ba/Sr) = –1.04 ± 0.24, n=37
17 log (Ba/Sr) = –0.74 ± 0.38; n=10
18 The original data were log transformed to aid comparisons and ranged from –1.12 to –0.055; log (Ba/Sr) = –0.385 ± 0.126; n=12

rather than negate, the main current conclusions that the Ballyhanna population consumed significant marine resources.

'Bia bocht' (poor man's food) and 'the king of fish'

In addition to historical records of medieval diet, some archaeological evidence exists relating to the use of regionally specific dietary resources during this period and of other aspects of diet which point to the exploitation of marine resources which could lead to low barium levels in human skeletons.

The consumption of shellfish is evidenced by the existence of shell middens in coastal regions of Ireland, dating from the Bronze Age through to the 10th century AD (Iomaire 2006, 220–2). Indeed, up until the 19th century, there is evidence that people gathered shellfish. The Gaelic terms given to this food were *cnuasach mara* (sea pickings) and *bia bocht* (poor man's food). The collection of this food requires no special fishing equipment or craft and it can simply be picked up at low tide. For this reason, it is rarely mentioned in history or records of commerce though the consumption of shellfish, particularly in times of hardship, is also recorded from 'archaeological digs, ancient writing and traveller's accounts' (ibid.).

Evidence of both seaweed and shellfish as components of the diet in the north-west of Ireland is also encountered in more recent accounts, such as that of the meal of seaweed and limpets known as crusach (translated as 'strength' or 'vigour') consumed by the last inhabitants of the island of Inishmurray, only 20 miles distant from Ballyhanna (Field 2006, 115). The name of this food is indeed apt since we now know that seaweed is a good source of both protein and essential vitamins at levels that would augment a balanced diet if consumed regularly (MacArtain et al. 2007, 541). Marine shellfish are also known to have a high protein content which contains all essential amino acids (Miletic et al. 1991; Zlatanos et al. 2009).

The proximity of the Ballyhanna burial ground to the famous salmon river of the Erne, referred to by a chronicler of the period, Lughaidh Ó Clérigh (Walsh 1948), as 'the place whence issues the famous river abounding in salmon' may also be significant regarding the diet of the population buried at

Ballyhanna. Salmon was revered as the 'king of fish' by Gaelic chiefs and the archaeological record of early monastic sites has provided evidence of fish traps and woven baskets for catching salmon (Iomaire 2006, 220–1). The low barium concentrations, and subsequent low barium to strontium ratios, encountered in the Ballyhanna individuals included in this study are consistent with the exploitation of these marine-sourced dietary resources (Illus. 8.3).

Illus. 8.3—Irish salmon (Northern Ireland Environment Agency).

A confounding factor in this interpretation, however, is that mineral consumption, such as that of sea salt, can also provide dietary calcium, strontium and barium. When considering bioavailable strontium sources in Viking Dublin, Knudson et al. (2012, 311) suggest that, as salt is traded over large distances, the individuals from Dublin may have been consuming salt from non-local, land sources or sea salt.

Sex and age variations

No significant difference was found in elemental bone concentration (i.e. barium, calcium, strontium) between males and females. Yoshinaga et al. (1995, 246), using elemental concentrations for modern bone from autopsy, reached a similar conclusion for the same elements. Since bone concentrations of strontium and barium reflect diet, this observation infers that the diets of both males and females buried at Ballyhanna were similar.

Strontium concentrations for the younger adult age groups (18–35 years) of both males and females at Ballyhanna are lower than that for the older groups (35 years and over) but only significantly different (i.e. 95% confidence) in the case of females. These results are consistent with research indicating that bone strontium concentration increases during life (Tanaka et al. 1981) and that females lose bone mineral during their childbearing years (Price et al. 1985, 425). Higher concentrations of strontium in bone are also associated with fewer bone related diseases (Yoshinaga et al. 1995, 251). However, when compared to modern bones obtained from autopsy (ibid.), the average Ballyhanna strontium concentration is greater by a factor of two, thereby implying generally superior bone health from this indicator relative to this modern population.

Conclusion

The multi-elemental and other analytical results have indicated a high degree of preservation and the occurrence of limited diagenesis within the bone of the Ballyhanna skeletal population. Methods have been described which can filter out trace element diagenetic interference, thereby optimising recovery of the true biogenic levels allowing archaeological interpretation.

Barium to strontium ratios, which are representative of all components in the diet, indicate a marine/aquatic component to the diet of the Ballyhanna population. Stable isotope ratios of carbon and nitrogen for a number of male bones indicate a mainly land-based diet with the consumption of some marine protein resources (Bashir 2012). The narrow range of trace element data infers a population that consumed a similar diet over several centuries. The inclusion of salmon, shellfish and other marine-sourced food in the diet may account for the low concentration of barium in the Ballyhanna bone and would also be consistent with the stable carbon and nitrogen isotopic ratios.

More research is required regarding the variety of locally available marine food resources consumed by the people of Ballyhanna. The source, use and consumption of salt also require further investigation. Further analysis of stable carbon and nitrogen isotope data for a larger, more representative group of the population is currently ongoing. The acquisition of strontium isotope ratios for bone would help resolve whether the strontium originated from land or marine sources. Stable carbon and nitrogen isotope ratio data for locally available marine shellfish would also be an essential part of the baseline data required for any future research which builds upon the Ballyhanna Research Project.

It appears that the poor of Ballyhanna, through their bones, are giving us insights into their lives which the written historical records may have largely overlooked. The chemical analytical techniques used here have provided a window into the lives of these lost and forgotten people.

9

CONCLUSIONS—ORDINARY LIVES: THE MEDIEVAL GAELIC PEOPLE OF BALLYHANNA

Catriona J McKenzie, Eileen M Murphy & Colm J Donnelly

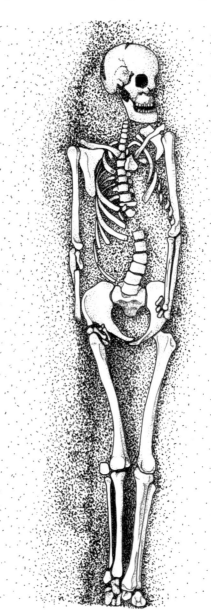

Stylised depiction of a young adult female, buried in a typical extended, supine position with the head to the west (SK 545) (Sapphire Mussen).

A biocultural research approach lay at the core of the Ballyhanna Research Project (BRP) from its earliest inception in 2006 when there was a realisation by the team members that the marriage of scientific methodologies with the archaeological and historical evidence had the potential to create a paradigm shift in our understanding of what life was like for the Gaelic people who lived in this region of north-west Ireland during the medieval period.

The extensive radiocarbon dating programme undertaken on the burials indicated that the graveyard was used by the community at Ballyhanna for almost a millennium, from the second half of the eighth century through to the early 17th century. The presence of a reliquary shrine, which perhaps contained the relics of a local saint, suggests that during its earliest phase of activity the site may have had monastic associations and that it may also have been a place of pilgrimage. A reduction in the level of burial activity in the period between the early 11th century and the second half of the 12th century, however, indicates that the graveyard's use was in decline during this period, perhaps as a consequence of flooding, but the reformation of the Irish Church that took place in the 12th century may have provided the catalyst which brought the site back into use. A stone church was constructed at some point after the mid 13th century (presumably a replacement for one or more earlier wooden churches), the foundations of which were encountered during the archaeological excavation, and this building was probably a chapel-of-ease for the newly established parish of Inishmacsaint in the diocese of Clogher. The estate would now have been in the control of the bishop, but he would have required someone to work the land. As such, Ballyhanna now became an erenagh estate, with its own erenagh lineage. By the turn of the 17th century we know that the lineage in charge was the McGockquins, but it is worth noting that not everyone who resided on the estate would have been members of this tenant group; the erenaghs would also have had their own sub-tenants and labourers, and it is this extended population that would have comprised the local people that were interred within the graveyard at Ballyhanna.

This was a rural population and a rural economy, and life on the estate would have been focused around the agricultural year—the sowing and harvesting of the oat crop, the grinding of the corn at the local mill, the breeding of cattle, the processing of dairy produce, the saving of turf for the winter fires, and the exploitation of local freshwater and maritime resources. The dental evidence from Ballyhanna certainly indicates that the people were eating a mixed subsistence diet of carbohydrates and protein. From the historical documentation it is evident that oats were the main cereal in the Gaelic diet, while meat and dairy products such as butter were probably an important source of protein. The Ó Domnaill lords facilitated foreign fishermen working off the west coast of Tír Conaill, but it is unclear the degree to which the fish caught in this manner would have been incorporated into the local Gaelic diet. We do know, however, that the erenagh estate at Ballyhanna had both eel and salmon traps and—significantly—the chemical analysis of the skeletal remains indicates that there was clearly a marine or aquatic component to the population's diet. The stable isotope ratios of carbon and nitrogen, for example, indicate that the people had a mainly terrestrial (e.g. cereal-based) diet, but that they were also obtaining protein from marine resources (e.g. salmon and shellfish). The food gathered and produced in this way would have fed the inhabitants of the estate, but would also have served to provide the rent that was to be paid to the bishop. In addition, there was also the upkeep of the little church to be considered by the erenagh, and the hospitality to be offered to travellers and visitors.

The diet at Ballyhanna would appear to have been wholesome, but we need to remain aware of the fact that there would also have been episodes of nutritional stress as, for example, in the run-up to the harvest when the previous year's oatmeal supplies would be running low, or in those years when the harvest was poor and famine threatened the community. The collective experience of prolonged nutritional stress and its associated poor health in a population can be gauged from the skeletal evidence. Relatively high levels (43.6%) of cribra orbitalia—pitting in the eye sockets—were apparent among the Ballyhanna juveniles, and deficiencies of vitamins B_{12}, C and D are thought to be a common cause of this condition. Similarly, high rates of cribra orbitalia were also noted among the adult individuals with 47.2% (59/125) of individuals with eye sockets affected.

Prolonged generational exposure to nutritional stress and its associated poor health, however, will also have an effect on the overall stature among a population. This was evident at Ballyhanna, but comparative data from other excavated skeletal assemblages would indicate that such factors were also at play throughout medieval Ireland and England. The study of the growth patterns of the juvenile individuals from Ballyhanna, for example, indicates that the children there were of comparable height to their contemporaries from Ardreigh in County Kildare and from Wharram Percy in Yorkshire, but that all of these children were substantially smaller in height when compared with modern individuals. When the statures of the 8–14-year-olds from Ballyhanna were compared with those of Irish children of corresponding age measured in 2002, for example, it was found that the latter were on average around 24 cm taller—almost the length of a ruler!

The church at Ballyhanna would have formed a focal point in the lives of the people living on the estate, through the religious services at Easter and Christmas, funeral services, marriages and baptisms, and beside it was the graveyard that contained the deceased members of the community— men and women, children and babies. The archaeological excavation did not identify any patterns to suggest that burials were placed in specific locations within the graveyard that might reflect the age, sex or social status of the deceased; it would appear that it was merely suffice that the dead body was buried somewhere within its confines. The dead were mostly buried wrapped in shrouds and— normally—in an extended and supine position, with their heads located in the west of the graves and their hands placed either by the sides of the body, or sometimes, placed together over the pelvic area. Occasionally, a piece of quartz was included in the graves, probably as some form of religious talisman, while beads from what may have been a rosary were recovered from the neck of one woman (SK 495).

We can envisage that the people living on the estate would have resided in thatched earthen-walled cottages, but—based on the historical evidence for the erenagh estates in the diocese of Derry—it may have been the case that the McGockquins had more substantial stone dwellings and perhaps even their own small castle. With Ballyshannon a centre of trade and commerce and a major Cistercian foundation located nearby at Assaroe, news would have come to Ballyshannon of what was happening in the wider world, and undoubtedly this would have formed the topics of conversation around the hearthsides—stories of plagues and famines, battles and wars, and the actions of the great, the good, and the not-so-good. Some of the inhabitants may even have journeyed far from home, availing of the foreign ships which would have harboured at Ballyshannon. We know that leading figures from the Gaelic aristocracy in the region went on pilgrimages to the Continent, but the scallop shell found placed over the right breast of a woman (SK 1175) may mark her out as someone who also travelled afar. The emblem of St James the Apostle, who was believed to have been buried at Compostela, the presence of this shell may indicate that this woman had been on a pilgrimage to north-west Spain, or—alternatively—that the shell may have been a souvenir brought back by a pilgrim as a gift for her. That the inhabitants of Ballyhanna would have witnessed stirring events on their own doorstep, however, is not to be doubted, given their proximity to Ballyshannon and the fording points across the Erne that provided access routes between Connacht and Ulster. They would certainly have witnessed—or perhaps even encountered—armed forces moving through their landscape; but what impact would this have had on their lives? The results of our study have revealed very little evidence for injuries indicative of interpersonal violence among Ballyhanna's dead; only 17 individuals of the 938 adults and adolescents displayed weapon trauma that was caused at or near the time of their death and this represents a rate of 1.8%. The vast majority (98.2%) of the people who lived in Ballyhanna, however, died for reasons that do not appear to have been associated with violence caused by weapons. We should not, however, be too surprised by this discovery given that we know from the historical evidence that raiding was the primary form of warfare used during the medieval period and that the objective of these raids was not to exterminate an enemy population and seize their lands but to force the submission of the lord of the territory under attack in order that they—and their people—might then provide their new overlord with tributes and services. In addition, the Church frowned heavily on attacks on women, children and clerics; within this context it is worth noting that only two women and two adolescents from Ballyhanna display evidence of weapon trauma.

The project has, however, revealed a notably high mortality rate, as 52.1% (281/539) of adult individuals died in young adulthood between 18 and 35 years of age. The implications of this are obvious. The poor health profile across the community's young adult population—those who should have been the healthiest and the most economically productive—would have caused social stress within the community; the typical family at Ballyhanna may have consisted of only two generations, with many children having lost one or both parents at a relatively young age. The high death rate among the young adults must also have meant that there was a considerable burden on those who survived to care for the dependent and sometime orphaned children. Accidents may have carried off some members of the community, and the osteoarchaeological study certainly identified a range of fractures that were presumably caused as a result of mishaps, but the majority of these injuries were relatively minor in nature and evidently not life-threatening since they had successfully healed. They do, however, serve as a reminder that life on the estate could be rough and it can be suggested that some of the more severe injuries among the menfolk may have been caused as a result of their working with large animals such as cattle. The case of SK 606 also comes to mind; this was a middle-aged man with a severe intra-pelvic dislocation of the thigh bone which was probably caused as a result of a heavy fall, perhaps from a horse or maybe even from a roof during its thatching! As we have seen, the level of interpersonal violence was low, but nutritional stress and its associated illnesses would have had an effect on the health profile of the Ballyhanna population since it would have left individuals susceptible to the onslaught of infectious diseases; it is here that we should look to see the cause of death among so many of the young adults. The osteoarchaeological analysis certainly identified evidence for tuberculosis in the skeletons of six adults and two children. Given that tuberculosis is only visible in the bones of a very small number of individuals affected by the disease (approximately 3% to 5%), this indicates that it is likely to have been present in endemic proportions in Ballyhanna. To provide further definition to this issue samples were taken from the six adult skeletons to identify whether it was possible to extract mycobacterial DNA and thereby provide additional support to the osteoarchaeological diagnosis of tuberculosis. Unfortunately, it was only possible to extract mycobacterial DNA from one of the skeletons and the result of the study proved inconclusive.

The BRP, however, also enabled the scientists to investigate for diseases that are not visibly evident among the skeletal remains. For example, cystic fibrosis is a genetic mutation that affects the lungs and the digestive system and has a high incidence rate in modern Ireland, but was this also the case in the medieval period? In order to answer this question a sample of 60 skeletons (4.6%; 60/1296 of the total population) were screened to see if they were affected. The results obtained from this exercise, however, would suggest that this was not the case and none of the individuals were shown to be carriers. The implication of this is that the mutation was not prevalent—or perhaps not even present—within the medieval population and, as a consequence, we should now look for some event that occurred in the past 400 years which triggered the mutation to develop.

Faced with these health problems was there any medical intervention that the Ballyhanna people might have called upon for assistance? The discovery of a woman (SK 1242) who had undergone a trepanation of her skull indicates that surgery of this type was being practised, but the radiocarbon date obtained from this skeleton indicates that she lived during the early medieval period; when we look at the situation in the late medieval period we do not find any comparable examples. While the ruling Ó Domnaill lineage in the late medieval period had their Mac Duinnshléibhe physicians to attend to their ailments, it is not clear how far down the social classes these individuals would have practised. As such, it is probable that it was folk-medicine that was practised among the general population at Ballyhanna, complete with wise-women and midwives. It is certainly the case that at least four of the women had died as a result of complications that had occurred during pregnancy and childbirth. A particularly poignant example of such a death was the case of a petite young woman (SK 978) who appears to have died shortly after the delivery of her twins (SK 986 and SK 979). She was buried with her arms around the newborn twins in a very careful and deliberate manner presumably by her bereaved relatives who mourned for all three lives. Genetic factors and poor maternal nutrition may have inflated the mortality profile among the babies who had survived the trauma of childbirth. Children would have been further susceptible to life-threatening ill-health during weaning, when they were introduced to new food types and deadly bacteria and, as they grew older and became more mobile and curious, they would also have been prone to everyday accidents. Suffice to say, the mortality profile of the youngest members of Ballyhanna's community indicates that there was a very high risk of death—some 46.4%—between the ages of one and six years of age.

In some cases we get glimpses of the attempts of families to look after and care for sickly children. One infant (6–8 months) and three young children (all 1–2 years) displayed evidence of rickets, which presents itself in the form of bone porosity and biomechanical changes among the skeletons of affected children and is caused by vitamin D deficiency. Such deficiency largely occurs as a consequence of a prolonged lack of exposure to sunlight and/or a lack of foodstuffs in the diet such as eggs, milk, liver and oily fish. A lack of exposure to sunlight is believed to be the most common reason for the development of rickets but it would be unexpected in a rural farming community, as would a lack of vitamin D-rich foodstuffs. The severe nature of the lesions in conjunction with the occurrence of only very young children with the condition at Ballyhanna led us to conclude that these four children had been sickly and, as a response to their poor health, they had been kept indoors as part of the care afforded to them by their families. Unfortunately, this course of action appears to have exacerbated their ill health, leading to the development of rickets which undoubtedly contributed to their untimely deaths.

It is impossible for standard osteoarchaeological analysis to accurately identify the sex of the children at Ballyhanna who had died prior to the onset of puberty, but it was recognised by the scientists that establishing the ratio of boys to girls among the dead might generate further insight into life at Ballyhanna. As such, an ancient DNA (aDNA) analysis was undertaken on a sample of 19 juveniles, comprising three younger children (1–6 years), eight older children (6–12 years) and eight adolescents (12–18 years). Results were returned for four of the individuals tested (comprising two of the older children and two of the adolescents) and this showed that all four were male. In addition, a further 10 of the study group were determined as probable males but only one was identified as a probable female. While the sample was admittedly both randomly selected and small in scale, the high preponderance of males and probable males returned through the exercise is nonetheless intriguing. Were boys in some way disadvantaged in Ballyhanna's society? Were they more susceptible to disease or death by accident than was the case for girls? Ancient DNA analysis is a new and evolving field of scientific research, but the results achieved from the Ballyhanna study indicate that future investigations on this theme from skeletons recovered from other ancient burial sites in Ireland may prove very illuminating.

Despite all of these young deaths, however, old age could be attained at Ballyhanna, although this was not without its own problems. Seven of the middle-aged and older females, for example, displayed light bones indicative of bone loss and two or more associated fragility fractures in their skeletal remains which were probably caused by the onset of osteoporosis. This was a community that looked after its less fortunate members, however, given that a number of people displayed evidence of physical impairments that would have rendered them in need of help and support. One individual whose bones were present within the disarticulated assemblage had suffered a chronic infection in their pelvis, while another had an anterior dislocation of his pelvis which had not been corrected (SK 606); in both cases these individuals would have had very poor mobility. In addition, there were the two men (SK 197 and SK 331) who were afflicted by multiple osteochondromas, a rare hereditary condition that involves the growth of benign bone tumours on the legs and arms during childhood and which can result in mobility problems for the affected person throughout their life.

If the contents of this chapter have tended to be gloomy then that is somewhat to be expected given that the text has been based on the results of a study of a dead people and what killed them. For all the hardship in their lives, however, there would undoubtedly have also been time for some laughter within this rural population. The distillation of whiskey in advance of holidays and fairs, perhaps, or the consumption of wine from far-off places at such events; folktales of Seannach and Aodh Ruadh mac Badhuirn, and ghost stories told by the old people to the children around the firesides on dark winters' evenings. Maybe even time for sport, since some of the menfolk displayed fractures in their hand bones which, while possibly sustained through work, may be indicative of their involvement in a game such as *camán* (winter hurling), and which serve to remind us of the 15th-century graveslab at Clonca Church in Inishowen, Co. Donegal, with its depiction of a *camán*. So life on the estate continued through the medieval period, decade after decade, generation after generation, until suddenly there was change; a new bishop and overlord, and a new tenant-in-chief.

The last people were laid to rest in the graveyard at Ballyhanna during the early decades of the 17th century, and it may have been the case that the local community were now forced to abandon their church and their graveyard, perhaps at the instigation of the new bishop or, more probably, his new tenant. Evidently the old church was not required by its new owners, the Church of Ireland, and this led to its abandonment and—in due course—its removal from the landscape. By that time, and in the area under investigation by the archaeologists, over 1,296 individuals had been laid to rest in its graveyard.

The BRP brought together the expertise of archaeologists and scientists based within the NRA (now TII), the Institute of Technology, Sligo and Queen's University Belfast to undertake a unique collaborative programme studying this human skeletal population from this location on the southern bank of the River Erne. As was originally envisaged, the painstaking study of these skeletons has now generated new information that has provided genuine insight into what life would have been like for this community of ordinary medieval Gaelic folk living on their small erenagh estate. This valuable insight is our project's enduring legacy.

APPENDIX 1
RADIOCARBON DATES FROM EXCAVATED SITES ALONG THE ROUTE OF THE SCHEME

Radiocarbon ages are quoted in conventional years BP (i.e. 'before present' at AD 1950) and the errors for these dates are expressed at the one-sigma (1σ) (68% probability) level of confidence. Calibrated date ranges are equivalent to the probable calendrical age of the sample material and are expressed at one-sigma (68% probability) and two-sigma (2σ) (95% probability) levels of confidence. The δ¹³C value indicates the difference between the sample's $^{13}C/^{12}C$ ratio and that of a standard. It can indicate if there is contamination in the sample or processing when the value is compared to similar material. Dates obtained from Beta Analytic in Florida (Beta lab code) were calibrated using the IntCal98 calibration curve (Stuiver et al. 1998). Dates obtained from Queen's University Belfast (UBA lab code) were calibrated with the CALIB REV 6.0.0 calibration programme, using the IntCal09 calibration curve (Reimer et al. 2009). These are all AMS (Accelerator Mass Spectrometry) dates.

Lab. code	Site	Sample/context	Yrs BP	δ¹³C ‰	Calibrated date ranges
Beta-200977	Magheracar 1 brushwood trackway	Hazel (*Corylus avellana*) from brushwood trackway	1520 ± 60	-26.1	AD 530–630 (1σ) AD 420–660 (2σ)
Beta-205182	Sminver 1a burnt spread	Hazel (*Corylus avellana*) and birch *(Betula)* charcoal from burnt spread	3620 ± 60	-25.6	2040–1900 BC (1σ) 2140–1780 BC (2σ)
Beta-205183	Ballynacarrick 1 hearth	Hazel (*Corylus avellana*) from hearth	2040 ± 50	-24.9	111BC–AD 21 (1σ) 177 BC–AD 64 (2σ)
Beta-205184	Ballynacarrick 1 settlement site	Pine (*Pinus sylvestris*) charcoal from pit	5170 ± 40	-24.6	3990–3960 BC (1σ) 4040–3940 BC (2σ)
Beta-205185	Magheracar 2 furnace	Oak (*Quercus sp.*) & birch (*Betula*) from furnace	1610 ± 50	-26.1	AD 400–530 (1σ) AD 350–560 (2σ)
Beta-206066	Magheracar 2 earthwork	Ash (*Fraxinus excelsior*) & willow (*Salix* sp.) from ditch	1790 ± 80	-27.4	AD 130–350 (1σ) AD 60–420 (2σ)
UBA-11440	Ballyhanna medieval graveyard	Bone from SK 30	469 ± 25	-18.0	AD 1427–1444 (1σ) AD 1415–1451 (2σ)

Lab. code	Site	Sample/context	Yrs BP	δ¹³C ‰	Calibrated date ranges
UBA-11441	Ballyhanna medieval graveyard	Bone from SK 182	338 ± 21	-23.5	AD 1494–1631 (1σ) AD 1477–1635 (2σ)
UBA-11442	Ballyhanna medieval graveyard	Bone from SK 197	1162 ± 24	-17.9	AD 783–940 (1σ) AD 779–965 (2σ)
UBA-11443	Ballyhanna medieval graveyard	Bone from SK 331	856 ± 24	-20.2	AD 1169–1215 (1σ) AD 1057–1254 (2σ)
UBA-11444	Ballyhanna medieval graveyard	Bone from SK 530	278 ± 24	-21.8	AD 1527–1654 (1σ) AD 1519–1791 (2σ)
UBA-11445	Ballyhanna medieval graveyard	Bone from SK 566	1160 ± 24	-22.8	AD 783–942 (1σ) AD 779–966 (2σ)
UBA-11446	Ballyhanna medieval graveyard	Bone from SK 670	529 ± 26	-20.5	AD 1402–1430 (1σ) AD 1324–1438 (2σ)
UBA-11447	Ballyhanna medieval graveyard	Bone from SK 857	1165 ± 24	-21.8	AD 782–936 (1σ) AD 778–961 (2σ)
UBA-11448	Ballyhanna medieval graveyard	Bone from SK 882	310 ± 29	-20.8	AD 1521–1642 (1σ) AD 1488–1648 (2σ)
UBA-11449	Ballyhanna medieval graveyard	Bone from SK 885	1168 ± 35	-23.3	AD 781–936 (1σ) AD 774–971 (2σ)
UBA-11450	Ballyhanna medieval graveyard	Bone from SK 984	302 ± 24	-21.3	AD 1522–1645 (1σ) AD 1495–1649 (2σ)
UBA-11451	Ballyhanna medieval graveyard	Bone from SK 1201A	347 ± 36	-20.2	AD 1484–1631 (1σ) AD 1460–1638 (2σ)
UBA-11452	Ballyhanna medieval graveyard	Bone from SK 1224	1138 ± 32	-19.3	AD 881–971 (1σ) AD 782–984 (2σ)
UBA-11453	Ballyhanna medieval graveyard	Bone from SK 1242	1286 ± 22	-23.7	AD 679–767 (1σ) AD 670–772 (2σ)

Lab. code	Site	Sample/context	Yrs BP	δ¹³C ‰	Calibrated date ranges
UBA-11454	Ballyhanna medieval graveyard	Bone from SK 1C	647 ± 22	-26.3	AD 1291–1386 (1σ) AD 1284–1391 (2σ)
UBA-11455	Ballyhanna medieval graveyard	Bone from SK 35	726 ± 21	-21.5	AD 1270–1283 (1σ) AD 1260–1291 (2σ)
UBA-11456	Ballyhanna medieval graveyard	Bone from SK 43	385 ± 21	-18.7	AD 1451–1611 (1σ) AD 1445–1620 (2σ)
UBA-11457	Ballyhanna medieval graveyard	Bone from SK 355	460 ± 22	-27.8	AD 1431–1446 (1σ) AD 1419–1453 (2σ)
UBA-11458	Ballyhanna medieval graveyard	Bone from SK 755	425 ± 23	-26.8	AD 1440–1463 (1σ) AD 1431–1607 (2σ)
UBA-11459	Ballyhanna medieval graveyard	Bone from SK 830	385 ± 21	-21.5	AD 1451–1611 (1σ) AD 1445–1620 (2σ)
UBA-11460	Ballyhanna medieval graveyard	Bone from SK 1029	415 ± 22	-22.7	AD 1443–1469 (1σ) AD 1435–1612 (2σ)
UBA-11461	Ballyhanna medieval graveyard	Bone from SK 1100	695 ± 19	-20.8	AD 1278–1292 (1σ) AD 1271–1381 (2σ)
UBA-11462	Ballyhanna medieval graveyard	Bone from SK 1117	381 ± 19	-20.4	AD 1453–1613 (1σ) AD 1447–1620 (2σ)
UBA-11463	Ballyhanna medieval graveyard	Bone from SK 1155	655 ± 20	-22.3	AD 1289–1384 (1σ) AD 1283–1389 (2σ)
UBA-14970	Ballyhanna medieval graveyard	Bone from SK 542	592 ± 31	-19.2	AD 1312–1402 (1σ) AD 1298–1412 (2σ)
UBA-14971	Ballyhanna medieval graveyard	Bone from SK 555	979 ± 38	-18.1	AD 1017–1151 (1σ) AD 994–1155 (2σ)
UBA-14972	Ballyhanna medieval graveyard	Bone from SK 787	708 ± 25	-21.1	AD 1273–1290 (1σ) AD 1263–1381 (2σ)

Lab. code	Site	Sample/context	Yrs BP	δ¹³C ‰	Calibrated date ranges
UBA-14974	Ballyhanna medieval graveyard	Bone from SK 24	437 ± 17	-21.3	AD 1439–1451 (1σ) AD 1432–1465 (2σ)
UBA-14975	Ballyhanna medieval graveyard	Bone from SK 153	776 ± 17	-21.1	AD 1228–1271 (1σ) AD 1223–1274 (2σ)
UBA-14976	Ballyhanna medieval graveyard	Bone from SK 84	429 ± 21	-21.4	AD 1439–1457 (1σ) AD 1432–1480 (2σ)
UBA-14977	Ballyhanna medieval graveyard	Bone from SK 111	654 ± 17	-23.9	AD 1290–1383 (1σ) AD 1284–1388 (2σ)
UBA-14978	Ballyhanna medieval graveyard	Bone from SK 102A	466 ± 19	-22.5	AD 1430–1444 (1σ) AD 1420–1449 (2σ)
UBA-14979	Ballyhanna medieval graveyard	Bone from SK 477	411 ± 30	-21.7	AD 1441–1486 (1σ) AD 1430–1620 (2σ)
UBA-14980	Ballyhanna medieval graveyard	Bone from SK 554	812 ± 24	-22.8	AD 1217–1256 (1σ) AD 1183–1268 (2σ)
UBA-14981	Ballyhanna medieval graveyard	Bone from SK 407	322 ± 22	-21.6	AD 1519–1635 (1σ) AD 1489–1643 (2σ)
UBA-14982	Ballyhanna medieval graveyard	Bone from SK 432	844 ± 23	-23.9	AD 1173–1220 (1σ) AD 1160–1254 (2σ)
UBA-14983	Ballyhanna medieval graveyard	Bone from SK 1134	397 ± 23	-24.2	AD 1447–1606 (1σ) AD 1441–1618 (2σ)
UBA-14984	Ballyhanna medieval graveyard	Bone from SK 1239B	849 ± 22	-20.0	AD 1174–1217 (1σ) AD 1158–1252 (2σ)
UBA-14985	Ballyhanna medieval graveyard	Bone from SK 70	656 ± 34	-21.6	AD 1285–1386 (1σ) AD 1277–1395 (2σ)
UBA-14986	Ballyhanna medieval graveyard	Bone from SK 931	297 ± 21	-22.6	AD 1524–1646 (1σ) AD 1515–1661 (2σ)

Lab. code	Site	Sample/context	Yrs BP	δ¹³C ‰	Calibrated date ranges
UBA-14987	Ballyhanna medieval graveyard	Bone from SK 1135	683 ± 23	-22.2	AD 1279–1378 (1σ) AD 1273–1386 (2σ)
UBA-14988	Ballyhanna medieval graveyard	Bone from SK 1009	438 ± 24	-22.8	AD 1435–1455 (1σ) AD 1425–1478 (2σ)
UBA-14989	Ballyhanna medieval graveyard	Bone from SK 1030	643 ± 19	-26.5	AD 1294–1386 (1σ) AD 1287–1391 (2σ)
UBA-14990	Ballyhanna medieval graveyard	Bone from SK 495	283 ± 27	-24.8	AD 1524–1654 (1σ) AD 1499–1791 (2σ)
UBA-14991	Ballyhanna medieval graveyard	Bone from SK 1054	707 ± 35	-29.1	AD 1266–1377 (1σ) AD 1229–1388 (2σ)
UBA-14992	Ballyhanna medieval graveyard	Bone from SK 824	480 ± 29	-24.6	AD 1422–1442 (1σ) AD 1409–1450 (2σ)
UBA-14993	Ballyhanna medieval graveyard	Bone from SK 809	681 ± 20	-24.2	AD 1280–1378 (1σ) AD 1275–1385 (2σ)
UBA-14994	Ballyhanna medieval graveyard	Bone from SK 1038	341 ± 17	-27.1	AD 1493–1630 (1σ) AD 1474–1634 (2σ)
UBA-14995	Ballyhanna medieval graveyard	Bone from SK 543	767 ± 17	-21.8	AD 1244–1276 (1σ) AD 1225–1276 (2σ)
UBA-14996	Ballyhanna medieval graveyard	Bone from SK 31	360 ± 29	-23.3	AD 1466–1624 (1σ) AD 1451–1634 (2σ)
UBA-14997	Ballyhanna medieval graveyard	Bone from SK 121	407 ± 28	-23.5	AD 1443–1606 (1σ) AD 1434–1619 (2σ)
UBA-14998	Ballyhanna medieval graveyard	Bone from SK 294	659 ± 18	-22.4	AD 1288–1382 (1σ) AD 1282–1388 (2σ)
UBA-14999	Ballyhanna medieval graveyard	Bone from SK 455	725 ± 19	-20.6	AD 1271–1283 (1σ) AD 1263–1289 (2σ)

Lab. code	Site	Sample/context	Yrs BP	δ¹³C ‰	Calibrated date ranges
UBA-15000	Ballyhanna medieval graveyard	Bone from SK 528	808 ± 24	-19.2	AD 1219–1256 (1σ) AD 1186–1270 (2σ)
UBA-15001	Ballyhanna medieval graveyard	Bone from SK 541	502 ± 19	-20.7	AD 1417–1433 (1σ) AD 1410–1440 (2σ)
UBA-15002	Ballyhanna medieval graveyard	Bone from SK 858	290 ± 29	-22.3	AD 1522–1650 (1σ) AD 1494–1661 (2σ)
UBA-15003	Ballyhanna medieval graveyard	Bone from SK 861	669 ± 28	-22.5	AD 1282–1383 (1σ) AD 1276–1390 (2σ)
UBA-15156	Ballyhanna medieval graveyard	Bone from SK 680	598 ± 19	-24.0	AD 1312–1397 (1σ) AD 1302–1405 (2σ)
UBA-15971	Ballyhanna medieval graveyard	Tooth from SK 150	470 ± 29	-18.4	AD 1425–1445 (1σ) AD 1410–1455 (2σ)
UBA-15972	Ballyhanna medieval graveyard	Tooth from SK 198	660 ± 23	-16.2	AD 1286–1384 (1σ) AD 1280–1389 (2σ)
UBA-15973	Ballyhanna medieval graveyard	Tooth from SK 295	773 ± 25	-10.9	AD 1227–1273 (1σ) AD 1220–1277 (2σ)
UBA-15975	Ballyhanna medieval graveyard	Tooth from SK 571	932 ± 27	-16.9	AD 1040–1154 (1σ) AD 1028–1161 (2σ)
UBA-15976	Ballyhanna medieval graveyard	Tooth from SK 850	361 ± 20	-17.8	AD 1469–1619 (1σ) AD 1455–1631 (2σ)
UBA-15977	Ballyhanna medieval graveyard	Tooth from SK 927	428 ± 24	-17.4	AD 1438–1462 (1σ) AD 1429–1606 (2σ)
UBA-15978	Ballyhanna medieval graveyard	Tooth from SK 1151	375 ± 30	-17.6	AD 1453–1617 (1σ) AD 1446–1632 (2σ)
UBA-15979	Ballyhanna medieval graveyard	Tooth from SK 1185	1215 ± 29	-20.4	AD 774–870 (1σ) AD 694–889 (2σ)

Lab. code	Site	Sample/context	Yrs BP	$\delta^{13}C$ ‰	Calibrated date ranges
UBA–15980	Ballyhanna medieval graveyard	Tooth from SK 936A	387 ± 36	-20.2	AD 1447–1617 (1σ) AD 1440–1633 (2σ)
UBA–15981	Ballyhanna medieval graveyard	Tooth from SK 86	469 ± 36	-20.8	AD 1421–1447 (1σ) AD 1403–1476 (2σ)
UBA–15982	Ballyhanna medieval graveyard	Tooth from SK 484	756 ± 46	-20.8	AD 1226–1281 (1σ) AD 1182–1379 (2σ)
UBA–15983	Ballyhanna medieval graveyard	Bone from SK 982	298 ± 26	-22.4	AD 1522–1647 (1σ) AD 1494–1653 (2σ)
UBA–15984	Ballyhanna medieval graveyard	Bone from SK 1113	664 ± 20	-20.1	AD 1286–1382 (1σ) AD 1280–1388 (2σ)
UBA–15985	Ballyhanna medieval graveyard	Bone from SK 1225	649 ± 20	-17.5	AD 1291–1385 (1σ) AD 1284–1390 (2σ)

APPENDIX 2
CREATING THE BALLYHANNA GARDEN

Gráinne Leamy

The unexpected discovery of the foundations of a stone building, thought to be the remains of Ballyhanna church, generated considerable interest among the local community in Ballyshannon (Illus. A2.1). The last recorded mention of Church lands at Ballyhanna was in the 17th century, but since that date the location of the church had disappeared from local memory. During the archaeological excavation a joint decision was made by Donegal County Council, the NRA (now TII) and the construction contractor to preserve the site. It proved possible to redesign the proposed junction at this location in order to avoid directly impacting on the site of the medieval church. Once the change in design was agreed, a plan was needed to establish the best way to preserve the site and present the remains of the church to the public.

Initial conservation work entailed the consolidation of the foundations by a stonemason to prevent erosion, as the site had been exposed to the elements as a consequence of the archaeological excavation. With the foundation walls stabilised, work then commenced on creating a design for the future.

The project involved a detailed consultation process with local interest groups, to give the community a voice in the future planning and design of the site. A series of meetings was held with representatives from the local town and county councils, and also with members of the local historical societies: Historic Ballyshannon, Donegal Historical Society and the Flight of the Earls committee. A public workshop was well attended by people from the town and a wide variety of ideas and opinions were proposed regarding their aspirations as to how the site should be developed. The high level of participation in the consultation process demonstrated the community's interest in, and commitment to, ensuring the best possible outcome for the preservation of the Ballyhanna site.

Based on the input from these consultations the decision was made to develop the site as a garden that would reflect the historical aspects of the church and graveyard in a respectful and sensitive manner, while also enabling the community to engage with the site on an ongoing basis. A design was created for the garden with the assistance of council architects and technicians, a landscape gardener and a sign-maker.

Illus. A2.1—Excavating a skeleton at Ballyhanna (Transport Infrastructure Ireland).

Several key objectives had been identified by the community and these were incorporated into the design. For example, the site was made accessible to all members of the community, including those with different levels of physical mobility, by incorporating recommendations made by an occupational therapist in the architect's design. A large sign with information about the history of the site was included within the design. Of particular importance to the local community was an artist's reconstruction drawing of how the church and graveyard may have looked in the medieval period, to help visitors understand the site. A small plaque was designed to commemorate Mr Lucius Emerson, a keen local historian who regularly visited the Ballyhanna site when the archaeological excavations were underway. Seating was provided, as it was felt that the garden would be an appropriate place to rest and reflect, as well as being a place of historical interest. Finally, it was considered fitting to include *Under the Grass* a poem by the 19th-century poet William Allingham, who was a native of Ballyshannon. The chosen verse seemed to be a remarkably apt reflection on the graveyard and its location.

> Where these green mounds o'erlook the mingling Erne
> And salt Atlantic, clay that walk'd as Man
> A thousand years ago, some Viking stern,
> May rest, or nameless Chieftain of a Clan;
> And when my dusty remnant shall return
> To the great passive World, and nothing can,
> With eye or lip, or finger, any more,
> O lay it there too, by the river shore.

William Allingham (1824–89)

The Office of Public Works, and the professional landscape gardener and sign-maker provided expert advice on key aspects of the design, particularly in terms of the implications for the upkeep and maintenance of the garden into the future. The durable and robust seating and signage shall withstand exposure to the elements. Planting was chosen with a view to complementing the other aspects of the design, while also requiring minimal maintenance.

At the request of the local community, the opening ceremony was held on 15 July 2007, to coincide with the Flight of the Earls commemorations being held in Donegal at that time (Illus. A2.2 and Illus. A2.3). The ceremony marked the completion of the conservation project and was an opportunity for the community to see the garden that they had designed. On that day, the site was formally returned to the people of Ballyshannon through Donegal County Council.

Since then, local groups are maintaining the garden in consultation with Donegal County Council, a clear demonstration of the sense of ownership that the local community has for the site. The conservation project has enabled the church to be re-integrated into the local community, ensuring that it will remain in the collective memory of the people of Ballyshannon. The enthusiastic participation of the community in the consultation and design process was crucial to the successful outcome of the project and it is hoped that the garden will be enjoyed by the people of Ballyshannon and visitors to the town into the future (Illus. A2.4).

Illus. A2.2—Official opening of the Ballyhanna garden in July 2007 (Eileen M Murphy).

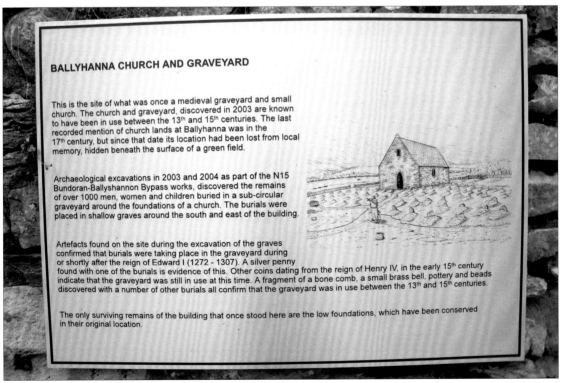

BALLYHANNA CHURCH AND GRAVEYARD

This is the site of what was once a medieval graveyard and small church. The church and graveyard, discovered in 2003 are known to have been in use between the 13th and 15th centuries. The last recorded mention of church lands at Ballyhanna was in the 17th century, but since that date its location had been lost from local memory, hidden beneath the surface of a green field.

Archaeological excavations in 2003 and 2004 as part of the N15 Bundoran-Ballyshannon Bypass works, discovered the remains of over 1000 men, women and children buried in a sub-circular graveyard around the foundations of a church. The burials were placed in shallow graves around the south and east of the building.

Artefacts found on the site during the excavation of the graves confirmed that burials were taking place in the graveyard during or shortly after the reign of Edward I (1272 - 1307). A silver penny found with one of the burials is evidence of this. Other coins dating from the reign of Henry IV, in the early 15th century indicate that the graveyard was still in use at this time. A fragment of a bone comb, a small brass bell, pottery and beads discovered with a number of other burials all confirm that the graveyard was in use between the 13th and 15th centuries.

The only surviving remains of the building that once stood here are the low foundations, which have been conserved in their original location.

Illus. A2.3— Information panel with reconstruction drawing of the church (Transport Infrastructure Ireland).

Illus. A2.4—People from the local community visiting the site (Transport Infrastructure Ireland).

APPENDIX 3
COMMUNICATING THE BALLYHANNA STORY

Deirdre McCarthy

From the time of its discovery along the route of the N15 Bundoran–Ballyshannon Bypass in 2003, it has been a priority of all involved with Ballyhanna that the story of the forgotten graveyard is communicated in a sensitive, open and informative manner. The story of the graveyard can be divided into two specific aspects—the initial discovery and excavation, and the subsequent establishment and findings of the Ballyhanna Research Project (BRP).

Upon its discovery and subsequent excavation, there was a lot of interest in the site from the local Ballyshannon community. The excavation director, Brian Ó Donnchadha, and his team from Irish Archaeological Consultancy Ltd enthusiastically conducted a number of tours of the site for individuals, groups and schools. A very important decision was made to not hide the excavations away behind hoarding; rather the excavation of the burial ground would be carried out in full view, allowing passersby to see the excavation in progress. This decision led to many exchanges during the excavation, all connecting the excavation, archaeologists, and those buried there with the local community. Following discussion with the local community and in respect of the sensitivity of the burial site, ecumenical services and prayers for the dead were led on site by local clergy prior to, and during, excavation of the human remains (Illus. A3.1).

Illus. A3.1—Service at Ballyhanna during the excavation of the site (Transport Infrastructure Ireland).

The contribution of the local community in providing local knowledge and folklore about the area, and their enthusiasm in helping to unravel the story of the forgotten graveyard, have ensured that the project has been a collaborative endeavour from its inception. The insights of some locals during the excavation were invaluable, most notably Lucius Emerson (†), a frequent visitor to the excavation, who remembered that, when ground works were being undertaken in the 1940s close to the existing site, a number of human bones were discovered. Anthony Begley, a distinguished local historian and author of a number of articles and books about the Ballyshannon area, has been very generous with his local knowledge, insightful comments on the site and his support for the project.

Ongoing liaison with local groups Historic Ballyshannon and Donegal Historical Society have proved fruitful in varying ways including introductions to locals with knowledge and unique insights into the history of Ballyshannon. They have also facilitated lectures by BRP team members over the years, which have given the researchers an opportunity to discuss their findings with the wider community. As part of the team's commitment to keeping the community informed of the development of the project, regular updates were sent to local councillors during the excavation, during the creation of the Ballyhanna garden (see Appendix 2), and during the development of the BRP.

An exhibition of the artefacts found during excavations along the route of the N15 Bundoran–Ballyshannon Bypass, including artefacts found on the Ballyhanna site, opened on 7 December 2006 in Donegal County Museum in Letterkenny (Illus. A3.2). This was coordinated with Judith McCarthy (Museum Curator) and her staff at Donegal County Museum who liaised with the National Museum of Ireland regarding the loan and display of the artefacts. Ballyhanna artefacts on

Illus. A3.2—Exhibition of the finds from the road scheme at Letterkenny Museum (Studio Lab).

display included medieval pottery, glass beads and metal artefacts. The exhibition used display panels and photographs to place the artefacts within the scientific context of archaeological excavation and post-excavation analysis, rather than simply presenting a display of finds. There was a particular focus on the Ballyhanna skeletons. A sample skeleton was displayed in a specially designed display unit as part of the exhibition, and the Donegal County Museum technical staff liaised with Dr Eileen Murphy (Queen's University Belfast) in relation to this (Illus. A3.3). The exhibition proved very successful and was visited by a large number of local students.

The foundations of the Ballyhanna site have been conserved and a garden created on the site of the graveyard. The garden was officially opened on 15 July 2007 as part of the Flight of the Earls commemorations in Donegal, marking 400 years since that historical event. There was a large crowd at the opening of the garden, which was preceded by a number of lectures from members of the BRP, during which the finding of the site, its excavation and updates on the research were outlined. The community aspect of the project was highlighted by the presence of many local dignitaries and the local brass band at the opening.

The unique cross-border nature of the BRP and the comprehensive research carried out on the human remains has attracted not just local but also national and international attention. In communicating the story of Ballyhanna to the wider community, the BRP team has given lectures and presented posters about the project at two NRA National Archaeology Seminars (2007 and 2010), the 6th World Archaeological Congress (2008), Institute of Technology, Sligo, Science Week (2009), the Institute of Archaeologists of Ireland Spring Seminar (2011) as well as at many science and archaeological conferences in Ireland and Europe (Illus. A3.4 and Illus. A3.5). The team have

Illus. A3.3—Opening of the Letterkenny Museum exhibition (Studio Lab).

Illus. A3.4—Michael MacDonagh (fourth from left), Tasneem Bashir (fifth from left) and Sheila Tierney (seventh from left) among the speakers at the NRA National Archaeology Seminar 2007 (Studio Lab).

Illus. A3.5—Sheila Tierney and a poster on her research, IT Sligo Science Showcase 2010 (IT Sligo).

contributed written articles about the project to a wide range of publications aimed at the general public as well as scientific publications aimed at the academic sector. Sheila Tierney won best overall poster at the Athlone Institute of Technology Posterfest 2011, featuring details of her research on the Ballyhanna assemblage (Illus. A3.6). A BRP website has been set up by Queen's University Belfast, which provides details of the researchers and their findings: http://www.qub.ac.uk/sites/Ballyhanna/

The discovery of the site and the subsequent findings of the BRP have attracted the interest of the media at local, national and international levels. The team have spoken to journalists from many newspapers and have been on radio and television speaking about their research and findings.

NRA archaeologists based in the Donegal National Roads Design Office ran an outreach programme with national and secondary schools in the region, where school visits were made to highlight some of the archaeological finds found on road schemes. The Ballyhanna excavation and BRP formed a large part of these talks, allowing the children to learn and speculate about the people who lived in Ballyhanna and how their lives may have differed from theirs. There was huge interest from children in the techniques of excavating the site, in death and human burial, and in the science behind the research results.

The BRP has, with the crucial oversight, approval and support of the National Museum of Ireland, provided a unique insight into the lifestyle of

Illus. A3.6—Posterfest 2011, from left to right: Dr Michelle Connolly, Research Office (ITS); Dr Joseph Ryan, Registrar, Athlone Institute of Technology (AIT); Ms Sheila Tierney (ITS); Ms Breda Lynch, Industry Programmes Manager (AIT) and Dr Alan Hernon, Postdoctoral Research Fellow (ITS) (Courtesy of Athlone Institute of Technology).

those who lived in Ballyshannon in the medieval period; from what they ate to how they lived and how they died. Engaging with community, making public the archaeology has been a critical element in the story of Ballyhanna, where the importance of such engagement, of listening to local concerns, and the benefit of public outreach have led to a harmonious project to the benefit of all involved. The excavation and research is simply the latest chapter in the history and story of a site that started back in the seventh century AD and that remained important for over 1,000 years. It is hoped that the transparent manner in which Ballyhanna and its people have been dealt with since the site's discovery has afforded people the chance to connect in some way with those people who were buried in Ballyhanna during medieval times.

APPENDIX 4
ARCHAEOLOGICAL DISCOVERIES ALONG THE ROUTE OF THE N15 BUNDORAN–BALLYSHANNON BYPASS

Deirdre McCarthy & Gráinne Leamy

In the summer of 2003 pre-development archaeological testing was undertaken by Irish Archaeological Consultancy Ltd (IAC Ltd) along the 10.5 km route of the proposed N15 Bundoran–Ballyshannon Bypass. This work led to the discovery of six archaeological sites in addition to the burial ground at Ballyhanna (Table A4.1). A seventh possible site (Sminver 2) was identified during monitoring in 2004 (see Chapter 1, Illus. 1.1). These sites were excavated under the direction of Brian Ó Donnchadha, Rob Lynch and Fintan Walsh for IAC Ltd.

Table A4.1—Archaeological sites discovered along the N15 Bundoran–Ballyshannon Bypass

Site name	Excavation ref.	Site type	Period
Ballyhanna	03E1384	Church and graveyard	Medieval
Ballynacarrick 1	04E0015	Temporary settlement site	Neolithic and Iron Age
Magheracar 1	04E0012	Settlement activity	Early medieval
Magheracar 2	04E0098	Linear earthwork	Iron Age
Rathmore and Finner 1	04E0016	House	Early modern
Sminver 1a	04E0017	Burnt mound	Bronze Age
Sminver 1b	04E0017	Holy well	Unknown
Sminver 2	A007/001	Possible megalithic structure	Unknown

Note: Rathmore and Finner 1 wholly lies within Finner townland. Archaeological excavations were also conducted at Coolcholly1 (04E0011), Finner 1 (04E0013), Finner 2 (04E0014) and Camp 1 (04E0096), but these sites proved to be of no archaeological significance.

While the Ballyhanna graveyard is the most prominent site excavated along the route of the N15 Bundoran–Ballyshannon Bypass, the other sites excavated during the course of the road development indicate a diversity of site types, including settlement, industrial and boundary markers spanning from the prehistoric through to the post-medieval period. Each site is summarised below according to its geographical position west to east along the N15 Bypass.

Settlement activity at Magheracar 1[19]

Magheracar townland stretches along the northern banks of the Drowes River. Two megalithic tombs are located in the townland (Record of Monuments and Places Nos DG106-011 and DG106-014) and these are evidence of prehistoric activity in this coastal area during the Neolithic and Bronze Age periods. Further evidence of activity in this area was uncovered during archaeological testing and excavations in 2003–4.

In an area of bogland in Magheracar a horizon of brushwood was discovered approximately 1 m below the surface of the bog. It is possible that this 5-m long structure was part of a trackway used to cross the wet bog or, alternatively, it was perhaps used as a platform for hunting waterside fowl or for fishing. The trackway or platform was constructed using branches of hazel which had been deliberately cut and laid down horizontally in the bog. The structure was dated to the early medieval period, AD 420–660 (Beta-200977).

Directly to the north of this feature was a scatter of 23 pieces of worked stone, mostly waste or debitage, resulting from the knapping of larger pieces of chert and flint to make stone tools. The tools may have been made to hunt or fish at the lakeside. A shallow pit was also present containing a small quantity of burnt animal bone.

Iron Age earthwork at Magheracar 2[20]

The Black Pig's Dyke is one of the most renowned linear earthworks in Ireland. Early writers described the Black Pig's Dyke as a single defensive earthwork stretching across the northern third of the island between Bundoran in the west to Dundalk in the east (Waddell 2010, 381). Sections of the Black Pig's Dyke are thought to survive in counties Leitrim, Cavan, Monaghan, Armagh and Down (ibid.). Archaeological excavations of a section of the Black Pig's Dyke earthwork at Aghareagh West, Co. Monaghan, in 1982 found evidence of a timber palisade and an external ditch with a double bank, with an intervening ditch. This structure was dated to the Early Iron Age, 390–70 BC (ibid.).

In the early 1900s Kane—a local antiquarian—suggested that a 2 m-high earthwork at Magheracar was part of the Black Pig's Dyke (Kane 1909, 320). This idea was rejected by archaeologists in the mid 20th century (Davies 1955, 32). The structure at Magheracar 2 remained unrecognised as part of the Black Pig's Dyke and to the archaeological record until archaeological works in 2003 rediscovered the feature and revisited this interpretation of the earthwork.

The linear earthwork ran for a distance of approximately 350 m on an east–west orientation. It comprised a bank, which was up to 2 m in height, and shallow U-shaped ditches on each side which ran parallel to the bank (Illus. A4.1). The material from the ditches had been up cast to build the bank, which seemed to have been constructed upon a small natural ridge. The preservation of the earthwork was variable—in some places it had been levelled. Charcoal samples taken from the ditches at Magheracar 2 have been dated to the Late Iron Age, AD 60–420 (Beta-206066). Also

---

19 NGR 181677, 358157; height 20 m OD; Excavation Licence No. 04E0012; Excavation Director Brian Ó Donnchadha.
20 NGR 182347, 358102; height 20 m OD; Excavation Licence Nos 04E0098 & 04E0108; Excavation Directors Brian Ó Donnchadha and Rob Lynch.

Illus. A4.1—Magheracar 2, showing excavation of the linear earthwork, the Black Pig's Dyke (Irish Archaeological Consultancy Ltd).

found within the earthwork were sherds of prehistoric pottery dating to the Late Neolithic/Early Bronze Age period (Illus. A4.2), earlier than the construction of the Iron Age boundary. The pottery is likely to have been residual—included in the bank material by accident.

The earthwork linked a small stream, the Sruhanafulla, at its east and west termini. The name of the stream Sruhanafulla is translated as the 'streamlet of blood' and it is recorded that this stream marked the border between Ulster and Connacht during the early medieval period (Kane 1909, 320). It appears that the earthwork was strategically built to act as a boundary marker in the higher ground above the bogland. In the lower boglands the wet terrain would have acted as a sufficient barrier without need for a reinforcing earthwork.

A British army issue 'Brown Bess' musket was found buried against the northern edge of the bank. The 'Brown Bess' was the slang term for a type of flintlock musket produced for the British army from about 1720 (Illus. A4.3). It was worn over the shoulder or back held by a white leather sling, or fitted to the saddle for mounted troops. The musket, which survived in fragmentary form up to 2.1 m in length, was carefully hidden at the base of the earthwork, but whoever hid the gun did not—or could not—return to retrieve it.

A short distance from the earthwork to the north was a small furnace which was also radiocarbon dated to the Late Iron Age/early medieval period, AD 350–560 (Beta-205185), roughly the same

Illus. A4.2—Artist's reconstruction drawing of the Late Neolithic/ Early Bronze Age pottery vessel found at Magheracar 2 (John Murphy).

period as the earthwork. The furnace was composed of a small pit with a linear flue-like gully. This feature contained a substantial quantity of slag and burnt clay.

Early modern dwelling at Rathmore and Finner 1[21]

Excavations at Rathmore and Finner 1 revealed the remains of a single-storey stone rectangular building, probably a house with two rooms, dating from the 18th–19th centuries (Illus. A4.4) The floor was made of packed earth and a hearth was present in the main room at the eastern end of the building. The smaller room at the western end was probably used to house animals—this was a common practice at this time as it ensured the animals were protected and provided additional warmth to the house. Slate and window glass found during the excavation show that the house

Illus. A4.3—A 'Brown Bess' musket, similar to the one found at Magheracar 2 (Enniskillen Castle Museums).

would have had a slate roof, and glass windows—and was therefore not the poorest of houses (Illus. A4.5). A large stone wall to the east of the house was identified as a probable field boundary. Evidence of spade furrows suggests agricultural activity around the farmstead.

Pottery found at the site dated from the 18th and 19th centuries, and included the unusual find of a piece of pottery from a 17th-century Spanish olive jar. A large quern-stone found in the house wall was originally the upper disc of a rotary quern, a small hand-mill for grinding grain, used in

---

21 NGR 185410, 359810; height 30 m OD; Excavation Licence No. 04E0016; Excavation Director Fintan Walsh.

Illus. A4.4—The post-medieval house at Rathmore & Finner 1 during excavation (Irish Archaeological Consultancy Ltd).

Ireland from before the first century AD up until the 19th century.

A second unexpected find from the house was a military button from a non-officer uniform of the 47th (The North Lancashire) Loyal Regiment of Foot, which was first stationed in Ireland during the famine period of 1846–51 (Illus. A4.6). No regimental records survive from this period, so it is not known exactly where they were stationed. It is possible that the farmstead, which would probably have been abandoned by the mid 19th century, was used as a temporary camp, or that the button was simply dropped by a passing soldier.

The house does not appear on the first-edition Ordnance Survey six-inch map of 1834–5, suggesting that it was probably already abandoned by that time. Ireland's population doubled between 1780 and 1830, leading to shortages of land and competition for resources. The result was extreme poverty and famine. Many tenants who were unable to pay their rent abandoned their farms.

Illus. A4.5—Artist's reconstruction drawing of the house excavated at Rathmore & Finner 1 (John Murphy).

188

Illus. A4.6—Military button of the 47th Loyal Regiment of foot, found at the house at Rathmore & Finner 1 (Richie Bromley).

Possible megalithic structure at Sminver 2[22]

A possible megalithic structure was excavated on the immediate south-eastern outskirts of Ballyshannon. This structure comprised a 'capstone' resting on three small (possibly outcropping) stones—an arrangement reminiscent of a portal tomb or boulder burial. The small 'chamber' defined by the stones did not contain any deposits of archaeological significance. The immediate area, which was characterised by extensive rock outcropping, was devoid of archaeological features and it is possible that the collection of stones was entirely natural in origin.

Prehistoric temporary settlement site at Ballynacarrick 1[23]

Excavation at Ballynacarrick 1 uncovered a circular structure which was formed by two shallow linear beam slots and up to 10 stake-holes. The beam slots may represent the location of a wall, and a stake-hole at the end of one of the slots could have been the socket for a doorjamb. Sherds of prehistoric pottery were found in the topsoil which covered the site—these represented three separate vessels. It was not possible to get an exact date for the pottery but sherds from one vessel, made by coil construction, were probably Bronze Age in date. There was a small hearth to the north of the structure which

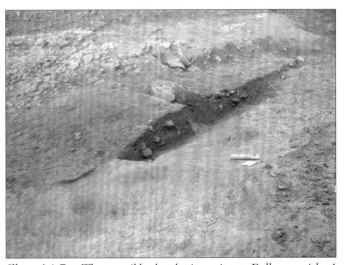

Illus. A4.7—The possible butchering pit at Ballynacarrick 1 during excavation (Irish Archaeological Consultancy Ltd).

was radiocarbon-dated to the Iron Age, 177 BC–AD 64 (Beta-205183).

Two pits were also identified at Ballynacarrick. The first was to the east of the circular structure. This sub-rectangular pit contained burnt material, and a large plano-convex flint knife, common

22 NGR 187970, 360700; height 23 m OD; Ministerial Direction No. A007/001; Excavation Director Fintan Walsh.
23 NGR 188140, 360840; height 40 m OD; Excavation Licence No. 04E0015; Excavation Director Fintan Walsh.

in the Early Neolithic. Pine charcoal dated the pit to the Early Neolithic, 4040–3940 BC (Beta-205184). The second pit was a round pit which was over 3 m in diameter, and two pieces of flint debitage, a piece of burnt bone and a piece of possible worked quartz were found in this pit.

Various activities were carried out at Ballynacarrick, over many generations. The large pit (Illus. A4.7) may have been a butchering pit, or even a corn-drying kiln. The evidence for tool production from the smaller pit is indicative of industrial activity.

The circular structure was probably a temporary shelter that could have been used by people working at the site. Bronze Age pottery and the Iron Age hearth show that the area was used and re-used over a long period of time. The site is located on well-drained soils, overlooking a small turlough (seasonal lake). A rocky bluff shelters it, and this protection from the weather would have made it an attractive place for living and working.

Bronze Age burnt mound at Sminver 1a[24]

A burnt mound, or possible *fulacht fia,* was discovered at Sminver 1a during test excavations. The mound measured 4 m by 8 m and during excavation was found to be approximately 0.1 m in height. *Fulachtaí fia* are the most common type of prehistoric monument in Ireland. Dating predominantly from the Bronze Age, they are composed of discarded heat-shattered stones and charcoal. The stones were heated in a fire, and placed in a pit or trough filled with water, to boil it. The water may then have been used for cooking, bathing or industrial purposes. There were no traces of a trough found associated with the burnt mound at Sminver. Charcoal from hazel and birch dated this feature to the Early Bronze Age, 2140–1780 BC (Beta-205182).

Holy well at Sminver 1b[25]

A holy well was recorded as 'Tobershannon', in the townland of Sminver, on the Ordnance Survey map of 1847–50, but could not be located during the Donegal Survey in 1983 (Lacy 1983). It was rediscovered during fieldwalking associated with the Environmental Impact Statement for the N15 Bypass. The holy well was identified as a natural spring with large stones placed around it to create a dry area for standing. A slight change in road design allowed the holy well to be preserved in situ (Illus. A4.8). There is a widespread tradition of holy wells in Ireland, some of which may have developed in the early medieval period or even during the pre-Christian era (O'Giolláin 2005). Water from holy wells was often believed to have healing properties, and many wells were associated with a patron saint. They became places of pilgrimage, where people travelled on certain 'pattern days', to pray and seek cures for various ailments.

---

24 NGR 188068, 360988; height 30 m OD; Excavation Licence No. 04E0017; Excavation Director Fintan Walsh.
25 NGR 188060, 360977; RMP DG107-057; height 20 m OD; Excavation Licence No. 04E0017; Excavation Director Fintan Walsh.

Illus. A4.8—Tobershannon holy well preserved adjacent to the new road (Richie Bromley).

BIBLIOGRAPHY

Agarwal, S C, Dumitriu, M, Tomlinson, G A & Gynpas, M D 2004 'Medieval trabecular bone architecture: the influence of age, sex and lifestyle', *American Journal of Physical Anthropology,* Vol. 124, 33–44.

Allingham, H 1879 *Ballyshannon: its history and antiquities; with some account of the surrounding neighbourhood.* Humphrey & Armour, Dublin.

Anderson, C M, Allan, J & Johansen, P G 1967 'Comments on the possible existence and nature of a heterozygote advantage in cystic fibrosis', *Bibliotheca Paediatrica,* Vol. 86, 381–7.

Anderson, T 2000 'Congenital conditions and neoplastic disease in British palaeopathology', *in* S Mays & M Cox (eds), *Human Osteology in Archaeology and Forensic Science,* 199–226. Cambridge University Press, Cambridge.

Andrews, J H 2001 'The mapping of Ireland's cultural landscape, 1550–1630', *in* P J Duffy, D Edwards & E FitzPatrick (eds), *Gaelic Ireland c. 1250 to c. 1650: land, lordship and settlement,* 153–80. Four Courts Press, Dublin.

Andrews, J H 2008 *The Queen's Last Map-Maker: Richard Bartlett in Ireland, 1600–3.* Geography Publications, Dublin.

Anon. (ed.) 1966 *Irish Patent Rolls of James I. Facsimile of the Irish Record Commission's Calendar Prepared Prior to 1830.* Irish Manuscripts Commission, Stationery Office, Dublin.

Arnay-de-la-Rosa, M, Gámez-Mendoza, A, Navarro-Mederos, J F, Hernandez-Marrero, J C, Fregel, R, Yanes, Y, Galindo-Martín, L, Romanek, C S & González-Reimers, E 2009 'Dietary patterns during the early prehispanic settlement in La Gomera (Canary Islands)', *Journal of Archaeological Science,* Vol. 36, 1972–81.

Aufderheide, A C & Rodríguez-Martín, C 1998 *The Cambridge Encyclopedia of Human Paleopathology.* Cambridge University Press, Cambridge.

Bailey, G 2008 *Detector Finds 4.* Greenlight Publishing, Witham.

Baraybar, J P & de la Rua, C 1997 'Reconstruction of diet with trace elements of bone at the Chalcolithic site of Pico Ramos, Basque Country, Spain', *Journal of Archaeological Science,* Vol. 24, 355–64.

Barrett, G F 1980 'A field survey and morphological study of ring-forts in southern County Donegal', *Ulster Journal of Archaeology,* Vol. 43, 39–51.

Bashir, T 2012 *Multi-elemental Analysis of a Medieval Irish Archaeological Assemblage from a Cemetery Located at Ballyhanna, County Donegal.* Unpublished PhD thesis, School of Science, Institute of Technology Sligo.

Begley, A 2009 *Ballyshannon and Surrounding Areas: history, heritage, and folklore.* Carrickboy Publishing, Ballyshannon.

Begley, A 2011 *Ballyshannon: genealogy and history.* Carrickboy Publishing, Ballyshannon.

Beneš, B, Jakubec, K, Šmíd, J & Spìvàèková, V 2000 'Determination of thirty-two elements in human autopsy tissue', *Biological Trace Element Research,* Vol. 75, 195–203.

Bertranpetit, J & Calafell, F 1996 'Genetic and geographical variability in cystic fibrosis: evolutionary considerations', *Ciba Foundation Symposium,* Vol. 197, 97–118.

Biddle, M & Hinton, D A 1990 'Copper-alloy bells', *in* M Biddle (ed.), *Object and Economy in Medieval Winchester. Artefacts from Medieval Winchester* (two volumes), 725–7. Oxford University Press, Oxford.

Bogin, B 1999 *Patterns of Human Growth* (2nd edn). Cambridge University Press, Cambridge.

Boylston, A, Holst, M & Coughlan, J 2000 'Physical anthropology', *in* V Fiorato, A Boylston & C Knûsel (eds), *Blood Red Roses: the archaeology of a mass grave from the Battle of Towton AD 1461,* 45–59. Oxbow Books, Oxford.

Bradshaw, B 1979 'Manus "the Magnificent": Ó Domnaill as Renaissance Prince', *in* A Cosgrove & D McCartney (eds), *Studies in Irish History Presented to R Dudley Edwards,* 15–36. University College Dublin, Dublin.

Bramanti, B, Sineo, L, Vianello, M D, Caramelli, D S, Hummel, S, Chiarelli, B & Herrmann, B 2000 'The selective advantage of cystic fibrosis heterozygotes tested by aDNA analysis: a preliminary investigation', *International Journal of Anthropology,* Vol. 15, 255–62.

Brewer, J S & Bullen W (eds) 1867 *Calendar of the Carew Manuscripts Volume 1, 1515–1574.* Longman, Green, Reader & Dyer, London.

Brickley, M 2000 'The diagnosis of metabolic disease in archaeological bone', *in* S Mays & M Cox (eds), *Human Osteology in Archaeology and Forensic Science,* 183–98. Cambridge University Press, Cambridge.

Brickley, M 2004 'Determination of sex from archaeological skeletal material and assessment of parturition', *in* M Brickley & J I McKinley (eds), *Guidelines to the Standards for Recording Human Remains,* 23–5. British Association for Biological Anthropology and Osteoarchaeology & Institute of Field Archaeologists Paper No. 7. British Association for Biological Anthropology and Osteoarchaeology & Institute of Field Archaeologists, Southampton & Reading.

Brickley, M & Ives, R 2008 *The Bioarchaeology of Metabolic Bone Disease.* Academic Press, London.

Bronk Ramsey, C 2005 OxCal Program v3.10 (http://c14.arch.ox.ac.uk/oxcal3/oxcal.htm).

Brown, K 2000 'Ancient DNA applications in human osteoarchaeology: achievements, problems and potential', *in* M Cox & S Mays (eds), *Human Osteology in Archaeology and Forensic Science,* 455–72. Greenwich Medical Media, London.

Buikstra, J & Ubelaker, D (eds) 1994 *Standards for Data Collection from Human Skeletal Remains.* Arkansas Archaeological Survey Research Series No. 44. University of Arkansas Press, Arkansas.

Burton, J H & Price, T D 1990 'The ratio of barium to strontium as a paleodietary indicator of consumption of marine resources', *Journal of Archaeological Science,* Vol. 17, 547–57.

Burton, J H & Price, T D 2000 'The use and abuse of trace elements for paleodietary research', *in* S H Ambrose & M A Katzenberg (eds), *Biogeochemical Approaches to Paleodietary Analysis,* 159–71. Kluwer Academic/Plenum Publishers, New York.

Burton, J H, Price, T D & Middleton, W D 1999 'Correlation of bone Ba/Ca and Sr/Ca due to biological purification of calcium', *Journal of Archaeological Science,* Vol. 26, 609–16.

Butler, J M 2001 'Commonly used STR markers', *in* J M Butler (ed.), *Forensic DNA Typing: biology & technology behind STR markers,* 53–81. Academic Press, London.

Cardy, A 1997 'The human bones', *in* P Hill, *Whithorn and St Ninian: the excavation of a monastic town, 1984–91,* 519–62. The Whithorn Trust and Sutton Publishing, Stroud.

Cashman, S M, Pation, A, Delgado, M G, Byrne, L, Denham, B & De Acre, M 1995 'The Irish Cystic Fibrosis Database', *Journal of Medical Genetics,* Vol. 32, 972–5.

Chamberlain, A 2006 *Demography in Archaeology.* Cambridge University Press, Cambridge.

Cipollaro, M, Galderisi, U & Di Bernardo, G 2005 'Ancient DNA as a multidisciplinary experience', *Journal of Cellular Physiology,* Vol. 202, No. 2, 315–22.

Cleary, R M 1996 'Medieval graveyard and boundary wall at Cove Street, Cork', *Journal of the Cork Historical and Archaeological Society,* Vol. 101, 94–111.

Colard, T, Gabart, N & Blondiaux, J 2008 'A palaeopathological case of a right maxilla's cemento-ossifying fibroma', *International Journal of Osteoarchaeology,* Vol. 18, 195–201.

Collins, F S 1992 'Cystic fibrosis; molecular biology and therapeutic implications', *Science,* Vol. 256, No. 5058, 774–9.

Conway, M 1999 *Director's First Findings from Excavations in Cabinteely.* Margaret Gowen & Co, Glenageary.

Consensus Development Conference 1991 'Diagnosis; prophlaxis and treatment of osteoporosis', *American Journal of Medicine,* Vol. 90, 107–10.

Corlett, C 2006 'The 1946 survey of the area flooded by the Erne Hydro-Electric Scheme, County Donegal', *Journal of the Royal Society of Antiquaries of Ireland,* Vol. 136, 50–98.

Cox, M 2000 'Ageing adults from the skeleton', *in* M Cox & S Mays (eds), *Human Osteology in Archaeology and Forensic Science,* 61–81. Cambridge University Press, Cambridge.

Cross, J F & Bruce, M F 1989 'The skeletal remains', *in* J A Stones (ed.), *Three Scottish Carmelite Friaries. Excavations at Aberdeen, Linlithgow and Perth 1980–86,* 119–42. Societies of Antiquaries of Scotland Monograph Series No. 6. Society of Antiquaries of Scotland, Edinburgh.

Crowe, C 1980 'A note on white quartz pebbles found in Early Christian contexts on the Isle of Man', *Proceedings of the Isle of Man Natural History and Antiquarian Society,* Vol. 8, No. 4, 413–15.

Cunha, E, Fily, M L, Clisson, I, Santos, A L, Silva, A M, Umbelino, C, Cesar, P, Corte-Real, A, Crubezy, E & Ludes, B 2000 'Children at the convent: comparing historical data, morphology and DNA extracted from ancient tissues for sex diagnosis at Santa Clara-a-Velha (Coimbra, Portugal)', *Journal of Archaeological Science,* Vol. 27, 949–52.

Cunningham, J B 1993 *The Letters of John O'Donovan from Fermanagh.* St. Davog's Press, Belleek.

Daniell, C 1997 *Death and Burial in Medieval England 1066–1550.* Routledge, London.

Davies, O 1955 'The Black Pig's Dyke', *Ulster Journal of Archaeology,* Vol. 18, 29–36.

Djingova, R, Zlateva, B & Kuleff, I 2004 'On the possibilities of inductively coupled plasma mass spectrometry for analysis of archaeological bones for reconstruction of paleodiet', *Talanta,* Vol. 63, 785–9.

Donnelly, C J & Murphy, E M 2008 'The origins of *cillíní* in Ireland', *in* E M Murphy (ed.), *Deviant Burial in the Archaeological Record,* 191–223. Oxbow Books, Oxford.

Donnelly, W (ed.) 1861 *Census of Ireland: general alphabetical index to the townlands and towns, parishes and baronies of Ireland*. Alex Thom, Dublin.

Donoghue, H & Spigelman, M 2006 'Pathogenic microbial ancient DNA: a problem or an opportunity?', *Proceedings of the Royal Society B,* Vol. 273, No. 1587, 641–2.

Donoghue, H D, Marcsik, A, Matheson, C, Vernon, K, Nuorala, E, Molto, J E, Greenblatt, C L & Spigelman, M 2005 'Co-infection of *Mycobacterium tuberculosis* and *Mycobacterium leprae* in human archaeological samples: a possible explanation for the historical decline of leprosy', *Proceedings of the Royal Society B,* Vol. 272, 389–94.

Donoghue, H D, Spigelman, M, Greenblatt, C L, Lev-Maor, G, Bar-Gal, G K, Matheson, C, Vernon, K, Nerlich, A G & Zink, A R 2004 'Tuberculosis: from prehistory to Robert Koch, as revealed by ancient DNA', *The Lancet Infectious Diseases,* Vol. 4, No. 9, 584–92.

Drancourt, M, Aboudharam, G, Signoli, M, Dutour, O & Raoult, D 1998 'Detection of 400-year-old *Yersinia pestis* DNA in human dental pulp: an approach to the diagnosis of ancient septicemia', *Proceedings of the National Academy of Sciences, USA,* Vol. 95, No. 21, 12637–40.

Dziadek, J, Sajduda, A & Boruń, M 2001 'Specificity of insertion sequence-based PCR assays for *Mycobacterium tuberculosis* complex', *The International Journal of Tuberculosis and Lung Disease,* Vol. 5, No. 6, 569–74.

Edwards, N 1990 *The Archaeology of Early Medieval Ireland*. Batsford, London.

Egan, G 2005 *Material Culture in London in an Age of Transition. Tudor and Stuart Period Finds c. 1450–c. 1700 from Excavations at Riverside Sites in Southwark*. Museum of London Archaeological Series Monograph No. 19. Museum of London Archaeology Service, London.

Eveleth, P B & Tanner, J M 1990 *Worldwide Variation in Human Growth* (2nd edn). Cambridge University Press, Cambridge.

Ezzo, J A 1994 'Zinc as a paleodietary indicator: an issue of theoretical validity in bone-chemistry analysis', *American Antiquity,* Vol. 59, 606–21.

Fabig, A & Herrmann, B 2002 'Trace elements in buried human bones: intra-population variability of Sr/Ca and Ba/Ca ratios–diet or diagenesis?', *Naturwissenschaften,* Vol. 89, 115–19.

Faerman, M, Kahila, Bar-Gal G, Filon, D, Greenblatt, C L, Oppenheim, S A & Smith, P 1998 'Determining the sex of infanticide victims from the late Roman era through ancient DNA analysis', *Journal of Archaeological Science,* Vol. 25, 861–5.

Fanning, T 1981 'Excavation of an Early Christian cemetery and settlement at Reask, County Kerry', *Proceedings of the Royal Irish Academy,* Vol. 81C, 67–172.

Farnum, J F, Glascock, M D, Sandford, M K, & Gerritsen, S 1995 'Trace elements in ancient human bone and associated soil using NAA', *Journal of Radioanalytical and Nuclear Chemistry,* Vol. 196, 267–74.

Farrell, J P 1886 *Historical Notes and Stories of the County Longford*. Dollard, Dublin.

Farrell, P M 2008 'The prevalence of cystic fibrosis in the European Union', *Journal of Cystic Fibrosis,* Vol. 7, No. 5, 450–3.

Farrell, P, Le Marechal, C, Ferec, C, Siker, M & Teschler-Nicola, M 2007 'Discovery of the principal cystic fibrosis mutation (F508del) in ancient DNA from Iron Age Europeans', *Nature Precedings* (http://hdl.handle.net/10101/npre.2007.1276.1)

Father Colmcille 1959 'Abbey Assaroe', *in* T O Donnell, OFM (ed.), *Father John Colgan, OFM, 1592–1658: essays in commemoration of the third centenary of his death,* 111–29. Assisi Press, Dublin.

Fazekas, I Gy & Kósa, F 1978 *Forensic Fetal Osteology.* Akadémiai Kiadó, Budapest.

Feldesman, M R 1992 'Femur/stature ratios and estimates of stature in children', *American Journal of Physical Anthropology,* Vol. 87, 447–59.

Ferembach, D, Schwidetzky, I & Stloukal, M 1980 'Recommendations for age and sex diagnoses of skeletons', *Journal of Human Evolution,* Vol. 9, 517–49.

Field, E 2006 'Irish seaweed revisited', *in* R Hosking (ed.), *Wild Food: proceedings of the Oxford Symposium on Food and Cookery 2004,* 114–21. Prospect Books, Devon.

FitzPatrick, E 2004 *Royal Inauguration in Gaelic Ireland c. 1100–1600.* The Boydell Press, Woodbridge.

FitzPatrick, E 2009 'Native enclosed settlement and the problem of the Irish "ring-fort"', *Medieval Archaeology,* Vol. 53, 271–307.

Foley, C & Donnelly, C 2012 *Parke's Castle, County Leitrim: archaeology, history and architecture.* Department of Arts, Heritage & the Gaeltacht Archaeological Monograph Series, No. 7. The Stationery Office, Dublin.

Garcia, J & Quintana-Domenque, C 2007 'The evolution of adult height in Europe: a brief note', *Economics and Human Biology,* Vol. 5, 340–9.

Gélis, J 1991 *History of Childbirth.* English translation. Polity Press, Malden.

Gilbert, R I 1985 'Stress, paleonutrition and trace elements', *in* R I Gilbert & J H Mielke (eds), *The Analysis of Prehistoric Diets,* 339–58. Academic Press, New York.

Gilchrist, R & Sloane, B 2005 *Requiem: the medieval monastic cemetery in Britain.* Museum of London Archaeology Service, London.

Gleason, A 1995 'Games', *in* S Duffy (ed.) *Medieval Ireland: an encyclopedia,* 193. Routledge, London.

González-Reimers, E, Velasco-Vázquez, J, Arnay-de-la-Rosa, M, Alberto-Barroso, V, Galindo-Martýìn, L & Santolaria-Fernández, F 2003 'Bone cadmium and lead in prehistoric inhabitants and domestic animals from Gran Canaria', *Science of the Total Environment,* Vol. 301, 97–103.

Goodman, A H & Martin, D L 2002 'Reconstructing health profiles from skeletal remains', *in* R H Steckel & J C Rose (eds), *The Backbone of History: health and nutrition in the western hemisphere,* 11–60. Cambridge University Press, Cambridge.

Goodman, A H, Martinez, D L & Chavez, A 1991 'Nutritional supplementation and the development of linear enamel hypoplasias in children from Tezonteopan, Mexico', *American Journal of Clinical Nutrition,* Vol. 53, 773–81.

Grandjean, P 1988 'Ancient skeletons as silent witnesses of lead exposures in the past', *CRC Critical Reviews in Toxicology,* Vol. 19, 11–21.

Griffin, R C & Donlon, D 2009 'Patterns in dental enamel hypoplasia by sex and age at death in two archaeological populations', *Archives of Oral Biology,* Vol. 54S, s93–s100.

Gwynn, A & Hadcock, R N (eds) 1970 *Medieval Religious Houses of Ireland.* Irish Academic Press, Blackrock.

Hagelberg, E, Bell, L S, Allen, T, Boyde, A, Jones, S J, Clegg, J B, Hummel, S, Brown, T A & Ambler, R P 1991 'Analysis of ancient bone DNA: techniques and applications', *Philosophical Transactions of the Royal Society of London Series B,* Vol. 333, No. 1268, 399–407.

Hall, S C & Hall, A C 1841 *Hall's Ireland: Mr & Mrs Hall's Tour of 1840,* Vol.3. Hall, Virtue & Co., London.

Hanawalt, B A 1986 *The Ties that Bound: peasant families in medieval England.* Oxford University Press, Oxford.

Haren, M & de Pontfarcy, Y 1988 *The Medieval Pilgrimage to St Patrick's Purgatory: Lough Derg and the European tradition.* Clogher Historical Society, Enniskillen.

Hershkovitz, I, Donoghue, H D, Minnikin, D E, Besra, G S, Y-C Lee, O, Gernaey, A M, Galili, E, Eshed, V, Greenblatt, C L, Lemma, E, Bar-Gal, G K & Spigelman, M 2008 'Detection and molecular characterization of 9000-year-old mycobacterium tuberculosis from a Neolithic settlement in the Eastern Mediterranean', *PloS ONE*, Vol. 3, No. 10, 1–6.

Hill, G 1877 *An Historical Account of the Plantation in Ulster.* McCaw, Stephenson & Orr, Belfast.

Hill, P & Nicholson, A 1997 'The utilised stones', *in* P Hill, *Whithorn and St Ninian: the excavation of a monastic town, 1984–91,* 464–74. The Whithorn Trust and Sutton Publishing, Stroud.

Hillson, S 1996 *Dental Anthropology.* Cambridge University Press, Cambridge.

Hofreiter, M, Serre, D, Poinar, H N, Kuch, M & Pääbo, S 2001 'Ancient DNA', *Nature Reviews Genetics,* Vol. 2, 353–9.

Hogan, J 1931–2 'The Irish Law of Kingship, with special reference to Aileach and Cenél Eoghain', *Proceedings of the Royal Irish Academy,* Vol. 40C, 186–254.

Horn, W, Marshall, J W & Rourke, G D 1990 *The Forgotten Hermitage of Skellig Michael.* University of California Press, Berkley.

Hurl, D 2002 'The excavation of an Early Christian cemetery at Solar, County Antrim', *Ulster Journal of Archaeology,* Vol. 61, 37–61.

Hurley, M F 1995 'The bone and antler artefacts', *in* M F Hurley & C M Sheehan, *Excavations at the Dominican Priory, St Mary's of the Isles, Crosse's Green, Cork,* 112–15. Cork Corporation, Cork.

Hurley, M F & McCutcheon, S W J 1997 'St Peter's Church and graveyard', *in* M F Hurley, O M B Scully & S W J McCutcheon, *Late Viking Age and Medieval Waterford. Excavations 1986–1992,* 190–227. Waterford Corporation, Waterford.

Iomaire, M M C 2006 'A history of seafood in Irish cuisine and culture', *in* R Hosking (ed.), *Wild Food: proceedings of the Oxford Symposium on Food and Cookery 2004.* Prospect Books, Devon.

Ivens, R J 1989 'Dunmisk Fort, Carrickmore, Co. Tyrone excavations 1984–1986', *Ulster Journal of Archaeology,* Vol. 52, 17–110.

Jay, M & Richards, M P 2006 'Diet in the Iron Age cemetery population at Wetwang Slack, East Yorkshire, UK: carbon and nitrogen stable isotope evidence', *Journal of Archaeological Science,* Vol. 33, 653–62.

Jefferies, H A 1996–7 'Bishop George Montgomery's survey of the parishes of Derry Diocese: a complete text from c.1609', *Seanchas Ardmhacha: Journal of the Armagh Diocesan Historical Society,* Vol. 17, 44–76.

Jefferies, H A 1999 'George Montgomery, first Protestant Bishop of Clogher (1605–1621)', *Clogher Record,* Vol. 16, No. 3, 127–9.

Jennings, T S 1989 *Handbells.* Shire Publications Ltd, Princes Risborough.

Jones, G 2001 '"Captain of All These Men of Death": the history of tuberculosis in nineteenth and twentieth century Ireland.* Clio Medica 62. Editions Rodopi B V, New York.

Jonge, J, Kingma, J, Van der Lei, B & Klasen, H J 1994 'Phalangeal fractures of the hand: an analysis of gender and age-related incidence and aetiology', *The Journal of Hand Surgery: British and European Volume,* Vol. 19, No. 2, 168–70.

Jurmain, R D 1991 'Degenerative changes in peripheral joints as indicators of mechanical stress: opportunities and limitations', *International Journal of Osteoarchaeology,* Vol. 1, No. 4, 247–52.

Jurmain, R D 1999 *Stories from the Skeleton: behavioral reconstruction in human osteology.* Routledge, London.

Kaestle, F & Horsburgh, K A 2002 'Ancient DNA in anthropology: methods, applications, and ethics', *American Journal of Physical Anthropology,* Vol. 119, Issue Supplement 35, 92–130.

Kane, W F 1909 'The Black Pig's Dyke: the ancient boundary fortification of the Uladh', *Proceedings of the Royal Irish Academy,* Vol. 27C, No. 14, 301–28.

Keenleyside A 2008 'Dental pathology and diet at Apollonia, a Greek colony on the Black Sea', *International Journal of Osteoarchaeology,* Vol. 18, 262–79.

Kerem, B, Rommens, J M, Buchanan, J A, Markiewicz, D, Cox, T K, Chakravarti, A, Buchwald, M & Tsui, L C 1989 'Identification of the cystic fibrosis gene: genetic analysis', *Science,* Vol. 245, 1073–80.

Kilby, J M, Gilligan, P H, Yankaskas, J R, Highsmith Jr, W E, Edwards, L J & Knowles, M 1992 'Nontuberculous mycobacteria in adult patients with cystic fibrosis', *Chest,* Vol. 102, 70–5.

Knodel, J & Kinter, H 1977 'The impact of breast feeding patterns on the biometric analysis of infant mortality', *Demography,* Vol. 14, 391–409.

Kohn, M J & Cerling, T E 2002 'Stable isotope compositions of biological apatite', *Reviews in Mineralogy and Geochemistry,* Vol. 48, 455–88.

Knudson, K J, O'Donnabhain, B, Carver, C, Cleland, R & Price, T D 2012 'Migration and Viking Dublin: paleomobility and paleodiet through isotopic analyses', *Journal of Archaeological Science,* Vol. 39, 308–20.

Lacy, B 1983 *Archaeological Survey of County Donegal.* Donegal County Council, Lifford.

Lacey, B 1995 'Prehistoric and early historic settlement in Donegal', *in* W Nolan, L Ronayne & M Dunlevy (eds), *Donegal: history and society,* 1–24. Geography Publications, Dublin.

Lacey, B 2003 'The battle of Cul Dreimne–a reassessment', *Journal of the Royal Society of Antiquarians of Ireland,* Vol. 133, 78–85.

Larsen, C S 2002 'Bioarchaeology: the lives and lifestyles of past people', *Journal of Archaeological Research,* Vol. 10, 119–66.

Lassen, C, Hummel, S & Herrmann, B 2000 'Molecular sex identification of stillborn and neonate individuals ("Traufkinder") from the burial site Aegerten', *Anthropologischer Anzeiger,* Vol. 58, No. 1, 1–8.

LeGeros, R Z & LeGeros, J P 1984 'Phosphate minerals in human tissues', *in* J O Nriagu & P B Moore (eds), *Phosphate Minerals,* 351–85. Springer, Berlin.

Lennon, C 1981 *Richard Stanihurst, The Dubliner, 1547–1618.* Irish Academic Press, Blackrock.

Lewis, M 2002 *Urbanisation and Child Health in Medieval and Post-Medieval England.* British Archaeological Reports, British Series 339. Archaeopress, Oxford.

Lewis, M E 2007 *The Bioarchaeology of Children: perspectives from biology and forensic anthropology.* Cambridge University Press, Cambridge.

Lewis, M E 2010 'Life and death in a civitas capital: metabolic disease and trauma in the children from Late Roman Dorchester, Dorset', *American Journal of Physical Anthropology,* Vol. 142, 405–16.

Lieverse, A R 1999 'Diet and aetiology of dental calculus', *International Journal of Osteoarchaeology,* Vol. 9, No. 4, 581–6.

Lillie, M C 1996 'Mesolithic and Neolithic populations of Ukraine: indications of diet from dental pathology', *Current Anthropology,* Vol. 37, 135–42.

Livingstone, P 1969 *The Fermanagh Story.* Cumann Seanchais Chlochair, Enniskillen.

Lockwood, F W 1901 'The remains of the abbey Assaroe, Ballyshannon, in the county of Donegal', *Ulster Journal of Archaeology,* Ser. 2, Vol. 7, 178–85.

Lovejoy, C O, Meindl, R S, Pryzbeck, T R & Mensforth, R P 1985 'Chronological metamorphosis of the auricular surface of the ilium: a new method for the determination of age at death', *American Journal of Physical Anthropology,* Vol. 68, 15–28.

MacArtain, P, Gill, C I, Brooks, M, Campbell, R & Rowland, I R 2007 'Nutritional value of edible seaweeds', *Nutrition Reviews,* Vol. 65, 535–43.

Macdonald, P 2005 *Excavations at Kilroot, Co. Antrim, 2003–04.* Centre for Archaeological Fieldwork Data Structure Report No. 36. Centre for Archaeological Fieldwork, Queen's University Belfast, Belfast (http://www.qub.ac.uk/caf/DSRs/CAFDSR36.pdf).

MacDonald-Janowski, D S 2004 'Fibro-osseus lesion of the face and jaws', *Clinical Radiology,* Vol. 59, 11–25.

Mac Giolla Easpaig, D 1995 'Placenames and early settlement in County Donegal', *in* W Nolan, L Ronayne & M. Dunlevy (eds), *Donegal: history and society,* 149–82. Geography Publications, Dublin.

Malcolm, E 2005 'Medicine', *in* S Duffy (ed.), *Medieval Ireland: an encyclopedia,* 323–5. Routledge, London.

Manning, C 2005 'Burials', *in* S Duffy (ed.), *Medieval Ireland: an encyclopaedia,* 53–5. Routledge, London.

Maresh, M M 1955 'Linear growth of long bones of extremities from infancy through adolescence', *American Journal of Diseases of Children,* Vol. 89, 725–42.

Marshall, J W & Rourke, G 2000 *High Island: an Irish monastery in the Atlantic.* Town House & Country House, Dublin.

Marshall, J W & Walsh, C 2005 *Illaunloughan Island: an early medieval monastery in County Kerry.* Wordwell, Bray.

Marshall, J W & Walsh, C 2009 'Illaunloughan: an early Iveragh monastery and its shrine', *in* J Crowley & J Sheehan (eds), *The Iveragh Peninsula: a cultural atlas of the Ring of Kerry,* 122–5. Cork University Press, Cork.

Mays, S A 1999 'Linear and appositional long bone growth in earlier human populations: a case study from mediaeval England', *in* R D Hoppa & C M FitzGerald (eds), *Human Growth in the Past,* 290–312. Cambridge University Press, Cambridge.

Mays, S 2003 'Bone strontium: calcium ratios and duration of breastfeeding in a mediaeval skeletal population', *Journal of Archaeological Science,* Vol. 30, 731–41.

Mays, S 2007 'The humans remains', *in* S Mays, C Harding & C Heighway, *The Churchyard. Wharram: a study of settlement on the Yorkshire Wolds, XI,* 77–192. York University Archaeological Publications 13. York Archaeological Publications, York.

Mays S 2010 *The Archaeology of Human Bones* (2nd edn). Routledge, London.

Mays, S & Cox, M 2000 'Sex determination in skeletal remains', *in* M Cox & S Mays (eds), *Human Osteology in Archaeology and Forensic Science,* 117–30. Greenwich Medical Media, London.

Mays, S & Faerman, M 2001 'Sex identification in some putative infanticide victims from Roman Britain using ancient DNA', *Journal of Archaeological Science,* Vol. 28, 555–9.

Mays, S, Brickley, M & Ives, R 2006 'Skeletal manifestations of rickets in infants and young children in a historic population from England', *American Journal of Physical Anthropology,* Vol. 129, 362–74.

McErlean, T 1983 'The Irish townland system of landscape organisation', *in* T Reeves-Smyth & F Hamond (eds), *Landscape Archaeology in Ireland,* 315–39. British Archaeological Reports, British Series 116. Archaeopress, Oxford.

McGettigan, D 2005 'Ua Domnaill (Ó Domnaill)', *in* S Duffy (ed.), *Medieval Ireland: an encyclopedia,* 476–7. Routledge, London.

McKenna, L 1919 'The historical poems of Gofraidh Fionn Ó Dálaigh', *The Irish Monthly,* January 1919, 1–5.

McKenzie, C 2010 *A Palaeopathological Study of the Adult Individuals from the Ballyhanna Cemetery, Co. Donegal.* Unpublished PhD thesis, Queen's University Belfast.

McKenzie, C J & Murphy, E M 2011 'Health in medieval Ireland: the evidence from Ballyhanna, Co. Donegal', *in* S Conran, N Roycroft & M Stanley (eds), *Past Times, Changing Fortunes,* 131–43. Archaeology and the National Roads Authority Monograph Series No. 8. National Roads Authority, Dublin.

McKerr, L 2008 'Towards an archaeology of childhood: children and material culture in historic Ireland', *in* L H Dommasnes & M Wrigglesworth (eds), *Children, Identity and the Past,* 36–50. Cambridge Scholars Publishing, Cambridge.

McKinley, J 2004 'Compiling a skeletal inventory: disarticulated and co-mingled remains', *in* M Brickley & J McKinley (eds), *Guidelines to the Standards for Recording Human Remains,* 14–17. British Association for Biological Anthropology and Osteoarchaeology & Institute of Field Archaeologists Paper No. 7. British Association for Biological Anthropology and Osteoarchaeology & Institute of Field Archaeologists, Southampton & Reading.

McSparron, C 2011 'The medieval coarse pottery of Ulster', *Journal of Irish Archaeology* Vol. 20, 101–21.

Meindl, R S 1987 'Hypothesis: a selective advantage for cystic fibrosis heterozygotes', *American Journal of Physical Anthropology,* Vol. 74, 39–45.

Miles, A E W & Bulman, J S 1994 'Growth curves of immature bones from a Scottish island population of sixteenth to mid-nineteenth century: limb-bone diaphyses and some bones of the hand and foot', *International Journal of Osteoarchaeology,* Vol. 4, 121–36.

Miletic, I, Miric, M, Lalic, Z & Sobajic, S 1991 'Composition of lipids and proteins of several species of molluscs, marine and terrestrial, from the Adriatic Sea and Serbia', *Food Chemistry,* Vol. 41, 303–8.

Minter, F 2009 'Great Barton, Suffolk: copper-alloy bell with heraldic arms', *in* Anon (ed.), *Portable Antiquities and Treasure Annual Report 2007,* 143. Department of Portable Antiquities & Treasure, British Museum, London.

Moorrees C F A, Fanning, E A & Hunt, E E 1963 'Formation and resorption of three deciduous teeth in children', *American Journal of Physical Anthropology,* Vol. 21, 205–13.

Morral, N, Bertranpetit, J, Estivill, X, Nunes, V, Casals, T, Giménez, J, Reis, A, Varon-Mateeva, N R, Macek, Jr M, Kalaydjieva, L, Angelicheva, D, Dancheva, R, Romeo, G, Russo, M P, Garnerone, S, Restagno, G, Ferrari, M, Magnani, C, Claustres, M, Desgeorges, M, Schwartz, M, Schwarz, M, Dallapiccola, B, Novelli, G, Ferec, C, de Arce, M, Nemeti, M, Kere, J, Anvret, M, Dahl, N & Kadasi,

L 1994 'The origin of the major cystic fibrosis mutation (delta F508) in European populations', *Nature Genetics,* Vol. 7, 169–75.

Murphy, E M 2010 'Trepanation and trephination in early modern Ireland', *in* M Davies, U MacConville & G Cooney (eds), *A Grand Gallimaufry Collected in Honour of Nick Maxwell,* 259–64 Wordwell, Dublin.

Murphy, E M 2011 'Children's burial grounds in Ireland (*cillíní*) and parental emotions towards infant death', *International Journal of Historical Archaeology,* Vol. 15, 409–28.

Murphy, E M & McKenzie, C J 2010 'Multiple osteochondromas in the archaeological record: a global review', *Journal of Archaeological Science,* Vol. 37, 2255–64.

Murphy E M, Chistov, Y K, Hopkins, R, Rutland, P & Taylor, G M 2009 'Tuberculosis among Iron Age individuals from Tyva, South Siberia: palaeopathological and biomolecular findings', *Journal of Archaeological Science,* Vol. 36, 2029–38.

National Library of Ireland Ms2656, Bartlett Maps ii, v, vi, ix and xi.

Newman, C 1992 *Castlederg Castle: excavations 1991.* Unpublished report prepared for Archaeological Development Services Ltd.

Newton, S M, Brent, A J, Anderson, S, Whittaker, E & Kampmann, B 2008 'Paediatric tuberculosis', *Lancet Infectious Diseases,* Vol. 8, 498–510.

Nicholls, K W 1971–2 'The register of Clogher', *The Clogher Record,* Vol. 7, No. 3, 361–431.

Nicholls, K W 1993 'Gaelic society and economy', *in* A Cosgrove (ed.), *A New History of Ireland, Volume 2: medieval Ireland, 1169–1534,* 397–438. Clarendon Press, Oxford.

Nicholls, K W 2003 *Gaelic and Gaelicized Ireland in the Middle Ages.* Lilliput Press, Dublin.

Ní Chonaill, B 1997 'Fosterage: child-rearing in medieval Ireland', *History Ireland,* Vol. 5, 28–31.

Ní Chonaill, B forthcoming 'Child-centred law in medieval Ireland', *in* R Davis & T Dunne (eds), *The Empty Throne: childhood and the crisis of modernity.* Cambridge University Press, Cambridge. [Available at http://eprints.gla.ac.uk/3812/]

Nic Suibhne, F 1992 '"On the Straw" and other aspects of pregnancy and childbirth from the oral tradition of women in Ulster', *Ulster Folklife,* Vol. 38, 1–13.

Norton, J & Lane, S 2007 'Clay tobacco-pipes in Ireland, c. 1600–1850', *in* A Horning, R Ó Baoill, C Donnelly and P Logue (eds), *The Post-Medieval Archaeology of Ireland, 1550–1850,* 435–52. Wordwell, Bray.

Ó Canann, T 1986 'Trí Saorthuatha Mhuinntire Chanannáin: a forgotten medieval placename', *Donegal Annual,* Vol. 38, 19–46.

Ó Canann, T 2003 'Carraig an Dúnáin: probable Ua Canannain inauguration site', *Journal of the Royal Society of Antiquaries of Ireland,* Vol. 133, 36–67.

Ó Canann, T 2004 'Mael Coba Ua Gallchobair and his early family background', *Journal of the Royal Society of Antiquaries of Ireland,* Vol. 134, 33–79.

Ó Carragáin, T 2003 'A landscape converted: archaeology and early church organisation on Iveragh and Dingle, Ireland', *in* M Carver (ed.), *The Cross Goes North: process of conversion in northern Europe, AD 300–1300,* 127–52. York Medieval Press, York.

Ó Carragáin, T 2010 *Churches in Early Medieval Ireland.* Yale University Press (for the Paul Mellon Centre for studies in British Art), New Haven.

O'Connell L 2004 'Guidance on recording age at death in adults', *in* M Brickley & J McKinley (eds), *Guidelines to the Standards for Recording Human Remains,* 18–20. British Association for Biological Anthropology and Osteoarchaeology & Institute of Field Archaeologists Paper No. 7, British Association for Biological Anthropology and Osteoarchaeology & Institute of Field Archaeologists, Southampton & Reading.

O'Conor, K D 1998 *The Archaeology of Medieval Rural Settlement in Ireland.* Discovery Programme Monographs 3. Royal Irish Academy, Dublin.

Ó Corráin, D 1973 'Aspects of early history', *in* B G Scott (ed.), *Perspectives in Irish Archaeology,* 64–75. Association of Young Irish Archaeologists, Belfast.

Ó Diobhlin, E 1998 *O'Neill's 'Own Country' and its Families.* Donaghmore Historical Society, Donaghmore.

Ó Doiblin, C & Hamill, T 1992 'Giolla Phádraig Ó Luchráin, circa 1577–1612', *Seanchas Ardmhacha: Journal of the Armagh Diocesan Historical Society,* Vol. 15, No. 1, 50–96.

Ó Donnabháin B 2003 'Trepanation and pseudotrepanations: evidence of cranial surgery from prehistoric and early historic Ireland', *in* R Arnott, S Finger & C U M Smith (eds), *Trepanation: history, discovery, theory,* 79–94. Swets & Zeitlinger Publishers, Lisse.

Ó Donnchadha, B 2006 *N15 Bundoran to Ballyshannon. Stage 2 Archaeological Services. Stratigraphic Report.* Unpublished report by Irish Archaeological Consultancy Ltd.

O'Donovan, J 1842 *The Banquet of Dun Na N-Gedh and the Battle of Magh Rath: an ancient historical tale.* Dublin University Press, Dublin.

O'Donovan, J 1856 *Annals of the Kingdom of Ireland, by the Four Masters, from the Earliest Period to the Year 1616* (7 volumes). Hodges, Smith & Co., Dublin.

O'Donovan, J 1862 *The Topographical Poems of John O'Dubhagain and Giolla na Naomh O'Huidhrin.* Irish Archaeological & Celtic Society, Dublin.

O'Dowd, M 1986 'Gaelic economy and society', *in* C Brady and R Gillespie (eds), *Natives and Newcomers,* 120–47. Irish Academic Press, Dublin.

Ó Gallachair, P 1958 'Where was Ó Domnaill's Fort at Murvagh?', *Donegal Annual,* Vol. 4, No. 1, 65–8.

Ó Gallachair, P 1960 'Coarbs and erenaghs of County Donegal', *Donegal Annual,* Vol. 4, No. 3, 272–81.

Ó Gallachair, P 1961 *Where Erne and Drowes Meet the Sea: fragments from a Patrician parish.* Donegal Democrat Ltd, Ballyshannon.

Ó Gallachair, P 1966 'The Erne forts of Cael Uisce and Belleek', *Clogher Record,* Vol. 6, No. 1, 104–16.

O'Gialláin, D 2005 'Revisiting the holy well', *Eire-Ireland: An Interdisciplinary Journal of Irish Studies,* Vol. 40, 11–41.

O'Kelly, M J 1958 'Church Island near Valencia, Co. Kerry', *Proceedings of the Royal Irish Academy,* Vol. 59C, 57–136.

O'Kelly, M J 1967 'Knockea, Co. Limerick', *in* E Rynne (ed.), *North Munster Studies: essays in commemoration of Monsignor Michael Moloney,* 72–101. The Thomond Archaeological Society, Limerick.

Ó Muirgheasa, É 1936 'The holy wells of Donegal', *Béaloideas,* Vol. 6, No. 2, 143–62.

O'Neill, T 1987 *Merchants and Mariners in Medieval Ireland.* Irish Academic Press, Blackrock.

Opie, H   2009   *Preliminary Report on Archaeological Investigations at Site 00E0156, on the Medieval Borough and Graveyard of Ardreigh, Athy, Co. Kildare* (4 volumes). Unpublished report for Kildare County Council.

O Rahilly, C   1998   'A classification of bronze stick-pins from the Dublin excavations 1962–72', *in* C Manning (ed.), *Dublin and Beyond the Pale. Studies in honour of Patrick Healey,* 23–33. Wordwell in association with Rathmichael Historical Society, Dublin.

O'Rourke, D H, Hayes, M G & Carlyle, S W   2000   'Ancient DNA studies in physical anthropology', *Annual Reviews Anthropology,* Vol. 29, 217–42.

Ortner, D J   2003   *Identification of Pathological Conditions in Human Skeletal Remains.* Academic Press, London.

Ortner, D J & Mays, S   1998   'Dry-bone manifestations of rickets in infancy and early childhood', *International Journal of Osteoarchaeology,* Vol. 8, 45–55.

OS   1834–5   Ordnance Survey of County Donegal, first edition, Sheet DL107 & FH007, scale 1:10,560.

OS   1900   Ordnance Survey of County Donegal, second edition, Sheet DL107-10 & DL107-11, scale 1:2,500.

OS   2005   High flown orthophotography, Sheet O586860 & O588860, scale 1:5000.

O'Sullivan A   1998   'Warriors, legends and heroes: the archaeology of hurling', *Archaeology Ireland,* Vol. 12, No. 3, 32–4.

O'Sullivan, A & Sheehan, J   1996   *The Iveragh Peninsula. An Archaeological Survey of South Kerry.* Cork University Press, Cork.

O'Sullivan, J   1994   'Excavation of an early church and a women's cemetery at St Ronan's medieval parish church, Iona', *Proceedings of the Society of Antiquaries of Scotland,* Vol. 124, 327–65.

O'Sullivan, J & Ó Carragáin, T   2008   *Inishmurray: monks and pilgrims in an Atlantic landscape, Volume 1: archaeological survey and excavations 1997–2000.* The Collins Press, Cork.

Pääbo, S, Poinar, H, Serre, D, Jaenicke-Després, V, Hebler, J, Rohland, N, Kuch, M, Krause, J, Vigilant, L & Hofreiter, M   2004   'Genetic analyses from ancient DNA', *Annual Review of Genetics,* Vol. 38, 645–79.

Peacock, P   1978   *Discovering Old Buttons.* Shire Publications, Aylesbury.

Perry, I J, Whelton, H, Harrington, J & Cousins, B   2009   'The heights and weights of Irish children from the post-war era to the Celtic tiger', *Journal of Epidemiology and Community Health,* Vol. 63, 262–4.

Pier, G B, Grout, M, Zaidi, T, Meluleni, G, Mueschenborn, S S, Banting, G, Ratcliff, R, Evans, M J & Colledge, W H   1998   'Salmonella typhi uses CFTR to enter intestinal epithelial cells', *Nature,* Vol. 393, 79–82.

Piontelli, A   2002   *Twins: from fetus to child.* Routledge, London.

Pollard, A M & Heron, C   2008   *Archaeological Chemistry.* Royal Society of Chemistry, Cambridge.

Poolman, E M & Galvani, A P   2007   'Evaluating candidate agents of selective pressure for cystic fibrosis', *Journal of the Royal Society Interface,* Vol. 4, No. 22, 91–8.

Power, C & O'Sullivan, V R   1992   'Rickets in 19th-century Waterford', *Archaeology Ireland,* Vol. 6, 27–8.

Price, T D, Schoeninger, M J & Armelagos, G J   1985   'Bone chemistry and past behavior: an overview, *Journal of Human Evolution,* Vol. 14, 419–47.

Rahtz, P 1978 'Grave orientation', *Archaeological Journal,* Vol. 135, 1–14.

Rand, N, Mosheiff, R, Matan, Y, Porat, S, Shapiro, M & Liebergall, M 1993 'Osteomyelitis of the pelvis', *Journal of Bone Joint Surgery,* Vol. 75, 731–3.

Rasmussen, K L, Boldsen, J L, Kristensen, H K, Skytte, L, Hansen, K L, Mølholm, L, Grootes, P M, Nadeau, M J & Flöche Eriksen, K M 2008 'Mercury levels in Danish medieval human bones', *Journal of Archaeological Science,* Vol. 35, 2295–306.

Reimer, P J, Baillie, M G L, Bard, E, Bayliss, A, Beck, J W, Bertrand, C J H, Blackwell, P G, Buck, C E, Burr, G S, Cutler, K B, Damon, P E, Edwards, R L, Fairbanks, R G, Friedrich, M, Guilderson, T P, Hogg, A G, Hughen, K A, Kromer, B, McCormac, G, Manning, S, Bronk Ramsey, C, Reimer, R W, Remmele, S, Southon, J R, Stuiver, M, Talamo, S, Taylor, F W, van der Plicht, J & Weyhenmeyer, C E 2004 'IntCal04 terrestrial radiocarbon age calibration, 0–26 Cal Kyr BP', *Radiocarbon,* Vol. 46, 1029–58.

Reimer, P J, Baillie, M G L, Bard, E, Bayliss, A, Beck, J W, Blackwell, P G, Bronk Ramsey, C, Buck, C E, Burr, G, Edwards, R L, Friedrich, M, Grootes, P M, Guilderson, T P, Hajdas, I, Heaton, T J, Hogg, A G, Hughen, K A, Kaiser, K F, Kromer, B, McCormac, F G, Manning, S W, Reimer, R W, Richards, D A, Southon, J, Turney, C S M, van der Plicht, J & Weyhenmeyer, C 2009 'INTCAL09 and MARINE09 radiocarbon age calibration curves, 0–50,000 years cal BP', *Radiocarbon,* Vol. 51, No. 4, 1111–50.

Resnick, D & Niwayama, G 1995a 'Degenerative disease of extra spinal locations', *in* D Resnick (ed.), *Diagnosis of Bone and Joint Disorders, Vol. 3* (3rd edn), 1263–372. W B Saunders, London.

Resnick, D & Niwayama, G 1995b 'Osteomyelitis, septic arthritis and soft tissue infection: organisms', *in* D Resnick (ed.), *Diagnosis of Bone and Joint Disorders, Vol. 4* (3rd edn), 2448–558. W B Saunders, London.

Riordan, J R, Rommens, J M, Kerem, B, Alon N, Rozmahel, R, Grzelczak, Z, Zielenski, J, Lok, S, Plavsic, N, Chou, J L, Drumm, M L, Iannuzzi, M C, Collins, F S & Tsui, L C 1989 'Identification of the cystic fibrosis gene: cloning and characterization of complementary DNA', *Science,* Vol. 245, 1066–73.

Roberts, C & Buikstra, J 2003 *The Bioarchaeology of Tuberculosis.* University Press of Florida, Florida.

Roberts, C & Manchester, K 2005 *The Archaeology of Disease* (3rd edn). Sutton, Stroud.

Roberts C, Boylston, A, Buckley, L, Chamberlain, A & Murphy, E 1998 'Rib lesions, tuberculosis and more support for the theory', *Tubercle and Lung Disease,* Vol. 79, 55–60.

Roe, H M 1969 'Cadaver effigial monuments in Ireland', *Journal of the Royal Society of Antiquaries of Ireland,* Vol. 99, 1–19.

Rodwell, W 1989 *Church Archaeology* (2nd edn). Batsford & English Heritage, London.

Rohland, N, Siedel, H & Hofreiter, M 2010 'A rapid column–based ancient DNA extraction method for increased sample throughput', *Molecular Ecology Resources,* Vol. 10, No. 4, 677–83.

Russell, C W & Prendergast, J P 1874 *Calendar of State Papers Relating to Ireland, 1608–1610.* Longman, London.

Saunders, S R 2000 'Sub-adult skeletons and growth-related studies', *in* M A Katzenberg & S R Saunders (eds), *Biological Anthropology of the Human Skeleton,* 135–62. Wiley-Liss, New York.

Saunders, S R & Hoppa, R D 1993 'Growth deficit in survivors and non-survivors: biological mortality bias in sub-adult skeletal samples', *Yearbook of Physical Anthropology,* Vol. 36, 127–51.

Saunders, S, Hoppa, R & Southern, R 1993 'Diaphyseal growth in a nineteenth century skeletal sample of sub-adults from St Thomas' Church, Belleville, Ontario', *International Journal of Osteoarchaeology,* Vol. 3, 265–81.

Scheuer, L & Black, S 2000 *Developmental Juvenile Osteology.* Academic Press, London.

Scheuer, L & Black, S 2004 *The Juvenile Skeleton.* Elsevier Academic Press, London.

Scheuer, J L, Musgrave, J H & Evans, S P 1980 'The estimation of late fetal and perinatal age from limb bone length by linear and logarithmic regression', *Annals of Human Biology,* Vol. 7, No. 3, 257–65.

Scorpio, A, Collins, D, Whipple, D, Cave, D, Bates, J & Zhang, Y 1997 'Rapid differentiation of bovine and human tubercle bacilli based on a characteristic mutation on the bovine pyrazinamidase gene', *Journal of Clinical Microbiology,* Vol. 35, No. 1, 106–10.

Scully, O M B 1997 'Metal artefacts', *in* M F Hurley, O M B Scully & S W J McCutcheon, *Late Viking Age and Medieval Waterford. Excavations 1986–1992,* 438–89. Waterford Corporation, Waterford.

Shafer, M M, Siker, M, Overdier, J T, Ramsl, P C, Teschler-Nicola, M & Farrell, P M 2008 'Enhanced methods for assessment of the trace element composition of Iron Age bone', *Science of the Total Environment,* Vol. 401, 144–61.

Shaw, H F & Wasserburg, G J 1985 'Sm-Nd in marine carbonates and phosphates: implications for Nd isotopes in seawater and crustal ages', *Geochimica et Cosmochimica Acta,* Vol. 49, 503–18.

Sheehan, J 2009 'A peacock's tale: excavations at Caherlehillan, Iveragh, Ireland', *in* N Edwards (ed.), *The Archaeology of the Early Medieval Celtic Churches,* 191–206. Society for Medieval Archaeology Monograph No. 29, Society of Church Archaeology Monograph No. 1. Maney Publishing, Leeds.

Simington, R C 1937 *The Civil Survey, AD 1654 to 1656: volume 3 – counties Donegal, Londonderry and Tyrone.* The Stationery Office, Dublin.

Simms, K 1975–6 'Warfare in the medieval Gaelic lordships', *The Irish Sword,* Vol. 12, 98–108.

Simms, K 1978 'Guesting and feasting in Gaelic Ireland', *Journal of the Royal Society of Antiquaries of Ireland,* Vol. 108, 67–100.

Simms, K 1987 *From Kings to Warlords.* The Boydell Press, Woodbridge.

Simms, K 1995 'Late medieval Donegal', *in* W Nolan, L Ronayne & M Dunlevy (eds), Donegal: *history and society,* 183–201. Geography Publications, Dublin.

Simms, K 1996 'Gaelic warfare in the Middle Ages', *in* T Bartlett & K Jeffery (eds), *A Military History of Ireland,* 99–115. Cambridge University Press, Cambridge.

Simms, K 2004 'Bardic schools, learned families', *in* S Duffy (ed.), *Medieval Ireland: an encyclopedia,* 35–7. Routledge, London.

Simms, K 2009 *Medieval Gaelic Sources.* Maynooth Research Guides for Irish Local History Number 14. Four Courts Press, Dublin.

Šlaus, M 2000 'Biocultural analysis of sex differences in mortality profiles and stress levels in the late medieval population from Nova Rača, Croatia', *American Journal of Physical Anthropology,* Vol. 111, 193–209.

Smith, B H 1991 'Standards of human tooth formation and dental age assessment', *in* M A Kelley & C S Larsen (eds), *Advances in Dental Anthropology,* 143–68. Wiley-Liss Inc., New York.

Smith, B N & Epstein, S 1971 'Two categories of $^{13}C/^{12}C$ ratios for higher plants', *Plant Physiology,* Vol. 47, 380–4.

Smith, M J, Efthimiou, J, Hodson, M E & Batten, J C 1984 'Mycobacterial isolations in young adults with cystic fibrosis', *Thorax*, Vol. 39, 369–75.

Southern, K W, Munck, A, Pollit, R, Zanolla, L, Dankert-Roelse, J, Castellani, C & the ECFS CF Neonatal Screening Working Group 2007 'A survey of newborn screening for cystic fibrosis in Europe', *Journal of Cystic Fibrosis,* Vol. 6, No. 1, 57–65.

Sponheimer, M, de Ruiter, D, Lee-Thorp, J & Späth, A 2005 'Sr/Ca and early hominin diets revisited: new data from modern and fossil tooth enamel', *Journal of Human Evolution,* Vol. 48, 147–56.

Stalley, R 1987 *The Cistercian Monasteries of Ireland.* Yale University Press, London.

Stanley, M 2010 'Death of a graveyard', *Seanda,* No. 5, 51.

Starley, D 1995 *Hammerscale.* The Historical Metallurgy Society Archaeology Datasheet No. 10. The Historical Metallurgy Society, London.

Stiner, M C, Kuhn, S L, Surovell, T A, Goldberg, P, Meignen, L, Weiner, S & Bar-Yosef, O 2001 'Bone preservation in Hayonim Cave (Israel): a macroscopic and mineralogical study', *Journal of Archaeological Science,* Vol. 28, 643–59.

Stirland, A J 2000 *Raising the Dead: the skeleton crew of King Henry VIII's great ship, the Mary Rose.* John Wiley & Sons Ltd, Chichester.

Stones, J A 1989 'The burials at Aberdeen, Linlithgow and Perth Friaries', *in* J A Stones (ed.), *Three Scottish Carmelite Friaries: excavations at Aberdeen, Linlithgow and Perth 1980-86,* 111–16. Society of Antiquaries of Scotland Monograph Series No. 6. Society of Antiquaries of Scotland, Edinburgh.

Stuiver, M, Reimer, P J, Bard, E, Beck, J W, Burr, G S, Hughen, K A, Kromer, B, McCormac, G, Van Der Plicht, J & Spurk, M 1998 'IntCal98 radiocarbon age calibration, 24,000–0 cal BP', *Radiocarbon,* Vol. 40, 1041–83.

Tait, C 2002 *Death, Burial and Commemoration in Ireland, 1550–1650.* Palgrave Macmillan, Basingstoke.

Tanaka, G I, Kawamura, H & Nomura, E 1981 'Reference Japanese man-II. Distribution of strontium in the skeleton and in the mass of mineralized bone', *Health Physics,* Vol. 40, 601–14.

Tanner, J M 1981 *A History of the Study of Human Growth.* Cambridge University Press, Cambridge.

Tanner, J M, Whitehouse, R H & Takaishi, M 1966 'Standards from birth to maturity for height, weight, height velocity, and weight velocity: British children, 1965 – Part I', *Archives of Disease in Childhood,* Vol. 41, 454–71.

Taylor, G M, Murphy, E, Hopkins, R, Rutland, P & Chistov, Y 2007 'First report of *Mycobacterium bovis* DNA in human remains from the Iron Age', *Microbiology*, Vol. 153, 1243–9.

Thomas, C 1971 *The Early Christian Archaeology of North Britain.* Oxford University Press (for the University of Glasgow), London.

Thomas, C 1998 'Form and function', *in* S M Foster (ed.), *The St Andrews Sarcophagus. A Pictish Masterpiece and its International Connections,* 84–96. Four Courts Press, Dublin.

Thompson, T J U, Gauthier, M & Islam, M 2009 'The application of a new method of Fourier Transform Infrared Spectroscopy to the analysis of burned bone', *Journal of Archaeological Science,* Vol. 36, 910–14.

Tierney, S N & Bird, J M 2015 'Molecular sex identification of juvenile skeletal remains from an Irish medieval population using ancient DNA analysis', *Journal of Archaeological Science,* Vol. 62, 27–38.

Troy, C 2010 *Final Report on the Human Remains from Ardreigh, Co. Kildare.* Unpublished report prepared for Headland Archaeology Ltd.

Trueman, C N 1999 'Rare earth element geochemistry and taphonomy of terrestrial vertebrate assemblages', *Palaios,* Vol. 14, 555–68.

Trueman, C N & Tuross, N 2002 'Trace elements in recent and fossil bone apatite', *Reviews in Mineralogy and Geochemistry,* Vol. 48, 489–521.

Trueman, C N, Behrensmeyer, A K, Potts, R & Tuross, N 2006 'High-resolution records of location and stratigraphic provenance from the rare earth element composition of fossil bones', *Geochimica et Cosmochimica Acta,* Vol. 70, 4343–55.

Turner-Walker, G 2008 'The chemical and microbial degradation of bones and teeth', *in* R Pinhasi & S Mays (eds), *Advances in Human Palaeopathology,* 3–29. John Wiley & Sons, Chichester.

Twiss, R 1776 *A Tour in Ireland in 1775 with a View of the Salmon Leap at Ballyshannon.* Messrs Sheppard, Corcoran, Cross, Potts, Chamberlaine and 13 others, Dublin.

Tykot, R H 2006 'Isotope analyses and the histories of maize', *in* J Staller, R Tykot & B Benz (eds), *Histories of Maize: multidisciplinary approaches to the prehistory, linguistics, biogeography, domestication, and evolution of maize,* 131–42. Elsevier, Burlington.

Ubelaker, D 2002 'Approaches to the study of commingling in human skeletal biology', *in* W D Haglund & M H Sorg (eds), *Advances in Forensic Taphonomy: method, theory and archaeological perspectives,* 331–51. CRC Press, Florida.

Van Klinken, G J, Richards, M P & Hedges, B E 2002 'An overview of causes for stable isotopic variations in past European human populations: environmental, ecophysiological, and cultural effects', *in* S H Ambrose & M A Katzenberg (eds), *Biogeochemical Approaches to Paleodietary Analysis,* 39–63. Springer, New York.

Waddell, J 2010 *The Prehistoric Archaeology of Ireland* (3rd edn). Wordwell, Dublin.

Waldron, T, Taylor, G M & Rudling, D 1999 'Sexing of Romano-British baby burials from the Beddingham and Bignor villas', *Sussex Archaeological Collections,* Vol. 137, 71–9.

Walker, P L, Bathurst, R R, Richman, R, Gjerdrum, T & Andrushkp, V A 2009 'The causes of porotic hyperostosis and cribra orbitalia: a reappraisal of the iron-deficiency-anemia hypothesis', *American Journal of Physical Anthropology,* Vol. 139, 109–25.

Walls, T & Shingadia, D 2004 'Global epidemiology of paediatric tuberculosis', *Journal of Infection,* Vol. 48, 13–22.

Walsh, P 1948 *Beatha Aodha Ruaidh uí Dhomhnaill: the life of Aodh Ruadh O Domhnaill. Transcribed from the book of Lughaidh Ó Clérigh.* Irish Texts Society, Vol. 42. Educational Co. of Ireland, Dublin.

Walsh, P 2010 *The Making of the Irish Protestant Ascendancy: the life of William Conolly, 1662–1729.* Boydell Press, Woodbridge.

Walsh, P & O Lochlainn, C 1957 *Life of Aodh Ruadh O Domhnaill: part 2.* Irish Texts Society, Dublin.

Waterman, D M 1979 'St Mary's Priory, Devenish: excavation of the east range, 1972–4', *Ulster Journal of Archaeology,* Vol. 42, 34–50.

Weiss, E & Jurmain, R 2007 'Osteoarthritis revisited: a contemporary review of aetiology', *International Journal of Osteoarchaeology,* Vol. 17, No. 5, 437–50.

Went, A 1945 'Fishing weirs of the River Erne', *Journal of the Royal Society of Antiquaries of Ireland,* Vol. 75, 213–23.

Wilde, W R 1843 'Report upon the table of deaths', *in Census of Ireland 1841,* i–lxviii. Alexander Thom, Dublin.

Witas, H W, Jatczak, I, Jedrychowska-Dańska, C, Żądzińska, E, Wrzesińska, A, Wrzesiński, J & Nadolski, J 2006 'Sequence of "ΔF508 CFTR" allele identified at present is lacking in medieval specimens from Central Poland. Preliminary results', *Anthropologischer Anzeiger,* Vol. 64, No. 1, 41–9.

Yang, D Y & Watt, K 2005 'Contamination controls when preparing archaeological remains for ancient DNA analysis', *Journal of Archaeological Science,* Vol. 32, No. 3, 331–6.

Yoshinaga, J, Suzuki, T, Morita, M & Hayakawa, M 1995 'Trace elements in ribs of elderly people and elemental variation in the presence of chronic diseases', *Science of the Total Environment,* Vol. 162, 239–52.

Zadzinska, E, Karasinska, M, Jedrychowska-Danska, K, Watala, C & Witas, H W 2008 'Sex diagnosis of sub-adult specimens from medieval Polish archaeological sites: metric analysis of deciduous dentition', *HOMO—Journal of Comparative Human Biology,* Vol. 59, 175–87.

Zapata, J, Pérez-Sirvent, C, Martínez-Sánchez, M J & Tovar, P 2006 'Diagenesis, not biogenesis: two late Roman skeletal examples', *Science of the Total Environment,* Vol. 369, 357–68.

Zlatanos, S, Laskaridis, K & Sagredos, A 2009 'Determination of proximate composition, fatty acid content and amino acid profile of five lesser-common sea organisms from the Mediterranean Sea', *International Journal of Food Science & Technology,* Vol. 44, 1590–4.

INDEX